Waiting for the Cemetery Vote

Waiting for the Cemetery Vote

The Fight to Stop Election Fraud in Arkansas

TOM GLAZE with Ernie Dumas

The University of Arkansas Press

Fayetteville • 2011

ISBN-13: 978-1-55728-965-0

23 22 21 20 19   5 4 3 2

Designed by Liz Lester

⊗ The paper used in this publication meets the minimum requirements of the American National Standard for Permanence of Paper
for Printed Library Materials Z39.48-1984.

LIBRARY OF CONGRESS CATALOGING-IN-PUBLICATION DATA

Glaze, Tom, 1938–
     Waiting for the cemetery vote : the fight to stop election fraud in Arkansas /
Tom Glaze, with Ernie Dumas.
          p.   cm.
     Includes index.
     ISBN 978-1-55728-965-0 (pbk. : alk. paper)
     1. Elections—Corrupt practices—Arkansas—History. 2. Elections—Corrupt
practices—Arkansas—Prevention. I. Dumas, Ernie. II. Title.
     JK5190.G53   2011
     364.1'324—dc22
                                                              2011013912

To Phyllis

CONTENTS

PREFACE

This book was on my mind for more than twenty-five years, a stretch when I served on three courts—the Chancery Court of Pulaski County, the Arkansas Court of Appeals, and the Arkansas Supreme Court—and after I had given up a usually bootless career as the scourge of election thieves. I imagined that the fine and careful science of judging discouraged the kind of reflection, writing, and passing of historical judgment that would be entailed in recounting a political era in which I had been involved, not altogether impartially, and which continued while I was on the bench. Besides, if I was going to be the calm and dispassionate judge that people expected me to be, I ought to subdue rather than rekindle the brooding rage that I had felt over the freebooting political bosses and election officials with whom I had jousted and the government's benign disposition toward them.

When I finally sat down after retirement to render the project to paper, the book evolved into something quite different from my original concept, which was to recount the heroic efforts of a band of women in one hill county to rend the veil of corruption and secrecy that had held their community in thrall since they were children and probably long before. Having co-opted my old friend Ernie Dumas into helping, I found myself yielding to his notions about what the narrative should be. He believed its commercial value would be raised if it were something of a memoir, a genre he thought was in fashion, and that its literary value would be improved by enlarging its historical perspective. Thus the book spends considerably more time reflecting on my personal strivings than I still find comfortable. It also takes a slightly longer look at the role of vote thieves in our state's political history and development than I first intended, and it tries to chronicle a political movement of about a dozen years that coincide roughly with the onset of the modern progressive era in Arkansas. That is the period in which I was involved in election reform, often to the exclusion of everything else.

The clean-election movement was led not by a party or by political leaders but by individual citizens who undertook to do what their public institutions persistently failed to do, which was to ensure that elections for public office were honest and that the will of the people was scrupulously obliged. If there is a moral to this story, it is that vigilant and courageous individuals can bring about institutional change when civic and political leaders are unwilling.

In writing this book, we have made every effort to set out documented accounts of Arkansas elections in which corruption was employed to win a race for political office or to influence the outcome of every race on the ballot. Readers will be astonished that such illegal acts occurred and went unpunished and that instead the perpetrators garnered power and money by using them. The practices can be traced far back into the state's history, to the Reconstruction era and before. The violations were so flagrant that they ought to have shocked the public conscience and impelled law-enforcement agencies and the courts to correct the fraud and hold the perpetrators accountable. Instead, corruption in many places became embedded in the political culture.

It would be foolish to pretend that other states have not experienced illegal voting, sometimes egregious and history making. Arkansas, however, is the one state where fraud was so dire and so perniciously ignored that citizens were forced to conduct their own investigations and file lawsuits to obtain an honest counting and tabulation of the votes. They did so sometimes under intimidation and threats to body and livelihood, and, on occasion, public officials turned the legal system against those who tried to unearth the fraud.

As an attorney for the citizens who surrendered their privacy and entered the lists to fight election thievery in Arkansas in the 1960s and '70s, the author unabashedly wishes that from this short history readers will take new devotion to the cause of honest and efficient elections, which are the foundation of our freedom. Ballot theft is not a mere issue of which among equally selfish factions will occupy the courthouse or city hall and exercise patronage and road-contracting privileges for the next two years. It can shape our destiny as a people. We need look no further than the presidential elections of 2000 and 2004, when irregularities cast a pall over the government of the United States and shook people's confidence in democratic institutions.

TOM GLAZE
October 2010

ACKNOWLEDGMENTS

My original premise in starting this book was to celebrate the courage and tenacity of a small clutch of women in Conway County, connected by family or friendship, who drew me into their struggle against the political machine that had held their community in thrall for years, partly through control of the ballot box. If I have an unpayable debt to anyone for any success that the book may achieve, it is to them. I am particularly grateful to the two who survived to see it, Dixie Drilling and Alidene Malone, and also Joan Paladino, whom we called "Tex," who died as this book was in production, because their records and memories have been invaluable in putting together the narrative of those battles. I only wish that the others —Katie Read, Faye Dixon, Helen Gordon, Jan Lynch, and Margie Brown—had lived to see the day or that it had not taken me decades to commit the story to paper. Wherever else we had some success in combating election fraud it was owing to people like them who chose at some personal risk to stand up to the bosses. Most of them are dead, too, but I ought to acknowledge their contributions, even anonymously.

Among the living, Dorothy Stuck, a high school history teacher who quit to help her husband run crusading weekly newspapers in northeast Arkansas and then devoted her life to equal justice, deserves special mention. Dorothy marked the sparrow's fall in Poinsett County politics, and her keen memory of the details of the voting fraud forty-five years later complemented my records on the investigation. Similarly, Fern Elliott of Marshall helped me reconstruct the crusade that she and her late husband, Rex, began to end the ancient system of vote buying in Searcy County (if, in fact, it ended).

Two prosecutors, Alex Streett and Tom Donovan, played a huge role, much bigger than my own, in pressing for a judicial remedy to the endemic election banditry in Conway and Faulkner Counties and were equally important in recounting the tale. Where my memory was fuzzy and the contemporary accounts indefinite, Alex's were sharp. He apparently never tossed away a file. The county powers tried to put Tom in prison for his work on election fraud, which seems to quicken his memory even now. The only other prosecuting attorney who evinced any interest in penalizing people who connived to flout election laws was Jim Guy Tucker, who served only two years before going on to higher things: attorney general, congressman, lieutenant governor and governor. I am grateful for his help in pinning down the details of investigations in North Little Rock and Little Rock in which I had a part. In a monumental miscarriage of justice, Tucker's career would be ended in 1996 by a highly politicized prosecution.

Richard Mays, who forsook his own struggling law practice to help me in the courtroom in several of the conflicts, helped again in reconstructing the events and legal strategies and focusing my mind on what was important. I am indebted to the lawyers, most of them law students at the time, who answered my call and served as poll watchers at the pivotal elections in Conway and Searcy Counties. The narrative is enriched by the colorful accounts of Mark Stodola, now the mayor of Little Rock; Jamie Cox, now a circuit judge at Greenwood; Joe Purvis, now a lawyer in Little Rock; and Robert Dittrich, the longtime prosecuting attorney at Stuttgart. Their remembrances have not dimmed, and I am grateful for their sharing them. I would be remiss if I did not also pay tribute to the other young lawyers who worked with me in our first venture into the labyrinth of Arkansas elections as John Haley's Election Research Council or its reincarnation as The Election Laws Institute, but I am afraid that my recollections are too feeble to name them all. I must mention two of them, my longtime good friend and adviser, Jim Wallace, and Ralph Hamner Jr., who often went where I could not go and who has continued to advise. Judge David Bogard of North Little Rock, my lifelong friend, supplied his keen insights into the history of election fraud and jurisprudence.

I wish that George Fisher, the keenest social critic of our time, were still around so that I could thank him for the indispensable contribution that he made to this book—and also so that I could still enjoy his genius every week. As it is, I can only thank the *North Little Rock Times,* the *Arkansas Democrat-Gazette*, and Rose Publishing Co. for permission to reprint a few of George's inspirations from his early days as a political cartoonist. Judi Woods, the proprietor of the Fisher legacy, guided me to the right places. Fisher's voluminous work is archived at the University of Arkansas's Mullins Library at Fayetteville, the Arkansas Arts Center, and The Butler Center for Arkansas Studies at the Central Arkansas Library System.

My grasp of Arkansas history and the insidious role of vote thieves was not exhaustive when I began election work in 1964, and I depended heavily on the research of real historians to raise my comprehension of the culture that winked at ballot fraud. I have borrowed heavily from several historians, mainly Michael Dougan, whose warts-and-all history, *Arkansas Odyssey,* is a gripping read. I may have exceeded scholarly limits in co-opting and condensing Dr. Kenneth Barnes's masterly book *Who Killed John Clayton?: Political Violence and the Emergence of the New South, 1861–1893,* which, it seemed to me, explained better than anything else how that culture developed. At any rate, I am indebted to him.

While I will refrain from making an inventory of all the people who helped, conscience will not permit me to ignore Mamie Ruth Williams and Winthrop Rockefeller. Mamie Ruth, I am quite sure, guided my destiny in all things, including this, before her death in 2003. She insisted that the book be done and, I think, made Ernie Dumas promise to help me. Ernie certainly kept his promise! His terrific writing and invaluable knowledge of Arkansas's political history made him the perfect person to work on this book from beginning to end. It was Rockefeller's vision of a better democracy in his adopted state and, yes, his willingness to commit a little of his vast wealth in the service of that goal that began and carried the clean-election movement. I shall always be thankful to both of them. Rose Moore helped me immeasurably with research on the supreme court years and by focusing my cluttered mind on the project at hand when the manuscript was in its final stages.

My daughter Julie Houlihan and son Steve Glaze took time from their busy careers to clear the cobwebs from my mind and help me focus on how the literary project should proceed. The inspiration, love, and encouragement of my daughters Amy Glaze and Ashley Glaze Russell and son Mike Glaze were indispensable.

Finally, this and about everything else that I have done the past thirty-five years would not have been possible without my wife, Phyllis. Her good humor, understanding, optimism, and generosity apparently have no limits. I have often strained the limits of her patience but have been allowed to get away with it.

Waiting for the Cemetery Vote

Tom Glaze

CHAPTER 1

· · · · · · · · · · ·

The Simple Expedient of Theft

"I consider it completely unimportant who in the party will vote, or how; but what is extraordinarily important is this—who will count the votes, and how."

—JOSEPH STALIN

Returning to my alma mater, the University of Arkansas, in September 1960 to enter law school, I found my senses refreshed by the gorgeous Indian summer that nearly always settles on the Boston Mountains at school time and also by a new curiosity about the peculiar state that I had begun to embrace as my permanent home. My knowledge of Arkansas, at least outside the immediate environs of the university campus, was limited and my opinions of it still a little unflattering. My high school at Joplin, Missouri, had integrated in 1955, and my glorious senior season in football was tarnished because two arch-rival schools in Arkansas, Fort Smith and Van Buren, canceled their games with us rather than have their boys play on the same field with a black youngster, the speedy running back on my team. I had followed, as acutely as a young sojourner from Missouri could, the confrontation between the governor and the United States government at Little Rock's Central High School and the gothic politics and legal struggles of its aftermath, all of which occurred while I was an undergraduate at the University of Arkansas. Arkansas was apt to be a good laboratory for a student of law, although at this point I was still not sure whether I wanted to be a minister, a coach, or a lawyer, which was my father's goal for me. But the story that dominated the statewide newspaper that September and October for a change was not school integration but a perverse judicial battle that was being waged in a couple of country courthouses in the Grand Prairie east of Little Rock. It afforded a colorful introduction to Arkansas election fraud and the quintessential Arkansas political boss, which would before very long become the twin objects of my career in the law.

The story, which was recorded sometimes humorously on the front pages of the *Arkansas Gazette,* involved the heroic attempts by the political boss of Prairie County and his foe, a politician from the adjoining county of Lonoke, to steal an election for the state Senate from each other.

State Senator Jerry J. Screeton was the prototype small-town Southern political leader, a bellicose segregationist who could deliver stem-winding speeches from the Senate lectern in Little Rock and go about town back home in Hazen as the mayor, school board president, bank chairman, and backslapping friend to all. Screeton's last hurrah as the Delta's pre-eminent demagogue would occur nine years later. In 1969, he deputized 120 auxiliary policemen armed with shotguns and hunting rifles and parked rice combines and barricades at the town's entrance to confront a skinny black youngster from Memphis with a lame arm calling himself "Sweet Willie Wine" (his real name was Lance Watson), who was going to traverse the main street of Hazen on foot on a hot August march from Memphis to Little Rock. It was a gesture that the young man thought would demonstrate to African Americans that even in the east Arkansas Delta they need not fear insisting upon their constitutional and God-given rights. Governor Winthrop Rockefeller, concerned that some harm might actually befall the young man on his highly publicized trek down old US Highway 81, dispatched state troopers to watch, but Wine/Watson sauntered through the steamy town unbothered. Screeton, a laughingstock owing to his overwrought stunt, pulled his men back before Willie got to town and was not to be seen, then or much afterward. "I came, I saw, I walked through Hazen," Willie pronounced as he exited the western edge of town.

In the late summer of 1960, Screeton faced oblivion from a more traditional force, the electorate. Prairie and Lonoke Counties had a sort of gentleman's agreement that they would share the seat in the state Senate from that district, a Prairie County man serving one term and a Lonoke County man the next. But Screeton calculated that the district needed his uninterrupted services and ran again. Lonoke County put up its finest, Joe T. Gunter from the town of Austin, and on the evening of the Democratic primary Joe Gunter seemed to have prevailed, at least according to the unofficial count, by 219 votes out of more than 15,000 cast. As I would rediscover personally a few years later, the days immediately after an election are sometimes more critical to a candidate's success than all the weeks preceding it. Gunter's lead dwindled the next two days to 139 as Lonoke, Prairie, and two other counties that were attached to the senatorial district jiggered their returns. By the third day, Friday, all counties were required by law to declare their official returns to Little Rock, but Prairie and Lonoke held back, each waiting for the other to certify its votes first. When Lonoke finally certified its results, Gunter picked up votes and Screeton lost votes, and Gunter surged ahead overall by nearly 500. Prairie County mailed its returns to Little Rock the next day. The County Democratic Committee reported finding a whopping 729 votes for Screeton that they had somehow overlooked the night of the election. Screeton retained the Democratic nomination, 8,185 to 7,939.

Gunter sued, claiming that Screeton's surrogates had stolen the election by manufacturing votes in the friendly precincts of Prairie. Circuit Judge J. W. Waggoner impounded the ballot boxes and a trial ensued, alternately at the Prairie County Courthouse at Des Arc and at the Lonoke County Courthouse in Lonoke. The trial and the coverage afforded the people of Arkansas and a young law student a rarity, a clear primer on just how their democracy can be subverted routinely by petty ambition and the complicity of citizens who are supposed to safeguard an important part of the people's business, their elections.

On the front page of the *Gazette* each day unfolded a small tragedy, the complete subversion of the people's voice, but you could not escape the feeling that for many, perhaps most, it was a comedy, at its most serious a soap opera. The paper reported one day that during a short recess Senator Screeton had bloodied the nose of the editor of the Lonoke weekly newspaper and that after a hasty mini-trial in the corridor conducted by a Lonoke justice of the peace, Screeton paid a ten-dollar fine and seven dollars in court costs for assault and battery and then muttered that for seventeen dollars he should have gotten in a better lick on the editor. It would be the only punishment meted out in the case although the evidence of crime was persistent and largely uncontested, including election officials wagering on the outcome of the election, breaking and entering, and ballot theft. When voter lists, tally sheets and ballots themselves turned up missing from many boxes, the county clerk of Prairie explained on the stand that a prowler had broken into his office and rifled the ballot boxes the night before the returns were to be canvassed and certified. I would discover later that the risk of burglary and fire at an Arkansas courthouse rises exponentially in the nights immediately following an election. When Screeton's lawyer got his turn, he demonstrated that Lonoke County had manipulated the results there in Gunter's favor. Lonoke's error was underestimating the scale of knavery that the situation required.

In the end, the Screeton-Gunter election merely joined the comedic chronicles of Arkansas's election hijinks. Nothing was settled by the courts, and nothing was achieved. Two weeks before the general election, Judge Waggoner stopped the trial and declared Screeton the default winner on a procedural miscue, and then a week later quashed that order and said he would turn the case over to a new judge for a fresh trial. The general election intervened. Screeton was defeated by a write-in candidate —the popular basketball coach at Cabot High, Charlie George—and everyone decided that the primary election contest was moot.

If the public airing of transparent election fraud and the resolution of it were shocking to fresh eyes, they hardly caused a stir in the body politic. That was because election fraud was an Arkansas tradition. My naiveté at the time was breathtaking. I knew little of Arkansas's history and nothing of its electoral traditions. I would discover over the ensuing years that from early statehood, ballot stuffing and theft or some form of manipulation were often the way to get things done. They were the methods by which you kept the malefactors out of power, prevented infidels who wanted to peddle whiskey from corrupting the morals of the people or else stopped the bluenoses from thwarting the free market and private freedom. (Wet-dry elections tended to be some of the dirtiest.) Voting fraud was more often the subject of jokes than of lamentations. You discovered this truth from personal experience and by the casual reading of Arkansas history.

Arkansas's return to the Union after the Civil War was built upon brazen voting fraud. The constitution of 1868, the ratification of which was the basis of the restoration of statehood, was drafted by carpetbaggers and scalawags and opposed by rank-and-file white natives, but the Republican-controlled state board of election commissioners announced that the vote on the new constitution was 30,380 for and 41 against. One observer noted that Republicans stuffed ballot boxes and "voted early and voted often, traveling from ballot-box to ballot-box." Augustus H. Garland, later the attorney general of the United States, said that an honest count of the ballots would have produced a defeat by at least 20,000 votes.

A lesson not lost on the Democrats, who returned to power after Reconstruction, was that whoever controls the voting machinery calls the shots. Four years later, in the election of 1872, Democrats turned to violence and intimidation to keep African Americans in line or else away from the polls altogether while the ruling Republicans resorted to the simple expedient of theft.

"Fraud, violence, intimidation and multiple voting were the order of the day," historian Michael B. Dougan would write. "Election day, November 5, 1872, reflected rather poorly on the democratic process."

But the low-water mark for Arkansas democracy must have been the election of 1888, which for embattled and disempowered whites assumed the character of Armageddon. The desperate, remorseless efforts to wrest back power and government in that bloody election cycle would be recycled for generation after generation by family legend, books, and scholarly articles, and the lore of those frightful but exhilarating days shaped public attitudes about election fraud far into the next century. People still boast about forebears who had roles in the criminal doings and vigilantism. Whichever side you were on, the vital issues involved in the accumulation or retention of power seemed to justify any level of skullduggery from vote theft to murder. Not merely your personal situation but the general welfare depended upon your side reaching and keeping the levers of power. Over the long course of the travails, from the beginning of Reconstruction until the dénouement after the 1888 elections, neither virtue nor sinfulness belonged exclusively to either side. That knowledge must have been the rationalization for whatever fraud or high-handedness, even murder, that anyone undertook. The other side was committing fraud, the reasoning went, or else it surely would if given half a chance. So do we, today, claim reason as the premise for crimes against the public trust like voting fraud.

A thorough and indelicate account of the events of 1888, particularly in Conway County, ought to be required in the curriculum of every school. I would suggest Kenneth C. Barnes's fearless and exhaustively researched chronicle of the election, *Who Killed John Clayton?: Political Violence and the Emergence of the New South 1861–1893* (Duke University Press, 1998). Barnes grew up in Conway County, where he heard the tales and boasts of forebears' cunning and bravery, and when he returned to teach European history at the University of Central Arkansas in the next county he set out to recover the full truth.

· · ·

I do not think it is out of place to briefly recapitulate the story. Much of this book will recount efforts seventy-five years later to combat voting fraud in Conway County and other scenes of the 1888 struggle, and I am convinced that the mindset and deeds of the desperate men of that year were hereditary.

The end of Reconstruction and the ratification of a new state constitution (our current one) in 1874, which restored voting rights to everyone and curtailed executive power, brought the Democrats back to power. But their hegemony was threatened in the 1870s and 1880s by two forces: the vast migration of African Americans into the state mainly from South Carolina and Tennessee and the radicalization of poor farmers and laborers in the great agrarian revolt of the '80s. Conway County, if you can believe it, was touted as the promised land for blacks, and hundreds settled in the town of Menifee. The *Arkansas Gazette* contemptuously referred to the county as "the Kansas county."

Elections were getting sticky for the Democrats by 1886 and winning again would test their cleverness. Election judges were about to count the ballots that fall at Plumerville, where blacks outnumbered whites by a margin of two to one, when Thomas C. Hervey and Robert Pate, leading Democrats, barged into the room and started a scuffle. They knocked over the table where the ballots were piled and extinguished the lamp. When order and light were restored, the judges found one hundred more ballots than there were people who had showed up to vote that day.

No degree of guile would be enough in 1888.

Poor farmers and laborers broke from the ascendant Democratic Party after Reconstruction and formed the Union Labor Party, which in 1888 nominated a one-legged Confederate veteran named C. M. Norwood for governor against the Democrats' James P. Eagle, a white planter. The

Republicans defaulted and supported the radical Norwood. Election day was particularly ruthless in the Delta, where intimidation of black voters reached the level of mayhem, a system popularly known as "the Mississippi Plan." In Crittenden County, white vigilantes drove out black officials and commandeered the election machinery. White Democrats, who had won local elections in many places in the Delta, acquired ballot boxes made in Memphis that were manufactured with false bottoms, the better to empty or stuff ballots. By the official count, Eagle won 99,650 to 84,273 but the Union Labor Party accused the Democrats of massive fraud and demanded a recount. The legislature said fine, as long as you deposit $40,000 for the cost, which was prohibitive for poor farmers and workers. In Pulaski County, officials counted 6,000 fraudulent ballots and then planted the evidence at the bottom of the Arkansas River.

Conway County was the focal battleground. Democrats formed a militia there, putatively to protect whites and polling places from blacks, and Governor Simon P. Hughes sent the County Democratic Club two boxes of guns and two thousand rounds of bullets. The militia paraded through the streets of Morrilton daily before the election. On his way to the polling place at dawn on election day, the Republican election judge, George W. Baker, was assailed by a neighbor, a paperhanger, who feigned drunkenness. Both were taken to jail. With the Republican judge absent, the Democratic militia took over the polling place, removed the Republican officials, installed Democrats in their places and announced that it would be the only polling place in town "under penalty of death if need be." When a Republican newspaper editor began handing out Republican ballots outside the polling place—that was the custom for both parties—militiamen beat him and the sheriff jailed him for his own protection. The township went Democratic by a margin of 6 to 1.

At Plumerville, where blacks outnumbered whites 2 to 1, the militia ousted the appointed Republican election judges and replaced them with Democrats because, the militia leader alleged, the Republicans were tardy at the polling place. The precinct, which had gone Republican two years earlier by five hundred votes, went Democratic by seventy-six votes. Democrats celebrated the victory that night with gunshots, a torchlight parade, and a mock funeral procession interring the Republican Party.

That was a tepid warm-up for the November federal election, in which John W. Clayton of Pine Bluff, the young brother of former governor and US senator Powell Clayton, was the Republican candidate for US House of Representatives from the Second District.* The first strategy was to keep black voters away from the polls. The sheriff and other Democrats cornered a black preacher behind a store in Morrilton and accused him of intimidating African Americans who wanted to vote Democratic or split their tickets. A Republican leader from Little Rock, Mason W. Benjamin, journeyed to Morrilton to organize Republicans and African Americans for the election. A mob met him at the train station, bludgeoned him to the ground, and yanked out most of his beard. Someone with a bean shooter let loose a lead ball that entered the man's head above an eye. A local doctor removed the ball and Benjamin was put on the next train back to Little Rock, where he died. No one was charged.

Owing to the September fraud, US Judge Henry C. Caldwell at Little Rock appointed Charles Wahl as a federal supervisor to watch over the voting and counting at Plumerville for the federal election. Sheriff Marcus Shelby countered by swearing in more than a dozen Democrats as special deputies to be sentinels at Plumerville, where blacks voted in big numbers, and at Solgohachia and Springfield, where the populist Agricultural Wheel was expected to turn out white voters against the Democrats. The two black Republican election judges who were blocked because they were late at the polls in September showed up well before dawn on November 6 but the assembled Democrats voted them out and elected all Democratic judges. Accompanied by Wahl, the federal agent, the Republicans went to a black barbershop to set up another precinct, but the sheriff's deputies threatened the barber with a hatchet and confiscated the ballot box. Back at the first voting place, deputies warned blacks away from the polls. Eighteen Democrats from Morrilton rode horseback through the rain to Plumerville after dark. Thirteen of them hung back at the railway depot while a posse of five, which included Walter P. Wells and brothers George and Oliver Bentley, rode into Plumerville to meet with other Democrats at a drugstore, and then went to the polling place. When Wahl and a Democratic election judge opened the ballot box, men wearing rubber slickers with handkerchiefs

*At that time, rather than a spring primary to decide party nominees for all offices and a fall general election to determine officeholders, September elections decided state and local offices and November elections determined federal offices. —E.D.

over their faces burst into the room and wrested away the ballot box and poll books, one of them muttering, "God damn you, turn it loose or I will blow your brains out. We will show you how Conway County goes." The posse took the ballot box and poll books back to Morrilton and burned them in a woodstove at Wells's store.

John Clayton lost the congressional race by 846 votes, a margin of two-tenths of 1 percent. Fraud was widespread but it was most egregious and decisive in Conway County. Clayton contested the election and hired a Plumerville man to collect the names of people who had voted for him. In the face of a looming congressional investigation, Democrats began an elaborate cover-up of the multiple crimes. One of the Democrats in the Morrilton posse turned state's evidence and outlined the whole plot in detail, including oaths to kill anyone who told the story. Before he could testify, he fled to Oregon with his wife and refused to return to Arkansas because he said he would be murdered. George Bentley, the elder of the brothers in the Morrilton posse, negotiated with the Pinkerton detective agency to be a government witness on the ballot theft. On the morning of November 27, Oliver Bentley shot his brother in the head point blank in the presence of another confederate in the five-man posse, the owner of a saddle shop. Oliver Bentley and the other man told the sheriff that they were examining a Smith and Wesson revolver in the saddle shop when the gun went off accidentally. The grandson of the dead man thought it strange that a gun would go off accidentally four times. The sheriff ruled the death accidental.

Wahl, the federal voting supervisor who would be the key witness, came to Plumerville to mill some grain on December 16 and stayed over to play poker with the town marshal and a couple of doctors. At the home of a local doctor that night, Wahl was standing near a glass door when a shot came through, blowing off part of an ear and grazing his head and neck. He fled bleeding to the home of a friend and left the next morning for Little Rock, never to return. His poker companions and others were indicted in federal court at Little Rock for trying to assassinate a federal witness, but they were not convicted. In Conway County, a grand jury indicted Wahl for gambling. He pled guilty from afar and sent the ten-dollar fine rather than risk his life by returning. No one else was charged.

Matters got serious for the Democrats in late January when Clayton, the losing congressional candidate, announced that he was going to

Conway County to personally investigate the election crimes. Republicans pleaded with him to stay away or take armed guards because he would be murdered, but he dismissed the peril. The only room Clayton could find in Plumerville was the rooming house of Mrs. Mary Ann McCraven on the edge of town, where for four days he took depositions from more than one hundred voters. Oliver Bentley tried to work out a deal with Republicans to have indictments for the attempted assassination of Wahl, a federal witness in the ballot-theft investigation, withdrawn and the investigation closed in exchange for allowing the county's disputed votes to be counted for Clayton, but it fell through. Democrats—the numbers and identities have varied over the years—gathered around the coal stove in A. D. Malone's general store in Plumerville and drew straws, the short one going to the designated killer. On the night of January 29, 1889, Clayton and a companion retired to the bedroom parlor along with another boarder, a traveling pottery salesman from Saline County who was working on his accounts. Two murderers—Kenneth Barnes identified them as brothers Robert and Charles Pate, one of whom had drawn the short straw—stood outside the boarding house in the cold. Clayton sat down six feet from the window and a load of buckshot nearly took off his head. He left a young widow and six children.

A congressional investigation of the election eventually concluded that Clayton had been elected, and the Democrat, Clifton R. Breckenridge, was removed for the rest of the term. He won the next election handily over the dispirited insurgents. As for Clayton's murder, one courageous Democrat, Circuit Judge George S. Cunningham, impaneled a grand jury and promised to bring the killer to justice. He lectured the community on the opening day of the grand jury. He called Clayton's killing a political assassination and said the guilty would be found among the most powerful men of the community, a rebuke to Democratic leaders, including the governor and the senior US senator, who had concocted absurd theories about a mistaken revenge killing by a man who turned out to have been lying on his death bed in California the night that Clayton was slain. Judge Cunningham said the killers and plotters should be found and hung regardless of their standing in the community.

"Political assassinations do not originate in the minds of men in the humblest walks of life," he said. "Men who earn their living by the sweat of their brows, whose lives are poems of honor and industry, do not find it in their minds and hearts to conceive assassination; but it is conceived and planned by more influential, fine-haired gentlemen who pretend to be respectable."

The grand jury produced no charges for the murder or for any of the election crimes. The community rallied around the plotters and supplied alibis for all the men involved. The crime wave surrounding the election continued. A Pinkerton detective hired a black man, Joseph W. Smith, to continue the investigation at Plumerville. Smith sent the detective a message saying he had found a man who could identify both Clayton's murderer and the ballot thieves and that he would bring them and other witnesses to Little Rock. That night, on a road a mile north of Plumerville, three white men on horseback corralled Smith while he was on his way home to his wife and five children and shot him in the head at close range. The killing was chalked up to rowdies whom Smith had verbally abused. Richard J. Gray, a mulatto physician and the township constable, found the killer and arrested him. A grand jury of Democrats freed the man and indicted the constable for breach of the peace because he had used insulting language in arresting the killer. Crime, indictments, and trials continued for another year but in the end no one was brought to justice. In 1893, a man named Hickey was charged with killing Clayton, but after a brief trial the jury deliberated a few minutes and acquitted him.

• • •

You might expect that the product of such calamity would be election reform, but it was the opposite. The freshly empowered Democratic government adopted sweeping new voting procedures aimed at excluding African Americans, a fourth of the population, from the political process. Senator W. S. Hanna, who had been elected in 1888 from Conway County, sponsored the first of a sequence of laws to disfranchise African Americans. The poll tax, the Australian ballot*, and the whites-only party primary were instituted. By 1895, the process was

---

*The Australian ballot, first used in 1856 in Australia, hence the name, created a secret ballot and one on which the names of all candidates appeared instead of only prominent contenders. While it was a progressive reform, it served in America to disfranchise blacks because ballots did not contain party symbols and required voters to mark a name. Many blacks were illiterate and tended to mark their votes based on party symbols, so the new ballot served to discourage them from voting and diminished black participation in political life. —E.D.

finished, and the voice of African Americans in the democracy fell silent for seventy years.

When political forces were strong enough or a disappointed candidate insistent enough to uncover election crimes, the institutions of government almost always lacked the will or the purpose to bring justice to bear. That was the case in the factional fight for the governorship in 1913 after newly elected Governor Joe T. Robinson resigned so that he could be chosen by the legislature to succeed US senator Jeff Davis, who died before beginning a new term.

Owing to his traditional strength in the Delta, Stephen Brundidge Jr., a progressive former congressman from Searcy, was the favorite in the special Democratic primary, but George Washington Hays won a slim victory on the strength of a big vote from Phillips County, which waited until all the other votes in the state were reported before delivering a big and surprising vote for Hays, who had the support of the powerful St. Francis River Levee Board. Fraud seemed rather obvious but the Democratic State Central Committee, which was controlled by Hays's faction, refused to allow time to collect poll books and pinpoint the fraud before certifying Hays as the winner. The Pulaski County Circuit Court ordered the committee to give Brundidge a fair hearing, but the Arkansas Supreme Court quickly quashed the injunction on the grounds that courts had no jurisdiction over party primaries. For another seventy-five years, the courts would nearly always find a way to wash their hands of voting fraud. Brundidge tried unsuccessfully to get the legislature to enact a law requiring the publication of poll-tax receipts before every election and jail sentences for people convicted of election fraud, but the House of Representatives defeated it. Voters approved an initiated act carrying some of the reforms in 1916.

But nothing really changed. With Arkansas resting at the bottom of the deepest economic abyss in the nation's history, the vote thieves during the Great Depression were not distracted from their work. Addressing the legislature for the last time in January 1935, Governor J. Marion Futrell said something just had to be done about crooked elections, which were undermining "the very foundations of government." All the election fraud, the governor lamented, was destroying "the good name of the state." In an amazing bit of understatement, Futrell said, "It seems to be conceded that fraud in elections is both possible and practicable without punishment." He said the poll tax had become a simple means for stealing elections. People who buy large blocs of poll-tax receipts own the balance of power in counties, he said. Futrell proposed a range of election reforms, including a voter registration system that would thwart the vote merchants. His plea went unheeded.

One instance in which the courts did play a pivotal role in curtailing election fraud was the GI Revolt in 1946, when Marine hero Sid McMath led a band of veterans in overthrowing the Leo McLaughlin machine at Hot Springs and capturing every county office. The GI Revolt is still the iconic movement that has inspired progressive reforms, such as they have been, for a half-century.

A 1942 grand jury had concluded that every provision of state law for preserving and protecting ballots in Garland County was routinely ignored. Mayor McLaughlin's merry men acquired large blocs of poll-tax receipts from the county collector and they were voted on election day at what were known to be collaborative precincts. McMath rounded up World War II veterans to retake the government from the machine by running for every office in the Democratic primaries. All but McMath, who was running for prosecuting attorney, were overwhelmed by the bloc votes. McMath managed to win narrowly on the strength of votes from little Montgomery County, which was part of the judicial district with Garland County. The telephone line to Mount Ida was down that evening, and McLaughlin's men didn't learn of McMath's solid vote in the outlying county in time to counter it with bogus votes in Hot Springs. But all the defeated GIs then filed as independent candidates for the general election. McMath wanted to challenge thousands of bogus poll taxes but needed to get the case out of the machine-controlled circuit court and into federal court. A friend of McMath, Pat Mullis, agreed to run for Congress as an independent, which would trigger federal jurisdiction if a conspiracy could be proved to have diluted the votes for a candidate for federal office. US District Judge John E. Miller conducted a trial on the challenged poll taxes. A nightclub operator admitted that he had been given two hundred poll-tax receipts, issued in alphabetical order, to vote in the election. Deadbeats, drifters, and drunks would be given drinks or cash to take the receipts around to various precincts to vote for the McLaughlin slate.

• • •

Judge Miller, who was likely to be sympathetic because he had himself been the victor in an independent campaign for the US Senate in 1937, eventually invalidated 1,607 poll-tax receipts, nearly a fourth of the vote in the primaries. The GIs swept every office in the general election. More than a half-century later McMath would write, "Thus, the freedom of the ballot box was returned to the people of Garland County, [and] the rights of dissent and political participation were restored."

Not every instance of election cheating made it into the history books or even into the contemporary public prints, but stories about writing poll taxes into the midwatches of election nights and voting them in absentee boxes or some clever bit of vote theft in this or that county were always the lore of campaigns.

Sid McMath

In every close statewide election, it was commonly understood that there were a number of counties where votes could be manipulated on election night or the days or even weeks afterward.

Recapitulating his first race for governor in an oral-history interview thirty years later, Dale Bumpers described his experience in the preferential primary of 1970, when he barely edged the state's attorney general to reach a runoff with former governor Orval E. Faubus. In the preferential primary, Bumpers was nursing a lead of only a few hundred votes at midnight.

Dale Bumpers

Faubus, who four years earlier had quit after six terms and was making a comeback, thought that the momentum of the newcomer Bumpers would be hard to stop in the two weeks before the runoff election.

I knew that Orval Faubus had a machine and that machine was going to start with a five-thousand-vote lead for me over [Joe] Purcell. I knew they were going to go to work to try to count me out. So at three o'clock in the morning, we began to call sheriffs all over the state in counties we knew that Faubus controlled, pleading with them to guard those ballot boxes with their lives. I remember talking with one sheriff and I won't call his name; he may still be living. I said, "I'm depending on you to watch that ballot box. I've got four hundred votes in your county. That's all I want, just those four hundred, but I want those." Strike that, I had nine hundred votes in that county.

He said, "Don't worry about it, Dale. There's only one little church precinct out here with thirty-two votes. We're going to bed, it's all over with here."

I said, "Well, sheriff, I sure hope you'll protect those votes anyway."

He said, "Don't you worry, you've got your nine hundred votes."

You know, by the following Thursday night I was down to four hundred votes in that county. Finally, they had me down to a nine-hundred-vote lead statewide over Purcell on Thursday night. The vote had to be certified by Friday noon. By Friday noon, they had decided that they couldn't get the other nine hundred votes [to put Purcell into second place instead of Bumpers]. Nobody wanted to go to prison on a federal charge of corruption, so they put the votes back in. When the final tally came in it was like 4,600 votes, right where it had been on Tuesday night.

Four days later, we had an apartment in the Quapaw Towers and we were letting people come from all over the state to give us money [for the runoff]. Here comes the sheriff with his delegation from his county. I think they brought maybe a thousand dollars or whatever, and it was all in cash. . . .

I said, "Sheriff, you promised me faithfully at three o'clock the morning after the election that you'd protect the ballot box up there. You got me down from nine hundred to four hundred votes in four days."

He said, "Next time we'll do it for you!"

That was the culture that I was only gradually starting to compre-hend as I steeped myself in the study of law at the dawn of the sixties. I do not think now that I was naïve. "Vote early and vote often," "wait for the cemetery vote," and all the other common jokes about election dishonesty were as familiar then to me as they were to people in the precincts where they were committed to serious practice. But I thought of those injustices as, if not apocryphal, at least historical and rare, not contemporary and commonplace. That would change abruptly when education gave way to career.

CHAPTER 2
• • • • • • • • • • •

The Boys of Summer

"I have been told and I am convinced that fifty thousand votes can be manipulated in any statewide election. My goal and the goal of my party ought to be to establish the sacredness of the poll once again."

—WINTHROP ROCKEFELLER

They called my father "Slick." Harry Glaze was a four-sport star in the brawling mining town of Joplin, Missouri, during the Depression, which I believe is how he earned the nickname. He also had a mischievous streak, which made it seem especially apt. He was proud of the name and so were his four sons, Tom, Dick, Harry, and the disappointingly named fourth, Larry, who was supposed to have been a girl named Ann (*see,* Tom, Dick, Ann, Harry).

My father was reared in an orphanage, from which he fled from time to time, and it must have been the source of his physical strength and mental toughness. Overcoming the odds of the circumstances may have accounted for the swagger that he carried into adulthood and fatherhood. As far as I could determine, he set out quite consciously to instill the qualities in all his boys. He didn't mind if any of his sons got whipped at school, but he did not want to hear that one of them backed down from a fight. We knew that a whipping would be our due if Dad heard about it so we might as well take it from someone at school and get our own licks in. No Glaze boy was ever to betray fear, and if a confrontation arose he was expected to land the first punch, preferably squarely on the nose.

Slick Glaze in his time was the personification of the town. Though it had undergone civilizing influences by the time he was growing up, Joplin in an earlier time was known for its lawlessness and meanness. It sprang up around the lead and zinc mines, and the miners, smelters, and railroad workers caroused and gambled in the many bars and cheap hotels around town. The place was named after a Methodist preacher, Harris Joplin, who organized the first congregation, but Rev. Joplin didn't leave his imprint on anything about the town except the name—certainly not his piety. A period in its early growing days was known as the Reign of Terror. The James and Younger gangs found the town hospitable from time to time. Bonnie and Clyde, the romantic gangsters of the Depression, hid out there for several weeks, robbed a few stores and then, when a neighbor tipped the police, shot their way out of town, leaving all their possessions and two dead lawmen behind. So toughness seemed to be a necessity if not the highest civic virtue when I entered Joplin High School.

Like my Dad, I went out for every sport, although boxing, which was one of his prized skills, was not in the curriculum. What I lacked in skill, which was immeasurable, I made up in fearlessness. I played end for the football Eagles at a time when you were expected to play both ways, on offense and defense. I relished defense and it was my goal to hit the running back or quarterback so hard that he would have to leave the game. Whenever I was on the field or in any competitive situation, I was infected with the impulse to earn my father's admiration in some way. Knocking another player out of the game, whether he was on my side or the other, gave my father something to brag about. As a senior, I injured one of our players in practice. The coach stopped the practice, put his arm around my shoulder and said, "Tom, you can't keep hurting our players. We don't have enough as it is." If they had conducted a personality test when I finished high school and asked me for one word to describe myself, it would have been "tough." If you think you are tough, the necessities to prove it are boundless.

I do not want to disparage my mother's influence on my character development. Mamie Rose Guterman was the daughter of a St. Louis labor boss, as the media and management have always called anyone who was in the leadership of a trade union. I always sort of liked the moniker. She and Dad and the rest of the family were always stalwart union people. Mamie Rose was nearly six feet tall and strong, towering over my father in more ways than physical dimension, and the boys, except me, inherited her height gene. She was as tough as Dad but not in a malevolent way. She abhorred violence and when she could she would restrain his hand, especially if it was about to be raised against one of us. The toughness manifested itself in a different way. Unlike my father's sometimes nonchalant approach to work, Mom's rule was that every task had to be finished and never put off, and you had to do it better than anyone else would do it. If others slack, you step into the breach and do the job. Much of her life she labored hard in an airless room of a Dur-A-Flex Corp. plant that molded polymer materials for airplanes. There was frequent sickness and she worked extra hours and extra hard to cover for those who were out. Eventually, the chemicals and fibers and emphysema got the better of her, too.

It would be some years and many life experiences later that I discovered that there are higher and even more rewarding virtues than the obdurate doggedness that I admired and strove so hard to achieve in my youth. I do not know but suspect that "tough" is not an adjective that colleagues and friends would quickly associate with me in my ripened years. But I am much surer that in my callow days that self-image shaped my ambitions and, either directly or obliquely, the opportunities that came my way, and determined whether I took them or shunned them.

An hour's drive down US Highway 71 from Joplin, the University of Arkansas was the surest place to satisfy the abiding passion of my life, which was athletics. Word of my prowess had not traveled the ninety miles to Fayetteville so in the fall of 1956 I walked on as a Razorback without a scholarship. I expected to make fans forget Bobby Proctor, the 150-pound captain of the "Twenty-four Little Pigs" who won the conference championship in 1954, and Bud Brooks, the pint-sized All-American guard from Wynne who won the Outland Trophy as the nation's best collegiate lineman and starred in the 1955 Senior Bowl.

The illusion was short-lived. It was Jack Mitchell's second and next-to-last season as the Razorback head coach, and if Mitchell was ever aware of my presence on the practice field that fall it was lost on me. Patience was not my best virtue and the frustrations grew with every practice. A freshman walk-on was not apt to get much playing time even in scrimmages, where the coaches were supposed to assay the talent pool that they had assembled before settling on the best two-dozen or so who would get the playing time. From the ranks of the scrubs on the sideline, I began to see plays that I would have made had I been on the field. I knew I was better than some of those guys, and I wanted to prove it. One afternoon I couldn't restrain myself. Without a nod from the coaches, I strapped on my helmet and dashed into the defensive huddle, tapping one of the linemen as if Coach Mitchell had sent me in. On the next play, Don Christian, the quarterback, faded back, and as he jumped up to pass I hit him in midair and drove him to the ground. As I was raising myself off Christian, I heard Coach Mitchell yell, "Who made that hit?" One of the other linemen waved a hand merrily and Mitchell shouted, "Good hit." Arguing the point would seem childish so I jogged back to the sideline and took my place with the scrubs. The incident, I thought, was a metaphor for my predicament. I had neither the reputation nor the physical dimensions to catch the coaches' attention, not that fall anyway, and I did not have the patience to wait. I returned to the dressing room, turned in my pads and helmet and said goodbye to a football career. Although I would not have admitted it, I think I dimly discerned that I had learned a valuable lesson, which was that I was not always going to be the best. Dad was disappointed and would not speak to me about my choices for a long time.

Baseball was another matter. It was the sport that best suited my modest physical attributes and I quickly found a home with the diamond Razorbacks as a catcher and reserve outfielder. The catcher my first year was Lamar Drummond, a multisport athlete from the mean streets of Strong, a tough sawmill town near the Louisiana border, who had averaged seven yards a carry as a reserve fullback for the Razorbacks in his single season with the football team. Drummond had the forearms of Popeye and, now that I think about it, a strikingly similar visage and the same affable fearlessness. A thirty-six-inch bat was like a twig in his hands and he could rifle the ball around the infield from his crouch behind the plate with more velocity than most of us could get from a running start. But Lamar left for the St. Louis Cardinals organization after his sophomore year and would have become a Cardinal star had the military not taken a couple of critical years out of his career. By his return, the Cardinals had invested in Tim McCarver, who would help them win three pennants, and Drummond retired from the sport. But his early departure from the Razorbacks gave me a leg up. I played three seasons.

I never achieved stardom but those were glorious springtimes. My ardor for the sport and fealty to the team never ebbed but grew stronger with the passing years.

Switching my affections from football to baseball was timely in other ways. The more leisurely training and the lower profile of collegiate baseball made it more congenial with scholarship. I studied far more assiduously than I had in high school and graduated with a bachelor's degree in business. I married my high school sweetheart, Susan Askins, when I was a sophomore. She worked at a church and I drove a truck part time to keep us and our rapidly growing family sheltered in Terry Village, an old Army barracks where a flat rented for thirty-five dollars a month plus utilities. But the life of scholar and breadwinner apparently had not planed my rougher edges, nor had it dislodged the chip from my shoulder. Not long ago, I went to a friend's office where several men were gathered. One was a contemporary at the university. He announced my presence by saying, "Here comes a judge who once slugged opposing players on the basketball court." During a fraternity basketball game at the field-house gymnasium, he had watched me walk up to an opposing player and flatten him with one blow to the jaw. There had been some rough play between us, which caused the fellow to mutter "bastard" as we jogged back down the court. My daddy's unbidden voice was always in my ear on such occasions. No one was going to call Slick Glaze's boy a bastard and get away with it. I discovered no pleasure in being reminded that I had been a rash and intemperate young man, although I am sure that on the court that day I was rather proud of myself.

Dad wanted me to be a lawyer—he thought there ought to be one in the family—and I had to resist the gravitational pull of the ministry. I looked into enrolling in the graduate seminary at Phillips University at Enid, Oklahoma, which was affiliated with the Disciples of Christ Church. The law also seemed to be a more practical option than coaching baseball, which was an enchantment of my fanciful moments, so, in the fall of 1960, I entered law school without a very clear notion about what I would do with the education I would get there. At least I was finally fulfilling my father's wishes on something.

I went to the hospital one semester and was diagnosed with hypertension, which forced me to withdraw from school for a while. It took seven and a half years to finish my college studies and get a law license, and I found myself in the spring of 1964 with a law degree, a growing family, military obligations, and no fetching job prospects. With a reserve officer's commission and a fresh promotion to first lieutenant, I awaited orders for active duty, probably in Vietnam, where the escalation of the American war effort was beginning, and I looked around for a temporary job to fill the interregnum. I actually yearned to go to Vietnam. In the spring of 1964 it was not yet the bloody quagmire that it would become, but for a young man who thought himself daring it held the promise of mystery, adventure, and fulfillment. Besides, after the hand-to-mouth struggles of the past several years, officer's pay was a powerful magnet. But by September, after the famous sea battles between American destroyers and North Vietnamese torpedo boats in the Gulf of Tonkin impelled President Johnson into a major buildup of forces in Southeast Asia, I had twice failed the Army's physical examination, which put a permanent hold on a warrior's career.

Arkansas's Byzantine politics had become a small but unavoidable fascination. In the early 1960s, it intruded upon every law student's studies, most conspicuously in constitutional law. Governor Orval E. Faubus, who had defied the federal courts' constitutional judgment that Little Rock's schools must begin to be integrated without delay, was running for his sixth and final term and it seemed certain that there would be a historic showdown that year between the old populist and the renegade scion of the great Hudson River clan, Winthrop Rockefeller. Rockefeller had moved to Petit Jean Mountain in Conway County ten years earlier to escape the notoriety of a gaudy divorce from Bobo Sears and the disapprobation of his Edwardian family. The word circulated at the law school that spring that John H. Haley, a lawyer with the Rose law firm at Little Rock (at that time called Rose, Meek, House, Barron, and Nash), was hiring young lawyers for an election-law research project, which seemed to be the kind of transitory work that would fit my uncertain situation. I did not know then, though I should have surmised, that Rockefeller largely underwrote the project. Soon after going to work there, I opened an envelope and found a cashier's check to the organization from the Chase Manhattan Bank, the Rockefellers' bank. I drove down to the Rose offices for an interview with Haley, and he hired me for a monthly salary of $450, which seemed princely enough for work that I expected to last only a few months.

The job proved to be longer than I intended, only partly because my military obligation ended abruptly owing to health issues. The labor of cleaning up elections became more than an employment convenience. It became a mission and, yes, maybe an obsession, which would propel about every turn I made in a legal career that spanned forty-five years.

John Haley's project was called the Election Research Council, and when I arrived in May 1964 we worked from offices in the Rose firm on Third Street four blocks west of the downtown business district. In August, we moved into an old frame building a block east of the Rose offices. Haley, a tanned, athletic man with a mordant wit, was a liberal Democrat, and indeed in every way but financially the Election Research Council was a bipartisan undertaking. Haley was the chairman, and the board comprised people who were nonpartisan or else Democratic officeholders or local party officials: state Rep. Hardy W. Croxton of Rogers, a reformer who had pushed a constitutional amendment through the legislature in 1963 replacing the poll tax with a system of permanent voter registration; former state Senator Sam Levine of Pine Bluff, a lawyer and a Democrat; Mrs. E. E. Elkins of Fort Smith, the state president of the League of Women Voters; Field K. Wasson of Siloam Springs, a lawyer, vice president of a bank and a Democrat; Dr. Don Clark of Arkadelphia, a dentist and a Democrat; Mrs. Dorothy Stuck of Marked Tree, editor of the *Marked Tree Tribune* and a liberal Republican; Rev. Sam J. Allen of Little Rock, executive secretary of the Arkansas Council of Churches; and Bob Fisher, editor of the *Crossett News Observer* and a Democrat who later became a supporter of Winthrop Rockefeller and then an assistant to four state attorneys general. Levine, one of a handful of state lawmakers who stood against the tide of bigotry in the aftermath of the constitutional collision at Central High School in 1957, died in the weeks after the council's formation.

Whether Rockefeller instigated the formation of ERC or whether Haley or others solicited his support I was never sure, but it was not the only time that he used his riches to bring about social and cultural change in his adopted state. At his direction, a considerable amount of his fortune was employed after his death in that pursuit. But in election reform he had personal as well as benevolent ends. At first an ally of Faubus when the young governor asked him to chair the Arkansas Industrial Development Commission, Rockefeller was deeply disillusioned by the governor's use of the state militia to prevent nine African American children from attending classes at Central High School and by the orgy of bigotry and regression that it begot. He had developed an idyllic fondness for the state after settling on the majestic mountaintop, and then experienced the dismaying discovery that it was a different place altogether than he had imagined. By 1960 he had begun to formulate a strategy for changing the state, and it involved his own election as governor, the only perch from which one could shape the laws and political institutions and bring some slight influence to bear on the social and cultural currents of the state. Politics was so corrupt and the Democratic Party, dominant for almost a century, so incestuous that his election would be possible only by the reconstruction of the moribund Republican Party for his own ends and by somehow reforming the machinery and conduct of elections. He was persuaded that fraud, intimidation, and sheer ignorance and carelessness in collecting votes would be sufficient to cost him the election. Haley would later calculate that the political powers when they were linked in common cause could manipulate fifty thousand votes in a statewide election. Seriously contested statewide elections typically fell within that margin.

The Election Research Council was only part of Rockefeller's strategy for bringing enough rectitude to elections that he might have a chance to win. That was not on my mind when I began to research the election code that spring, although there would come a time when I quite consciously and earnestly joined that cause.

At the outset, the Election Research Council had an educational mission and, in a sense, even the subsequent investigations of election fraud that roiled the political establishment were intended only to inform voters about how their democracy functioned, or malfunctioned. Haley assembled a team of mostly recent law graduates—Jim Moser, Troy Wiley, Charles D. Matthews, Robert J. Brown, Norman Smith, and me—along with a young newspaperman, Kenneth Cole Danforth, who had worked at the *Arkansas Gazette* and would subsequently go to Washington and Vietnam for *Time* magazine. Kay Collett, a young political scientist and an excellent researcher, joined the team in the summer. We were to research the state's crazy quilt of election laws, which had been amended helter skelter over a century, and find out what actually went on in the election precincts—how well those laws were observed by the county officials and precinct judges and clerks. We sent detailed questionnaires to election officials about how voting was required to be conducted and how voting was conducted and how the ballots were handled, counted, reported, and preserved. When he announced the survey, Haley said he expected it to show that election officials often did not know what the law required them to do and frequently were not equipped to comply even if they knew. The secret ballot, for instance, was a revered doctrine but it existed only in the Fourth of July bombast of the politicians. People marked their ballots at tables, on fire hoses or against the wall in clear view and often with the assistance of election judges and fellow voters. For three-quarters of a century, the law required counties to furnish a voting booth for every one hundred voters in each precinct, but it was universally ignored. Bob Brown designed a collapsible corrugated paper booth and took it to Hoerner Boxes, Inc., of Little Rock, which said it could produce the booths for three dollars fifty cents each. With wonderful flourish, we offered to provide the booths at cost to every county in the state and when county officials showed little ardor for the concept—they couldn't afford it or there was no place to store them, they said—we urged private citizens to order them for their precincts, and we would have them delivered. A handful of counties eventually signed on. State Rep. David Pryor of Camden, just beginning a storied political career, urged every civic organization in Ouachita County to sponsor a booth or two.

We prepared a little booklet explaining in simple terms what the law required election judges and clerks to do and exactly how ballot boxes were to be opened and the ballots counted, how votes were to be reported and how ballots were to be stored. We printed five thousand of them and tried to get them into the hands of judges and clerks of all seventy-five counties, but we could not ensure that they were read or followed.

That was the popular phase of ERC's civic service. John Haley had his suspicions about how elections really functioned, founded on anecdotes and the few instances where election disputes went to court, as in the Screeton-Gunter election fraud suit four years earlier, but we decided to make a serious examination of our own in the party primaries and general election. By late summer, the pleasantries of civic action were over. Messing with a hoary tradition like vote thievery, we would discover, is very dangerous business.

CHAPTER 3

• • • • • • • • • • • •

Absentee Democracy

"When a hound dog can freely vote in seventy-five counties, the laws are in sad shape."

—JOHN HALEY

Investigating elections can be hazardous, Arkansas history having recorded a few violent deaths that were associated with election inquiries. The prospect for violence often could be measured in direct proportion to the availability of alcohol, as either a lubricant or a prize. But I was barely conscious of the risk when Jim Moser and I set off in late July 1964 to monitor the Democratic primary in Yellville, the county seat of sparsely populated Marion County on the Missouri border, which was just beginning to experience growth from the creation of Bull Shoals Lake. Haley dispatched law graduates to other counties where anecdotal evidence from recent elections raised strong suspicions of voting fraud. The Democratic primaries were lackluster affairs in 1964 because Faubus, who was running for his sixth term, faced no serious opponent in his party for the first time in his career, and no other major statewide race was on the ballot. But local elections were often the most contentious and invited the most skullduggery. Kenneth R. Smith, a friend and classmate in law school, was running for state representative in the Democratic primary and was in a tough race with the incumbent establishment candidate. Haley had complaints about the elections in Marion County and he told us to go up to Yellville the day before the election and keep tabs on the balloting and the vote counting in the town boxes. Another old classmate, Don Adams, had joined Smith in law practice at Yellville, and we drove to his home on Monday evening. We were sipping coffee in his living room and talking about the race when Smith barged in unannounced. He walked past us without a word and asked Don if he had a gun.

"Yes," Adams said, "it's in the bedroom."

"Get it and meet me at the square," Smith said.

He asked if we were spending the night and we said we were. He told us to go with Adams and left. Adams returned from his bedroom with a pistol and the three of us jumped in his car and drove the few blocks to the courthouse, a native-stone English Medieval building in the middle of town. Adams said that Smith's opponent and his supporters customarily distributed bottles of liquor the night before an election and that if Smith could prevent that from happening, he thought there was a good chance of winning. Giving away whiskey at elections was a time-honored vote-getting tactic in many counties. In hopes of containing ballot fraud, the Republicans who ran things for a period after the Civil War passed a law in 1868 prohibiting the free distribution of liquor on election day.

Adams angled his car up to a low stone wall that kept the waters of Crooked Creek out of the courthouse during spring storms. A man with a gun approached Adams's door.

"Where are they?" Adams asked.

Suddenly, two cars sped off in opposite directions and Adams said, "You take one and we'll take the other." We roared off in pursuit of one of the cars. Adams said the men we were chasing were giving away free liquor for votes and Smith wanted to stop the exchange. The chase lasted for more than an hour. We raced around the twisting mountain roads through Marion and Baxter Counties. Seated nervously in the back seat, I wondered what we would do if we caught them. Shoot them? It was our good fortune, I think, that they navigated the back roads better than we did. While Smith lost that precinct, he narrowly won the election. He believed, however, that he would have lost if the whiskey barter had not been stopped.

We spent the next day at a precinct where election officials were suspected of playing cavalierly with the ballot box. We were distinctly not wanted there, but Moser and I could not enter the polling room anyway until the polls closed, the law at that time not permitting observers inside the polls. The legislature would rectify that a dozen years later after a contentious special election in Conway County in which poll observers were authorized by a United States district judge.

Although several of us had joined the project in May or June 1964, not until August, two weeks after the preferential party primary, did we announce the formation of the Election Research Council. Governor Faubus said he was more than slightly suspicious that Winthrop Rockefeller might be behind the organization. Haley disputed it. Ten days later, Haley offered a brief review of what he had found from our observations at a handful of precincts around the state in the Democratic primary and from investigations of reports on the voting that came into the office. He said there had been widespread double voting (people voting more than once, usually in different counties), an almost universal lack of voting booths in spite of the law's requirement that they be furnished at every polling place, illegal issuance of poll-tax receipts, electioneering closer to the polls than the law permitted, unauthorized people counting ballots, haphazard ballot counting generally, and failure to post voting results as the law required. We would get a much clearer, and sometimes more harrowing, picture of election conduct in the fall.

For the first time since 1890, the high-water mark of the farmer-labor revolt and the beginning of the disfranchisement of African Americans, the Arkansas general election in 1964 amounted to more than a rote drill for the counties, mainly because Rockefeller was the first non-Democrat to contend seriously for governor or for any other statewide or regional office. For seventy-five years, only in the rural zones and small towns of the central Ozarks where secession had not been popular in 1861— Benton, Marion, Searcy, Newton, Madison, Van Buren, and Carroll Counties—had Republicans competed even in local races. In all those years, the lonely GOP cohort in the legislature rarely rose to five out of 135 seats.

Faubus acted during the spring like he would not run again, finally yielding to a carefully staged draft. Sheriff Marlin Hawkins and some of his friends from Conway County brought Faubus's filing fee in a potato sack to the capitol. All right, Faubus said, he would run if people insisted, but the sixth term would be his last. He clearly relished a campaign against Rockefeller because it gave him the chance to rekindle the idealistic embers of his youth and of his socialist father, Sam, who had named him Orval Eugene after the great Socialist Party leader Eugene V. Debs. In the next election after Faubus's birth, the five-time Socialist candidate for president had polled nearly 7 percent of the vote in Arkansas, much of that in the Ozarks countryside. Faubus could run against Winthrop's grandfather, John D. Rockefeller, and the barons of Standard Oil, who had driven the price of coal oil to ten cents a jug and who in Faubus's itinerant youth, as he told it, had cruised the streets of Northern metropolises in black limousines. At every junction where he could draw a crowd, Faubus recounted riding on the back of his daddy's wagon from Huntsville back to Combs squeezing the coal-oil can between his knees and keeping a raw potato plugged firmly into the spout to prevent the spilling of a single drop of Coal Oil Johnny's precious elixir, which lit the kerosene lamps in the Faubus cabin on Greasy Creek.

In Faubus's telling, Rockefeller was the pampered and divorced scion of a family that never knew want like an Arkansawyer did, and the rich

man did not understand or appreciate the homely values of people reared in hard work and reverence for family and forebears. It would turn out to be a remarkably close race until the final weeks, when someone tipped Faubus that a tractor operator clearing brush for a Rockefeller grass farm in Lonoke County seemed to have tipped over a couple of grave markers in an old untended cemetery. It seemed to be the perfect metaphor for the arrogance and disdain that Faubus wanted people to imagine was the Yankee's soul. He accused Rockefeller of "cemetery desecration." Rockefeller first scoffed at the accusation, then prepared an elaborate television commercial rebutting it, which merely gave the issue new legs. Faubus confided to reporters at a post-election party at the Governor's Mansion that the tombstone issue gave him what proved to be a comfortable margin on election night.

The presumed peril to Faubus's reign and to the political status quo that fall was enough to crank up the deviant election machine in numerous counties where it functioned whenever the need arose. Two other issues, constitutional amendments that were placed on the ballot by initiative petitions, also supplied incentives for the machine to gin up the extra votes that the electorate did not feel obliged to supply.

What would become Amendment 51 raised a direct challenge to the whole culture of election theft by outlawing the poll tax as a requirement for voting and erecting in its place a system of permanent voter registration, where people signed up to vote in person once in a lifetime and earned the right to vote thereafter without tribute or favor. The poll tax had been instituted as a way to discourage the black franchise—you had to purchase a poll-tax receipt for one dollar every election year—and also to control large blocs of votes. Someone, a plantation owner or a nursing home operator, for example, could buy big blocs of receipts in the names of his sharecroppers and farm workers and the residents of his nursing homes. The poll tax already was doomed. The Twenty-fourth Amendment to the US Constitution barred states from using a poll tax to restrict people's voting in federal elections and was ratified in January 1964. The federal courts two years later would apply the ban to state and local elections as well, but the Arkansas initiative moved the process of free voting ahead of the courts. The Arkansas legislature chose not to join forty other states in ratifying the US amendment. Privately, Rockefeller had helped fund the voting initiative but the drive was led publicly by progressive forces such as the League of Women Voters, the Arkansas State AFL-CIO, the United Steelworkers Union, and state Rep. Hardy Croxton, one of ERC's founding directors.

The other initiative would have legalized casino gambling in Garland County. Rev. Roy Galyean, a Baptist preacher from Gravette who served three somnolent terms in the state House of Representatives, had a sudden seizure of piety and goaded the House into voting ninety-one to three to adopt a resolution demanding that gambling at Hot Springs be curbed. In March 1964, Faubus sent the state police to the resort to shut down the slot machines and blackjack tables that had been running wide open on Central Avenue. The gambling forces quickly gathered petitions to put an amendment on the ballot permitting ten casinos in Garland County, and Faubus's press secretary, Bob Troutt, helped run the campaign for its ratification.

Publicly, Faubus gave the voter initiative a lukewarm endorsement and the gambling amendment a noncommittal shrug—he personally opposed gambling, he said, but it ought to be a local matter. Privately, he circulated the word that he would not be unhappy to see the voter amendment defeated and legalized gambling ratified. Indeed, when the big bloc votes in absentee boxes were analyzed after the general election, Faubus and gambling carried the day, and the voter law failed by big and amazingly similar margins. In the overall count, however, gambling failed decisively, and over the next year the slots and card tables were brought out of storage at The Vapors, Southern Club, Black Orchid, and other gambling dens and the games returned on the same sub-rosa basis as before. Three years later, Rockefeller's state police director would shut them down for good—that is, until 2005, when the legislature, with Governor Mike Huckabee's assent, gave the pari-mutuel parlors at Hot Springs and West Memphis a green light to install gambling machines.

Arkansas voters ratified the voter-registration amendment at the 1964 general election, and the poll tax died an unlamented death, which did more than anything else, starting with the next election, in 1966, to spawn an era of real and broad reform. It would not vanquish the vote thieves but it would make their labors harder.

This last general election under the poll tax provided a good primer on its evils and also on the hardiness of vote fraud and the difficulty of tracking it down and bringing it to justice. Even with the small band of

election observers dispatched by the Election Research Council and Republican agents that Rockefeller recruited in a number of counties to monitor the voting, detecting fraud while it was in the making proved nearly impossible, and obtaining evidence of it after the fact was difficult and often dangerous.

Nowhere did it prove harder than in Faubus's home county of Madison, where, unlike anywhere else in Arkansas, Republicans and Democrats had struggled in rough parity since before the Civil War, when one of the county's two delegates to the secession convention demurred alone in the final vote to leave the union, and then served after the war as the state's first Republican and Reconstruction governor. As a young teacher and even then a political activist, Faubus had watched as Democrats, who thought the Republicans were about to steal an election that was rightfully theirs, lined up at the courthouse to do battle with local Republicans, who were arrayed across the square. Men came to town from the hills and creeks armed with rifles, pistols, shotguns, and clubs, Faubus remembered. The sheriff, who had somehow come into possession of a couple of machine guns, set up in a second-story window of the courthouse. As Faubus told it, when the election commission chairman came out with the election certificate to read the results (the Democrats had won), a handkerchief covered a pistol in his other hand. Everyone returned home unscathed.

In the 1964 election, however, Madison County Republicans were pretty sure that the Democrats were stealing the election. A clue to the importance that they attached to the election was that more poll-tax receipts were issued than there were voting-age people in the county, according to the 1960 census. The county had established a reputation for an unusually high quotient of citizenship. In the runoff primary for governor in 1954, the locally reared upstart, Orval Faubus, had received a vote that was 107 percent of the county's eligible voters, which were those who had met the law's requirement that they obtain a poll-tax receipt before the election.

Joe Gaspard of Fayetteville, a paid worker for Rockefeller, went to the county clerk's office the day before the 1964 election and asked to examine the absentee-ballot applications, but the clerk said he could not see them. Gaspard telephoned John Haley, and on Tuesday morning Haley drove to Huntsville. Perhaps knowing of the penchant for hooliganism around elections he took with him Bob K. Scott, another young lawyer who had gone to work for Rockefeller and who would later become the governor's commissioner of revenues. At the courthouse they met up with Dotson Collins, a farmer who chaired the Republican County Committee. About three o'clock all three men went into the office of county clerk Charles Whorton. The *Arkansas Gazette* reported that about forty people, including county judge Clarence Watson and circuit clerk Wayne McChristian, both Democrats, were milling around the office. Haley exchanged pleasantries with Whorton and asked to see the absentee-ballot applications. Whorton said they were locked in his safe and he was not going to open it with so many people around.

Let the *Gazette* reporter tell it from there:

> The conversation became crisp. McChristian presently suggested that Haley and his companions could be locked up for 48 hours for investigation.
>
> Watson said, "We'll just get the sheriff over here to lock up you boys."
>
> Haley stood up to leave. An unidentified younger man told him, "He told you to stay in this room. Sit back down."
>
> Haley asked the man, "Are you a deputy?"
>
> The man replied, "I can be in a minute."
>
> Another person, also unidentified, said, "Stick around tonight and you might be dead."
>
> The crowd outside had begun to mutter. A small group of Republicans, having heard of the trouble from their headquarters a short distance away, arrived at the courthouse. They looked ready for a fight. Tension began to build up rapidly.
>
> Then two state police troopers who had been waiting nearby entered the clerk's office and went into the room with Haley and the others. Haley left and walked to the Republican headquarters. The troopers arrived a few minutes later and asked them not to return to the courthouse. They said a crowd of people was waiting for him and his companions there and they did not think two troopers could handle the situation.
>
> Before leaving for Fayetteville, Haley left instructions with the Madison County Republicans on how to check the absentee-ballot counting and how to challenge votes.

Needless to say, no Republican ever got to see the Madison County absentee-ballot applications, or any other election records. A month after the election, Republicans obtained an order from Chancellor Thomas F. Butt allowing them to copy the list of people who had voted in the election, but Whorton appealed the order to the state supreme court. The Republicans went to Whorton's office from time to time to see the absentee-ballot applications but the clerk never had the time to open the vault where he said they were stored. On January 11, 1965, Carl White of

Springdale, a Republican field worker, went to the clerk's office and asked Whorton to be allowed to photograph absentee voting records. He said an unidentified man slugged him and threatened him with a paperweight. Before going to a Fayetteville hospital for treatment of an ear injury, White reported the incident to the sheriff, who had been standing in the doorway when the roughhousing occurred. But the sheriff told a reporter later that he was not looking in that direction when the incident occurred, and White could not identify the man except that he was in his fifties, so the sheriff said he was not going to investigate it. Several Republican women returned the next day to ask to copy the records, but a deputy clerk slammed the door on them. Whorton said the women had followed his deputy around the office making catty remarks so she got fed up with them. The women said they would be back.

The authorities, whoever they were, took care of the matter with finality. That night, someone broke into the courthouse and stole the records of the election: absentee-ballot applications, absentee-ballot list, lists of those who voted, tally sheets, and the election certificates. The door to the walk-in vault in Whorton's office was latched but had been left unlocked for several years because, he explained, the lock was cranky and often took a long time to open. Whorton said he had no idea who stole the voting records or why. Money and everything in the vault except the election records were undisturbed.

"I can't comprehend this thing," Whorton said. "It beats me."

The state police prowled around the offices the next day but the thief left a cold trail. The FBI sent an agent to Huntsville to check on the theft because it could also have been a federal crime. Farrell Faubus, the governor's son, was the deputy prosecuting attorney for the county. The crime mystified him. No charges were ever filed; no suspect was ever identified.

It would be another nine months, on October 18, before the Republicans won a hollow victory. The supreme court ruled that Judge Butt was right and that the Republicans should have been able to see the voting records, a doctrine so elemental that it beggared challenge by the state. Associate Justice Jim Johnson, the former White Citizens Council leader who had helped foment the resistance at Central High School in 1957 and who in a few months would be the Democratic nominee for governor, wrote the unambiguous opinion.

"The denial of the public of reasonable access to public records is not conducive to the perpetuation of our form of government," Johnson wrote.

By that summer, the Republicans had thought of another route: the voter lists that were stored in the individual ballot boxes. But the Madison County Election Commission took care of that. It voted two to one to destroy the records, the single Republican demurring. One of the two Democratic commissioners was the governor's brother. They acted on the advice of Attorney General Bruce Bennett, who had called the Election Research Council's election investigations "Hitler-type smears." When the destruction of the records came to light, Bennett explained to a reporter for the *Gazette* that he recalled his office having written a legal opinion to an official of some county saying that it would be all right to destroy ballots six months after an election if there were no election dispute. He guessed it must have been Madison County. In the parlance of mountain politics and the quaint jurisprudence of General Bennett, a quarrel over access to election records and their ultimate theft did not involve an election dispute.

• • •

If you want to steal an election, the absentee box is the place to begin, and if you want to calculate the likelihood of fraud in a county, first figure the percentage of its total vote that is cast in absentia. The higher the percentage, the greater the chance that bogus votes are being cast in substantial numbers. In the intervening years since the 1964 election, many states, including Arkansas, have tightened the procedures for obtaining and counting absentee votes while making it easier to vote absentee. Flexible early-voting schedules also have lessened the need to vote by absentee ballot. But absentee boxes are still the battleground of election disputes. The seating of a United States senator from Minnesota in 2009 was held up for six months while election officials and then the courts tried to determine which of tens of thousands of absentee ballots were legitimate votes under Minnesota law.

The absentee vote was particularly vulnerable to fraud in tandem with the poll tax. In a tight and spirited race in 1958 between Congressman Brooks Hays and Dr. Dale Alford, a segregationist write-in candidate who eventually won, the sheriff was reported to be holed up in one room of the Conway County Courthouse late on election night writing out poll-tax receipts, which were ferried to another room, where a deputy filled out the ballots for the phantom voters and deposited them in the absentee box, all marked for the sheriff's longtime friend, Congressman Hays. We found that to be a common practice in other Arkansas counties. Dorothy Stuck, who was a member of the Poinsett County Library Board (and a founder of the Election Research Council), tells of an election evening when the library had a one-mill tax on the ballot. It was winning in the rest of the county but the vote was close in Trumann. She was told that when a certain key county official, who happened to oppose the tax, came in, she should low-ball the pro-tax vote in the rest of the county by one hundred votes or so. That way, the official would underestimate the number of poll-tax receipts and absentee ballots they would need to manufacture during the night to ensure the tax's defeat. She did and the tax overcame the absentee tide and passed by about fifty votes.

Election laws and the observance of them were so lax that anyone with a willful intent to corrupt the election had no trouble finding a way to multiply the votes for his favorite candidates. The day before the general election in 1964 Haley held a news conference at Little Rock to warn that ten thousand to fifteen thousand absentee votes were almost certain to be cast illegally the next day. In a random search in Conway County we had found twelve persons holding poll taxes who were below the legal voting age and others who were listed as the wives of known bachelors. Haley showed photographs of absentee-ballot applications of seven people who had voted illegally in the county two years earlier and who had poll-tax receipts ready to vote again illegally the next day.

"I can take my pet basset hound, Harvey, get him a poll tax in every county in this state and he could vote by absentee ballot in every county," Haley said. "When a hound dog can freely vote in seventy-five counties, the laws are in sad shape."

Four counties—Madison, Perry, Poinsett, and Conway—were far ahead of the rest in the share of votes that were cast by people who could not make it to the polls on election day 1964. At least one in every ten votes in those counties was cast absentee. In Tyronza in Poinsett County, one in every six people on the eligible voting list got an absentee ballot. In a typical county, three or four out of a hundred votes might be absentee, a true reflection of the share of voters who expected to be discommoded on election day. Lacking the resources and staff for a wider investigation, Haley's little band of poll sleuths (by that time, I was the executive director of the organization) concentrated on the absentee votes in the run-up to the general election and afterward.

Days before the election, we reported instances of fraud in absentee balloting to several prosecuting attorneys. The prosecutors performed cursory investigations here and there, but no one was ever convicted.

Our men did not originate every complaint. A few brave souls helped. Dorothy Stuck, a high school history teacher who had quit to help her husband, Howard, run the family's three newspapers in Poinsett County, had watched with rising anger as the election count was manipulated year after year. Everyone knew how it worked. Big farm owners and other estimable men of the community acquired poll-tax receipts for workers, patients, or just phantom residents and then voted them, usually by the absentee ballot. One man patted his hip pocket and told her, "I can deliver you five hundred votes right here."

Shocked by Governor Faubus's exploitation of racial bigotry and by the defeat of Congressman Hays in 1958 and enraged by Faubus's cynical manipulation of welfare recipients—a five-dollar monthly raise in the cash benefit the month before every election—Stuck became a Republican, albeit a liberal Republican, which was not then an oxymoron. She would later serve as regional director of the US Office for Civil Rights for the decade of the seventies, the critical period of compliance with school-desegregation orders, the Voting Rights Act, and the fair-housing law in the states of the South and Southwest.

"I had seen the election fraud go on for so long over there," Stuck said later. "I just decided that I was going to do whatever I could to fix it."

A few days before the 1964 election, she copied the names of everyone who had applied for an absentee ballot for the general election and published them in the *Marked Tree Tribune*, the family's flagship paper. (They also owned the *Trumann Democrat* and the *Lepanto News Record* in Poinsett County.) People began to tell her that this person had been dead for years and that person had been gone for years. Several lived in Memphis. Clearly, hundreds of people were going to be voted without their knowledge or consent. She called me to report her findings and suspicions. I told her that she needed to get affidavits from as many people as she could. Stuck took her little portable typewriter, tracked down a number of people, including nonresidents, typed their statements that their signatures on ballot applications were forgeries, and got their signatures on the affidavits.

County clerk Max J. Edens mailed more than 175 absentee ballots to PO Box 256 at Trumann and another large batch to PO Box 27. The recipients included nonresidents who later signed affidavits saying they had not voted or intended to vote in the county although their names were on absentee-ballot applications and on the list of people who purportedly voted. As the commissar of elections in Poinsett County for twenty years, Edens moved all the wheels of the election machine.

The town of Tyronza, famous as the founding place in 1934 of the Southern Tenant Farmers Union, an uprising by tenant farmers and sharecroppers that spread across the Delta, was a particularly productive place for Democrats of the right persuasion. Every sixth voter from the farm hamlet voted absentee. The lone physician in Tyronza, Dr. L. H. McDaniel, who happened to be chairman of the Democratic Central Committee, took poll-tax books with him when he made house calls and when welfare recipients came to his office for treatment. He got them to sign poll-tax applications and kept the receipts for future use.

Perry County was the smallest county in Arkansas (1960 pop. 4,927) but it always came up big on election day, thanks to an absentee turnout that regularly swelled to 10 percent of the votes or more. We drove to Perryville before the election to check on the absentee applications and the poll-tax receipts that were current for the election. The 1960 Census recorded the voting-age population (age twenty-one and above at that time) as 2,974, but the sheriff and collector had issued 3,187 poll-tax receipts. That would be a level of voter participation that exceeded that of any totalitarian country where voting was mandatory and limited to the slate of party candidates. We reported it to the prosecuting attorney, John T. Jernigan, who telephoned the sheriff. The sheriff told him that the 1960 Census was flawed and, besides, the county had begun to grow a little over the previous three years, explanations that satisfied the prosecutor. While trying futilely to find many on the poll-tax rolls, we checked names with townspeople, who could not identify registrants who listed the same tiny ward or the same street as their domicile.

ERC hired Earl Davenport, a handwriting expert from Memphis, to analyze signatures on poll-tax applications across the state. In Perry County, it appeared the same person filled out numerous applications for ballots and the ballots were mailed to people in other counties or outside the state for their signatures. All listed "work" as the reason for their absence on election day.

These were not isolated episodes. In Garland County, more than one hundred people who voted in the Democratic primary in July were listed in the 1963 poll book as having the same address, which was a post office box, and the 1964 list of actual voters carried all the same names with the same post office box as their addresses. We calculated that at least a fourth of the absentee votes in Garland County were illegal. Requests for ballots came in all kinds of ways besides the forms that the law required, including unsigned mimeographed statements or simple letters.

In Lonoke County, forty absentee-ballot applications were signed with an X but no witness to the X as the law required for voters who were unable to sign their names.

In Faulkner County, a person who had been dead for six months cast an absentee ballot in the Democratic primary.

In Desha County, our handwriting expert identified seventy-three instances of signatures on absentee-ballot applications that did not match the signatures on voter-registration affidavits that all voters were required to sign.

In Conway County, we found voters from Michigan who had cast ballots in Arkansas as well as in Michigan, where they lived. In one county, our workers found 150 names listed in alphabetical order in a duplicate poll-tax receipt book, which indicated that they had been taken from a telephone book or similar listing.

In Madison County, our work found that county election workers went into nearby counties recruiting people to sign up for poll taxes and absentee-ballot applications. With the theft or destruction of all the Madison County election records we could never pinpoint the violations.

Despite its history of ugly racial enmity, Phillips County was then as it is now a biracial carrier of ballot viruses. (The culture of election connivance remains as vibrant there in the twenty-first century as it was in 1964.) When we examined the list of those who had voted absentee, we found the names of 835 voters, but 209 names were either illegible or else they were not in the poll books and thus were ineligible to vote. Of the verifiable names, 223 were white and 403 were African Americans. But instead of 835 applications for absentee ballots, county clerk Warfield Gist had only 301 on file. The other 534 were allowed to vote without making the legal application. Of the 835 ballots cast, only 744 came with a voter statement, which, again, was required by law.

Nearly all the absentee ballots for African Americans came from Helena's Fourth Ward, and the clerk told us that he gave them to Jack and Amanda Bryant, proprietors of the Dream Girls Beauty Shop. Our handwriting analyst determined that a hundred of the voter statements, which are supposed to be signed by the absentee voter, were forged by the same person. We identified the forger and informed the prosecuting attorney, from which nothing came. The absentee African Americans voted amazingly alike: for Governor Faubus (and not for the champion of equal rights and justice who was his opponent), for legalized gambling, and against the permanent voter registration amendment that at long last would lift the yoke of the poll tax from the beleaguered blacks of the Mississippi Delta.

Next to the subservient blacks of the Delta, the most abused people in the election calamity of 1964 were the residents of nursing homes. It was not uncommon for nursing home operators to buy poll taxes for their patients and manage their votes, but it was done that year with unusual zeal and thoroughness.

In the late fall, Charles A. Stewart, the executive secretary of the Arkansas Nursing Home Association and a big supporter of the governor, sent a letter to all the nursing-home operators. It was attached to a memorandum that he had written to Faubus suggesting a nice increase in the state's monthly reimbursement rate of $105 a bed to the nursing homes. In the letter to his members, Stewart said they could bring about the increase with "a 100 percent effort" from all the nursing homes in Arkansas. They would need to see that the governor was re-elected and the right people elected to the legislature.

Stewart further set out what the operators needed to do:

> We may and we will ask you to do some things which will require some work and a little money, but we cannot stress strongly enough that this is a must. We must have your help. One of the first things that must be done is that we need your help in securing a poll tax for each of your nursing home patients who do not have

a new poll-tax receipt and a poll-tax receipt for each of your employees. . . .

> After making this survey of your own nursing home or nursing homes then we ask you to go to your county court house and secure poll taxes for every patient and every employee who does not have one. After doing this it is most important that we have, in this office, a list of these patients and employees with their poll-tax numbers. There are about 7,000 nursing home patients in Arkansas at this time and an estimated 5,000 employees, you can see how effective, politically, that a stack of these listings with poll-tax numbers will be to us. This is an effort that requires the help of every nursing home in the state. Cooperation by half of the nursing homes simply will not get the job done.

Stewart said such an effort by the nursing homes would succeed in changing "the entire regulation of both the Health Department and the Welfare Department and effect a complete new pay scale which will more equitably reimburse you for the care you are now giving your patients." In addition to a copy of the memo to Faubus, the operators received a brochure favoring the gambling amendment. Somehow the operators also got the message that the permanent-voter-registration law needed to be defeated. It would, after all, make such deceits as the bloc nursing-home votes much harder.

To what extent the nursing-home operators complied, we could never discern, but it was substantial. The overhaul of the reimbursement system for nursing-home residents passed handily in the legislature the next spring and Governor Faubus signed it into law. The administrator of the GPW nursing home for African Americans in Jackson County was charged with a felony after forging the absentee-ballot applications of patients, one of whom had been dead for a considerable time. That was the single instance of charges being lodged against anyone for corrupting the election.

The *Pine Bluff Commercial* published a story the month after the election about the practices of the Kilgore Nursing Home in Jefferson County. The home kept a political folder containing all the poll-tax receipts of patients along with Stewart's letter, the Faubus memo, and gambling propaganda. The company paid for sixty of the poll taxes. We gave copies of the poll-tax receipts, absentee applications, and voter statements to our handwriting expert, who concluded that many of them were forged, eighteen by one person and thirteen by another. In the absentee box where Kilgore patients voted, the vote was overwhelmingly for Faubus and gambling and against the voter-registration law, all of which ran counter to the countywide votes.

Election officials disqualified all the absentee ballots cast for patients at the Doyle Shelnutt Nursing Home at Benton because they had been delivered to the county clerk by the proprietors, which was unlawful. Our handwriting analysis of forty-nine applications for absentee ballots from the Pioneer Nursing Home in Izard County showed that signatures on forty-seven of the forty-nine forms had been forged by the same person and the other two by another person. The same person who had forged the forty-seven signatures on the applications forged the signatures on thirty-four of the voter statements. Handwriting analysis demonstrated that eleven of the absentee-ballot applications and twelve of the voter statements for patients from the Twin Lakes Nursing Home in Mountain Home carried forgeries by the same person and that another person signed six applications and six voter statements.

The absentee boxes were not the only source of corruption; we had little time for other exploration. We did discover that one gentleman from the Arkansas River Valley traveled to at least four northwest Arkansas counties on election day to cast his vote. He had a poll tax in each.

Conway County, however, was the real home of the nonresident voter. People who had not lived in those parts for many years, or ever, restored their loyal citizenship on election day, casting ballots for the good sheriff and the host of friends and issues that he embraced. That would be the field of future battles.

CHAPTER 4

• • • • • • • • • • • •

Throw the Rascals Out

"In the end the party would announce that two and two made five, and you would have to believe it."

—GEORGE ORWELL, 1984

For all that we could grasp at the time, the election of 1964 was a thorough repudiation of electoral and political reform. Faubus defeated Rockefeller to win an unprecedented sixth term more convincingly than many of us had imagined, and the public seemed to countenance widespread and documented voting fraud with astonishing equanimity. It was clear that no one would pay the smallest price even for the most blatant criminal cover-up—the wholesale theft of a county's election records. It was my first real taste of politics, and I felt both personal remorse over the seemingly futile work that I had done and, for a while, an abiding pessimism that significant change could occur. But the election did shift the tectonic plates under the Arkansas political order, although that would not become clear for a while.

Except for a special bond election three months later in which a smattering of voters would stomp a Faubus road-building program, the '64 general election was the last under the poll tax, ending seventy years of manipulation and repression of the votes of poor blacks and whites across nearly half the state. A vote analysis showed that most African Americans who voted in 1964 had their votes counted, amazingly, for Faubus, the man known around the world for resistance to their civil rights. That, at least, would not likely happen again since people's voting rights were no longer tethered to a poll tax and less apt to be controlled by the boss, their doctor or the proprietor of the general store. Cast in the light of the counterintuitive black vote for Faubus, Rockefeller's 43 percent of the votes in '64 should have been read as a powerful message.

The one person who probably read it that way was Orval Faubus. In late November, after the election, Faubus did something uncharacteristic and, in a way, prophetic. He threw a party for the press, the men and the single woman from newspapers and broadcast stations who had covered his triumph over Rockefeller. The Faubuses entertained far less than any other administration since World War II, maybe because they suspected that the "silk-stocking crowd," as Faubus had called the capital's social elite, had always looked down upon the rustic couple from Madison County. Alta Faubus enjoyed a small coterie of friends but she found the social expectations of being first lady of the state vexing. Also, the media were among the last that could expect to be feted at the Governor's Mansion. Except for three men whose reporting he found sympathetic, the press was never an object of the governor's geniality. But on this occasion, the reporters and cameramen who had worked either the Faubus or Rockefeller campaigns or both were invited over for an evening to reminisce over fruit punch and snacks about the great battle, so epic in the governor's own mind.

Faubus was not prone to impulsive or frivolous behavior like an evening of mirth with the boys of the press. He apparently sensed, if vaguely and incompletely, that the election had been a demarcation in Arkansas history, that things would never be the same for the state and, as it would turn out, certainly not for him. (He would run for governor three more times but never come close again.) But in the media, Faubus divined, it had been just another brawling Arkansas election. For him it was certainly a season of relief and satisfaction, but the great victory had not been properly celebrated or recognized for what it was. The poor boy from Greasy Creek had defeated a Rockefeller, the rich scion of one of the original Robber Barons whom Faubus's father had despised.

A reporter for the *Pine Bluff Commercial* showed his slides of the campaign and, to the governor's great amusement, shared some humorous commentary on a few photographs of Rockefeller campaigning. Then for the dozen or so reporters and cameramen, Faubus analyzed the election: his own shrewd decisions, Rockefeller's blunders, and the stroke of luck that brought the Lonoke County gravestone travesty to his attention when the race seemed to be tightening. He was not embarrassed at all about having exploited a laborer's carelessness in an unattended cemetery. And, yes, a few of his supporters might have been overzealous in using the election machinery to help him on election night but those things always happen on both sides on a small scale, and he did not believe the election chicanery was decisive in his election. Despite the sizable margin at the end, he said, Rockefeller was actually fairly close to being elected two weeks before the voting, and he said Rockefeller might yet be elected governor. For the first time that anyone knew about, Faubus talked candidly, even proudly, about his father's leftist passions. With the two reporters from the *Gazette* who lingered after the party at his request, he boasted of his own progressive impulses. He was, he said, the most liberal governor in the South in modern times and he ticked off the things he had done for poor people, government workers, the mentally ill, public education, and African Americans. He was not the hidebound conservative that the press made him out to be. Roy Reed, one of the *Gazette* men present, reminded him that he had used the police power to prevent nine black teenagers from attending school with whites, hardly the measure of a Southern liberal. Yes, Faubus replied with a smile, "but in politics one must trim his sails to the prevailing wind." Had he not catered to the momentary passions of people, he said, Bruce Bennett, the race-baiting attorney general, would have defeated him in 1958. To achieve good works for people, he explained, one has to do what is necessary to grasp and keep the reins of government. It was the classic rationalization for expediency. It is the fond doctrine of every demagogue and every ballot thief. You do the grimier work of democracy so that people might benefit from your superior vision.

Faubus's purpose was to make the media and a hoped-for wider audience realize the magnitude and meaning of his victory over a Rockefeller, but there also was evidence of some reflection and foreboding. Although it had been Rockefeller who had talked about a progressive agenda, Faubus again wanted to think of himself as a liberal without using the word in any public way. For the rest of his life he would alternately adopt the language of Southern reactionaries and then offer himself as a man who fought for the poor and dispossessed. Trying to make a comeback in the late summer of 1970 against a young liberal named Dale Bumpers and facing a rematch with Rockefeller if he won, Faubus called both men "bogus liberals" and insisted that he was the only "true liberal," which he described as someone who actually achieved progressive things rather than merely promising them. In 1988, he endorsed Rev. Jesse Jackson for president and a year later went to a tribute to Daisy Bates, the civil rights leader who had shepherded the nine black students through Central High School in 1957 to praise her dedication to the cause.

In the months after the press party, Faubus placed himself on the side of President Lyndon Johnson's War on Poverty. Johnson's Great Society, he thought, was something like his own agenda. In the fall, he had tersely endorsed Johnson against Senator Barry Goldwater, who would carry most of the South, and he may have been surprised that Johnson and his liberal running mate, Hubert Humphrey, had gotten the same share of the Arkansas vote on that November day that he had. Rockefeller had announced immediately after the election that he would be running again in 1966, and Faubus seemed to contemplate another race in which he might fly this time with the better angels of his populist nature.

It was not to be. Within a year, the weight of a decade of cronyism, lethargy, and self-dealing had reduced his administration to wreckage. One scandal seemed to follow another with rhythmic force.

Driven out by tough regulatory enforcement in Texas and other neighboring states, insurance and securities swindlers found easy prey in Arkansas and hospitable refuge under Faubus's tender regulators.

In the summer of 1966, a lawmaker let slip that the administration and the legislature had set up secret pensions for seven cronies of the governor who had gotten brief appointments over the years to quasi-judicial commissions—Workers Compensation, Public Service, and Transportation. The Quasi-Judicial Retirement Act had seven baffling sections, each one, as it turned out, dedicated to a political pal. One pal was William J. Smith, the governor's powerful legal adviser, who had served a short spell on the Workers Compensation Commission in the 1940s. The act became known as "Pensions for Pals."

Faubus was generous with his friends in many ways, often helping them get family members and friends out of the penitentiary. When his rich horse-fancying friends were going to have to dig into their own pockets to pay the accumulated debts of the extravagant Arkansas Horse Show, Faubus transferred $20,729 from an emergency fund set aside for unexpected public crises to his brother Doyle at the state livestock and poultry commission, who paid the debts of the show-horse fanciers.

One check went to Bob Troutt, the governor's press secretary, who had done a little work on the side for the horsemen's club. The biggest went to Harry Parkin, a close Faubus friend whose commercial printing company did printing for the group. All that was in addition to $15,000 a year that the state sent the horsemen's group regularly after Faubus became governor to pay for its show prizes. Faubus explained that his friend Dr. T. J. Raney, the group's president, would have paid the bills himself if he hadn't died.

Periodic exposés of illegal gambling at Hot Springs under the nose of his state police would stir the administration to action, but the slots and croupiers never stayed in hiding long.

In 1965, Faubus sent his longtime friend and chief political operator, Mack Sturgis, from the state purchasing department over to the highway department, where Faubus's appointed commissioners were getting a little too independent. Working late at night and with Faubus's knowledge, Sturgis and an assistant, Young William Whelchel, set substantial pay raises in motion for some 2,100 of the agency's 3,500 employees, all apparently unbeknownst to the highway commissioners. Most were clearly illegal. Pundits labeled it the "Midnight Pay Raises."

Rumors persisted at the capitol and in western Arkansas (later confirmed) that his administration had given the green light to a banking scam headquartered at Van Buren called Arkansas Loan and Thrift, in which my old nemesis Bruce Bennett thrived. Federal regulators and the United States District Court stepped in after Faubus left office and padlocked the place, but not before more than two thousand people had lost most of their life savings.

Finally, a state police investigation of the state penitentiary exposed widespread extortion, bribery, and torture. A torture device known as the Tucker Telephone—it was employed at the Tucker Unit of the penitentiary—became a symbol of the corruption. Wardens and inmate trusties would wire a recalcitrant inmate's genitals to an old magneto-operated telephone and crank it vigorously, sending an electrical shock through the prisoner's privates. Inmates feared it more than the whip.

His reputation battered by the scandals, Faubus decided that it was time to spend more time with his family and announced that he would not run again in 1966 and would instead retire to his new stone-and-glass home, designed by the famous architect E. Fay Jones. A subscription

"I wear the chains I forged in life."

campaign among state employees helped defray the cost of the governor's dream home, which was perched on a mountaintop ledge overlooking the town of Huntsville a few miles north of his boyhood home on Greasy Creek.

In the spring of 1965, the prospects for change did not seem so evident when I went to work for Rockefeller in his political offices at Little Rock. The Election Research Council was on the verge of disbanding. After com-

For the first time in twelve years, Faubus's name was not on the ballot.

piling and releasing a summary of the irregularities in the fall election and the shortcomings of the election procedures both as they were defined in the law and as they were practiced in the counties, we had nothing to do but await the next election. Haley closed the Election Research Council and returned full time to his practice at the Rose law firm, to be summoned again two years later when the new governor, Rockefeller, needed someone to reform the scandal-ridden prison system.

I was not yet at loose ends when I was approached about working for Rockefeller's political operation. Rockefeller wanted me to develop his next campaign for governor, in 1966, and to manage what amounted to his political operations on the fifth floor of the Tower Building, which was then Little Rock's only skyscraper. I did not consider myself a Republican or give much thought to party allegiance when the offer came, but Rockefeller seemed to be the only antidote to the corruption and injustice that I believed were rampant. I consulted with my friend and confidante in all things, Mamie Ruth Williams, who I suspected had something to do with my getting the offer. Mamie Ruth, whose great heart dwarfed her ample girth, had been a hard worker in the Democrats for Rockefeller organization on Little Rock's east side in 1966. She told me that I should tell Rockefeller that I would work for $1,000 a month. She said he would be offended if I asked for anything less. That seemed outrageous so when Rockefeller asked what salary I needed I wondered if $700 a month would be all right.

"Fine, it's done," he said.

Rockefeller was convinced more than ever that his election would depend as much as anything on an unimpeded vote and an honest counting of the ballots, but he also figured that he would need a far more sophisticated campaign effort than the one that had been thrown together in some haste in 1963 and 1964. Everyone from Rockefeller down had been a neophyte at politics. Elsewhere, political organizations were beginning to apply modern communication and marketing technology to elections. Rockefeller wanted to see if an extensive database of voters and better ways to communicate with them could be developed in Arkansas in time for the next election, which was only eighteen months away. It would be another year before there would be records of voters registered under the new permanent system created by Amendment 51 of 1964.

My own knowledge of politics was hardly acute. In my one season I had focused on the wheels of election machinery, not on how you go about winning the hearts of voters and getting them to the polls. As general counsel and office manager for the Rockefeller campaign organization in Little Rock, I would still work on assuring a clean election, and I became peripherally involved with Rockefeller's private attorneys, G. Thomas Eisele and Marion B. Burton, in the continuing imbroglio in Conway County, where the political bosses were trying to put the crusading local newspaper out of business for its reporting of election fraud. But my main task was to develop a modern campaign organization and a strategy for what we all thought would be a rematch with Orval Faubus in 1966.

Since Oral Roberts University at Tulsa had developed one of the first computer-based data systems in the country, I went there to see how it was done. Later, an IBM employee, Ray Waters, and I went to Lincoln, Nebraska, to study the Cole Directory, which was on the cutting edge of information technology. Since 1947, Cole Information Services had been putting together directories that cross-referenced listings by names, addresses, and telephone numbers, and it was generating sophisticated computer letters for business customers. Using public records, we could build an efficient and rapid-response communication system for the Rockefeller campaign. I would leave before the operation was perfected but Burton, who took over my work, had a fascination with and an affinity for the new information technology. He would manage Rockefeller's race for governor in 1966, and Rockefeller's ability to communicate directly with a wide audience made a big difference. In the summer of 1966, people in Little Rock's big apartment complexes and at the forks of the creek in Calhoun County began getting letters with their names in the salutation and Winthrop Rockefeller's distinctive scrawl at the bottom. Most of them had never seen anything like it. No one else was doing that in the region, and it would be some years before the Democratic Party or any other political organization caught up.

Not for long would I last in the campaign organization. Egotism and envy are endemic afflictions of political organizations, whether the campaign is for president or justice of the peace. People want to be at the right hand of the man, to be his one indispensable adviser. As far as I can tell, jealousy and suspicion among staff and advisers dog every candidate for office. Rivalries, turnover, and dismissals of top advisers form the inevitable stories of every presidential campaign. I do not know, but I have no doubt, that on the other side the view in 1966 was that mine was the insatiable ego.

At any rate, the friction began early. Everett Ham, a former government farm agent, was Rockefeller's first political aide and from the first until the end he considered himself as Rockefeller's vicar. He talked to Rockefeller and everyone else talked to him. Anything that anyone had to report to Rockefeller had to be passed through the prism of Ham's fevered cogitations, which over time branched into ever-greater expanses of paranoia. Eventually, Ham became such an affliction that Rockefeller himself connived to have him offered a can't-refuse job at a high salary with the Republican National Committee in Washington, DC. Ham turned it down. But in my first real job, only a year out of school, I was not wise or rugged enough to shed the tension. Rockefeller had told me that I was to report directly to him, but Ham told me that I had to stop going to Rockefeller and pass on my reports and advice to him instead. That was the chain of command and I either followed it or I would be gone. Ham thought I was going behind his back and undermining his authority. Burton seemed to concur that Ham, not Rockefeller, was my boss. They said this line of authority was necessary to insulate Rockefeller from people who constantly approached him for money or favors. The tension was so palpable that I dreaded going to work each day. For weeks in the evenings, sometimes in the midwatches of night, I would be awakened by the ringing telephone and greeted with silence except for the measured breathing of the caller. On a Saturday morning, I arose and wrote a letter of resignation to Rockefeller, forgetting in my anxiety to sign it before posting it. My anxieties over the wee-hours telephone calls may have been paranoia, but they stopped after I resigned.

The next Monday morning I received a call from the director of the adjudication office of the Veterans Administration at Little Rock asking whether I might go to work there. With my big and hungry family—I had three children by then—it seemed heaven-sent and I took it without asking many questions. It was a ritual desk-bound job, poring over veterans' case files, but for a while it was a pleasure to go to a workplace each morning where no snarls or petty intrigues confounded your labors and where you were thanked for your work. Still, I had been infected incurably by politics and yearned to put my legal training to work on something challenging and where the days did not run together in numbing succession. I told my boss and he said he had not believed that the work would enthrall me for long.

Burl C. "Buddy" Rotenberry, an old friend from undergraduate and law school days, was running the fledgling Legal Aid Bureau of Pulaski County, and in the late summer of 1966 offered me a job. President Johnson's War on Poverty created local legal-service agencies in 1965 to provide representation to people who could not afford to hire a private attorney, and Rotenberry opened the Little Rock office that fall with a

$35,000 grant from the Office of Economic Opportunity. A few agencies, like California's, created a sensation nationally by filing class-action suits against local and state officials, but in Arkansas we toiled on the most basic legal terrain: divorce and other domestic-relations issues, traffic fines, evictions and tenancy squabbles, employment issues and, occasionally, the denial of public services. They were the kinds of clients lawyers normally hated to see walk through the door because the issues were grubby, stressful, and sometimes even dangerous, and the remuneration pitiful if it came about at all. The clients were on the cusp of survival, where matters that would be trifling annoyances for most people made a critical difference in their lives. In a matter of weeks I went from representing the richest man in Arkansas to representing the poorest.

Except for an occasional appearance with Tom Eisele in the endless court battles over election fraud and attendant crimes in Conway County, in the nearly two years since leaving law school I had not entered a single pleading or conducted myself in a courtroom when I joined Legal Aid. Legal Aid offered plenty of experience in the municipal courts, and in the Pulaski County Chancery Court, where divorce, custody, and other contentious domestic quarrels found a resolution or at least a conclusion. It was a valuable precursor to my own service on the chancery bench a dozen years later. My brief and deeply disillusioning introduction to the court system had been in Conway County, where the judge and nearly all the officials of court were part of the political apparatus. Whether you were a litigant or a lawyer, how you fared in the courts of Conway County depended 100 percent upon your terms with the political machine. The Legal Aid work afforded me the chance to study the bearing of real judges and see how they went about achieving justice when the constitution and the statutes did not settle it.

You also discovered that men usually did not shed their private passions and peccadilloes when they became learned men of the judiciary. One of my first clients was a beautiful African American woman who was terrified of her estranged husband. We went to Chancery Court for a hearing to get a restraining order, and before the hearing began she leaned over and whispered that maybe she should bring up her husband's insatiable sexual appetite. No, I said, we had plenty of evidence without it. But on the stand she couldn't help herself and said her husband would demand sex ten or twelve times a day. I interrupted her to say that we need not go into that. Chancellor Kay L. Matthews had been in deep repose behind the bench, but he sprang forward in his chair and asked, "Did I hear the witness say something about sex?" I started to say that it was irrelevant.

"Let the witness tell her story, counselor!" he barked. She did. When I took the restraining order for him to sign, Matthews said: "That was a good one, wasn't it?"

• • •

This was my fourth job in a little more than two years, which did not augur well for my stability or sense of purpose, but I was soon as restless as ever. It was not the pay. While poverty law was at the bottom of the scale for even freshly minted lawyers, the wages seemed sufficient for my circumstances. The nobility of providing civil legal assistance to people who could not afford it sustained Buddy Rotenberry, Hobson Mahon, John Choate, and the other young lawyers at Legal Aid who had been infused in college with the egalitarian impulses of the freedom and civil rights movements. My own defining experience had been the election work that summer and fall after law school, and I was impatient to get back to that and the wider world of politics. Six months after Buddy hired me, I told him I was leaving to work for Joe Purcell, an obscure municipal judge in Saline County who had been elected attorney general.

It was a particularly fortuitous development because after leaving Rockefeller's political staff early that year I had not been involved at all in the tumultuous elections, even in Purcell's seemingly quixotic run for attorney general against my nemesis Bruce Bennett in the Democratic primary. Purcell may not have been indebted to me even for my solitary vote because I cannot be sure that I voted in the Democratic primary, owing to my recent involvement with the campaign of the Republican candidate for governor. Joe did not owe many people because few imagined that an obscure, underfinanced, and terminally bland politi-

Joe Purcell

cian could defeat Bennett, a silver-haired Bilbo who was the model for the Claghorn politician that every Southern state was electing.* Joe's campaign was memorable for one moment. He ran a big advertisement in the *Arkansas Gazette* listing the names and telephone numbers of hundreds of people in Saline County. The ad copy said simply, "Please call us collect if you want to know more about this fine man."

Mamie Ruth Williams was one person to whom Joe was deeply indebted, and upon her advice he asked me to be assistant attorney general.

Mamie Ruth was part of the "Throw the Rascals Out" movement of 1966. That romantic little campaign, popularized by the political caricatures of George Fisher, a commercial artist who a decade later would become the editorial cartoonist for the *Arkansas Gazette,* was put together by a band of liberals in Pulaski County who coalesced around the women who had thrown out the segregationists in the Little Rock school board battles of 1958 and 1959. They targeted politicians who were cogs in the political machine: Bennett, state Rep. Paul Van Dalsem of Perryville, and two Pulaski County representatives who were resilient allies of Faubus in the legislature, Glenn F. Walther, a former Speaker of the House of Representatives, and J. H. Cottrell Jr., who was the reigning Speaker. Governor Faubus and Nathan Gordon of Morrilton, who had been Arkansas lieutenant governor since mustering out of the Army with a Medal of Honor for battlefield heroism in World War II,

Paul Van Dalsem

---

*Theodore Bilbo, a Mississippi Democrat who served in the US Senate in the 1930s and '40s, was a symbol of racism and hatred during his tenure and the model for the satirical character Sen. Beauregard Claghorn on the Fred Allen Show, a popular weekly radio program. —E.D.

would have been targets but they felt the tremors in the electorate and decided to spend more time with their families.

The "Rascals" campaign targeted the Little Rock media, mainly the two daily newspapers, but it rippled across the state. Representative Van Dalsem did the movement immeasurable good, and his fellow rascals incalculable harm, by making himself an icon for boorish behavior. With his barrel chest and broad shining pate, Van Dalsem was the physical template for a bully. He was the literal boss of the House of Representatives, and in 1964, faced with court-ordered reapportionment that would forcibly expand his tiny Perry County base, he got the state board of apportionment (Faubus, Bennett, and Secretary of State Kelly Bryant) to lump him with Pulaski County's fourteen representatives, all of whom would run at large in the two counties in the next election in 1966. He argued to the Pulaski County business establishment that he could use his power and savvy to deliver for them what he had delivered for the country folks since 1941. It might have worked, but in a speech to a Little Rock civic club in late 1964 Van Dalsem embroidered on his theme of country cunning. He joked that up in the cocklebur country they didn't have any trouble with educated and uppity womenfolk meddling in politics. They kept the women barefoot and pregnant and gave them a cow to milk, he said. Barefoot and pregnant became a metaphor for the old political order. Fisher's satirical caricatures became a statewide celebration.

Herbert C. Rule III, a young lawyer with Rose, Meek, House, Barron, Nash, and Williamson, the oldest law firm in the state, defeated Van Dalsem in a walkaway in the 1966 primary. Liberal opponents Charles D. Matthews and Paul Meers defeated Walther and Cottrell, who had a combined thirty-two years in the legislature. Purcell's landslide in central Arkansas swamped Bennett's tide from South Arkansas's faithful precincts.

"Throw the Rascals Out" was only the visible crest of the wave. Few of us had recognized it after the dismal 1964 campaign, but people had had enough. It was my hopeful belief that a year of revelations about electoral fraud had helped. In the Democratic free-for-all for governor, the progressive candidates, former Congressman Brooks Hays and Sam W. Boyce, a Newport trial lawyer, had finished a disappointing third and fourth behind two supreme court justices, Jim Johnson and J. Frank Holt. Johnson was a throwback to Jim Crow populism and the Lost Cause. A founder of the White Citizens Council, Johnson had exploited the state's virulent strain of racial bigotry in three statewide races in the 1950s, but only the last one, for the supreme court in 1958, was successful. Holt was an agreeable man with profoundly temperate impulses, both in politics and in judging, but his late entry into the race after the Associated Press spotted him in consultation with the kingmakers of the Faubus era across the street in the Stephens, Inc., offices cast him unfortunately as the candidate of the old order.

Jim Johnson

Confronted with the choice of a bigot who was against the establishment and someone they feared was a minion of the powers, the voters took the bigot. Three months later, in the 1966 general election, they opted for the bona-fide anti-establishment candidate, Rockefeller. Jim Johnson was hurt by division in the old party establishment. Governor Faubus worked quietly for Rockefeller against his own party's nominee, as he would do again four years later when Dale Bumpers was the party's nominee. The rivalry with Johnson and then Bumpers was deeply personal. Sheriff Hawkins, the Conway County boss, wrote in his memoir that Faubus had called to beseech him to throw the county's votes to Rockefeller, which Hawkins refused to do.

Since Faubus and Lieutenant Governor Nathan Gordon weren't running, Bennett furnished the only outlet for the voters' spleen. He was the only person on the ballot who had a visible role in the election scandals of 1964–65. He had furnished timely legal opinions that enabled the ballot thieves, including an opinion to Madison County election officials in 1965 that they could legally and properly destroy all the county's election records and thus evade responsibility for the wholesale fraud that came to light. He opined officially that a person's residence for voting purposes depended entirely on his own whim, an open invitation for election officials to stuff the ballot boxes with the votes of nonresidents who might or might not have any knowledge of their votes. Your domicile and voting home, Bennett opined, could be wherever you wanted it to be, whether you lived there or not. Three months after becoming an assistant attorney general, I had occasion to reverse that opinion. I said the act and intent of residency must combine.

Although I had done nothing to help Joe Purcell's cause or to bring down Bruce Bennett, I found it particularly satisfying to be on the team that cleaned up after him. Bruce and I had jousted for much of a year over the residency requirements for voting and the rights of mobile residents of the state to vote. He had issued an array of opinions on election procedures in the summer and fall of 1964 that baffled election officials. One opinion said that a person who moved from one county to another during the election season could vote in his new county as long as he did not mark his ballot in local races. I had moved from Fayetteville to Pulaski County in the early summer of 1964 and I realized that, under his opinions, I could wander about the state and vote in any number of counties as long as I didn't mark a ballot in any city or county race. How would election officials keep up with that and how would they know which races I voted in? (We would discover that traveling voters were indeed a problem.) Represented by John Haley, I sued in the fall of 1964 in Pulaski County Chancery Court to overturn Bennett's opinions and have my voting rights and those of thousands of other peripatetic residents clarified. We argued the case in the courts for most of a year. Bruce handled the case personally rather than having an assistant attorney general appear, which was his usual manner. He appeared in court personally only in highly publicized cases like evolution, where reporters and cameras were likely to be present.

Election chicanery, as it turned out, was one of Bennett's more innocent pursuits. He would become by the decade's end the emblem of the cronyism and self-dealing that had infected government during the long Faubus saga. When he faced the voters in the late summer of 1966, rumors were circulating that Bennett, key legislators, and others in the government were enmeshed in a shady banking operation called Arkansas Loan and Thrift Corporation (AL&T), which under the benign gaze of the Faubus administration was siphoning millions of dollars from widows and churches with offers of high interest rates and deposit guarantees that banks and thrifts could not match. Bennett had insisted that his wife had briefly owned a few shares of stock in the company that she had obtained from a broker in 1965 but that he had no connection with it.

On January 23, 1967, only six days after taking office, Joe Purcell filed a lawsuit in Pulaski County Chancery Court seeking to shutter the Van Buren-based company or else make it stop representing itself as a bank, trust company, or savings and loan association, which would have the same result. The case was assigned to Judge Kay Matthews, my judicial exemplar at the courthouse the previous fall. Matthews had been appointed to the seat a year earlier by Governor Faubus, for whom he had been an adviser and shipping regulator. The morning after Joe filed the suit on behalf of the state bank commission, Ernest A. Bartlett Jr., the president and chief executive officer of AL&T, appeared at the West Seventh Street office of Claude Carpenter Jr., Matthews' business and law partner, with a check for $23,000, for which Carpenter would later testify he did nothing but chat with Bartlett about the Arkansas Razorbacks and accompany him on a drunken pleasure flight to Las Vegas. Joe's suit floundered in Matthews' court while the judge gave the company one continuance after another. It would turn out that besides the work-free retainers, Judge Matthews' partner had insider dealings with Arkansas Loan and Thrift.

Eighteen months later, convinced that Joe's lawsuit would never go anywhere in Matthews' court, Governor Rockefeller's securities commissioner, Don Smith, begged the federal Securities and Exchange Commission to look into the company's activities. Two SEC attorneys arrived at Van Buren to examine the records, and in short order US District Judge John E. Miller padlocked the company and ordered its liquidation. An audit showed that AL&T and a phony insurance company that was set up to guarantee the safety of people's deposits were hopelessly insolvent. The assets, the life savings of more than two thousand people, had been squandered on loans and fees to the operators and to insider government officials who had gathered at the trough at the founding. The receiver eventually recouped about a quarter of each dollar that people had entrusted with AL&T's thieves. When the federal investigators moved in on the company, Judge Matthews at Little Rock suddenly discovered that AL&T had rented an office in a building that he and Carpenter owned and he recused from any other proceedings. For his part, Bennett manfully decided to make a political comeback and ran for governor in the Democratic primary while the auditors were poring over AL&T's books. He finished a distant fourth behind Rep. Marion H. Crank, who would fall to Rockefeller in the general election.

AL&T's files provided a fuller portrait of Bennett's involvement with the company. The incorporation papers were drawn up in his offices in the Justice Building by one of his assistants, who was given stock in the company for his pains. AL&T's board organized in the attorney general's office, and the minutes reflected that the old attorney general was the company's general counsel. Bennett held a large block of stock in the name of his wife, took regular legal fees from the company, and collected some $200,000 in loans from AL&T and a sister company in Baton Rouge, Louisiana Loan and Thrift Corp., which collapsed about the same time with nearly identical repercussions. The Louisiana attorney general, Jack P. F. Gremillion, a pal of Bennett, spent fifteen months in prison on perjury charges arising from the thrift scam, a fate that Bennett would manage to escape. Bennett also sold a defunct casualty insurance company, of which he was president, to AL&T for $64,000. The casualty company, renamed Savings Guaranty Corporation, became the faux guarantor of everyone's deposits although the sum total of its capital assets was a quantity of worthless stock in AL&T. The company's files also yielded copies of three official opinions from Bennett, which his office had never made public, advising Governor Faubus's banking, savings and loan, and securities regulators that they should keep their hands off AL&T because its hybrid operations were legal and not subject to their monitoring.

A federal grand jury at Fort Smith indicted Bennett on twenty-eight counts of securities, mail, and postal fraud and named Ernest A. Bartlett Jr. and two other officials of the company, Afton and Hoyt Borum, in a range of indictments. The other three were convicted and spent a few years in the penitentiary. US District Judge Oren Harris, who hailed from Bennett's hometown of El Dorado, severed Bennett's case from the others, and when Bennett announced that he had throat cancer the judge postponed his trial. Bennett never went to trial and died ten years later.

• • •

I would spend more than three years in the attorney general's office, first as an assistant attorney general and then as deputy attorney general, Special Projects Division. Although I had never met Joe before he hired me, it quickly became clear that I was expected to develop programs in the new division that would build Joe's résumé for a future race for governor. It was not a repugnant objective for me, although I would eventually leave him just as the goal seemed to be in sight.

Joe grew up in the same South Arkansas environs as Jim Johnson, a contemporary, but he didn't carry the baggage of prejudices that so many from that time and place did. Until he ran for attorney general, he had not evinced either ambition or a gift for high-level politics. City attorney and municipal judge in a midsize South Arkansas town were not career paths for a middle-aged man aiming for high office. So clumsy were his political skills that, upon his statewide election, Joe did not seem destined for political stardom, but he was a simple, honest and conscientious public servant. Over and over he uttered the same platitude—he intended to do the best job he possibly could for the people—until reporters mimicked him. But he was earnest about it. That was the extent of his political philosophy and his wisdom about governance. He wanted us to interpret the law as precisely and rigidly as possible, and if he got the chance he would have a government that was honest, efficient and compassionate. He was one of those lucky men whose self-image became the public one. He was Honest Joe. George Fisher caricatured him in a stovepipe hat like Honest Abe. When Orval Faubus briefly faced the prospect of running against Joe in a run-off for the Democratic nomination for governor in 1970 he confided to Jack Gardner, his campaign manager, that it would be hard to concoct a campaign issue against Joe in two weeks because no one in Arkansas thought he could ever do anything dishonest. No one would get excited about voting for him but no one would believe anything bad about him. That image of impeccable rectitude was all that he had going for him politically. It was almost but not quite enough to get him to the top.

There was a stubborn streak in him that could be aggravating but that you sometimes had to appreciate. He was not pushed around easily, at least in his first term. I had joined up with a group of mavericks in North Little Rock who wanted to make changes in the city government, which was the fief of Mayor William F. "Casey" Laman. Casey was the closest thing to prototypical big-city political bosses Pendergast and Tweed that

Arkansas had seen.* He got plenty of things done in city government, only some of it self-serving, but he was ruthless. Then-Prosecuting Attorney Jim Guy Tucker had a grand jury look into suspicions about the mayor's relationship with the owners of a nightclub where gambling flourished, but the grand jury handed down no indictment. Several of us formed a group called Up-Grade '68 and we began a highly publicized campaign to unseat a couple of Casey's automatons on the City Council and replace them with men of high principle and intellect whom we had chosen. Casey set out to remove us, one by one, from the fray. Our chairman, my friend Richard Longing, resigned after Casey persuaded his boss, Jess P. Odom, the president of National Investors Life Insurance Co. and the developer of Maumelle, that it wouldn't be in Odom's best interest to have an employee working against Casey. Laman went down the line until

Casey Laman

Henry Ketcher, a roofing contractor, and I were left. Someone untethered Henry's houseboat on the North Little Rock shore and put it adrift. He marched into Casey's office, told the mayor to follow him and they drove the few blocks from City Hall to the harbor where Henry's boat drifted. Henry pulled a pistol from beneath the driver's seat and told the mayor that if anything happened to his family, his boat or any of his property he would be coming after Casey. They drove in silence back to City Hall.

As I was leaving the attorney general's office one after-

---

*William "Boss" Tweed was in charge during the 1870s of the New York County Democratic political machine, which had worked to alter elections and maintain power there since the late 1700s. Tom Pendergast headed in the 1930s a political machine in Kansas City that wielded statewide election influence in Missouri. —E.D.

noon, John T. Harmon, a young lawyer and Laman acolyte, went into Joe's office. I knew what was up. The next morning I went to see Joe and told him that if he wanted me to pull back from the North Little Rock campaign I would instead have to resign from his office. Joe puffed on the pipe that he always kept at hand when he was at his desk. "No," he said, "I don't want you to resign. Do what you have to do over there, but keep your head down." Our little campaign to clip Casey's wings was only partly successful. Casey's man won one seat and , a reform-minded barber named Travis Hartwick, won the other.

At a conference of attorneys general at Portland, Oregon, I heard an assistant attorney general for Missouri, Christopher Bond, give a presentation about the office's new consumer-protection program. Some thirty states had consumer programs in their attorney general's offices. I told Joe that given Arkansas's record of victimization by consumer frauds, this could be a valuable service for the attorney general to perform. Not coincidentally, having achieved it would be a nice asset for a future race. We got back to Little Rock and readied a bill creating a consumer division for the legislature, which was in session. Governor Rockefeller supported the bill, which probably was not an advantage in the overwhelmingly Democratic legislature, and the bill got buried. Although it had no statutory powers of investigation, we set up a modest consumer program under Clair Reece Gladden of Benton, a mother of four. (Ray Thornton, who succeeded Joe in 1971, would pick up the legislation and get it passed although without giving the consumer office subpoena powers.)

· · ·

Joe's ambition grew with his flourishing confidence. Editorials in the *Arkansas Gazette* and *Pine Bluff Commercial* praised him regularly and he began to talk to me more and more about running for governor. He probably missed his best chance. That was 1968, when the Democrats had no obvious or very credible candidate for governor and Joe was the top Democratic officeholder. But he had been in office only 18 months when the filing started and he thought it would seem presumptuous to leap at the first chance to quit the office that he had so earnestly sought. He chose to run for a second term, and I took a leave of absence to manage his campaign. It was a lark of a job because he had no Democratic opponent and the Republican did not mount a serious challenge. The race for governor exposed all the Democrats' problems. State Rep. Marion Crank of tiny Foreman in Little River County was the Old Guard candidate and he enjoyed the financial support of all the men who had bankrolled Faubus and other Democratic luminaries. Crank was eminently qualified because he was smart and the most knowledgeable candidate of either party on the mechanics of government. He had voted with Witt Stephens on Stephens's Fair Field Price Act, which sailed through the legislature in three days in 1957 and created fortunes for Arkansas Louisiana Gas Co. officers and shareholders. For that and other services, Crank got a lifetime job as a public-relations specialist for Arkansas Cement Corp., a subsidiary of the gas company.

But Crank's liabilities exceeded his considerable abilities. Dyspeptic and reserved, he could contrive to smile only at great effort and he avoided any show of exuberance. He survived the Democratic primaries with luck and cunning. His chief opponents were Virginia Johnson, the wife of the old race-baiter Jim Johnson, who was himself running for the US Senate against J. William Fulbright, and Ted Boswell, a silver-haired trial lawyer whose eloquence in front of juries had won the biggest personal-injury judgment in Arkansas history. Boswell, who was unknown when the race

Marion Crank

began, seemed to have edged out Johnson for the second spot on election night but during the early morning hours, the vote shifted to Johnson by 409 votes. A Crank campaign official would say years later that the votes for Johnson and Bruce Bennett, who finished a distant fourth, were transposed in a few South Arkansas boxes to produce the more salutary result. The newcomer Boswell would have swamped Crank in the runoff. Johnson barely scratched.

Crank might still have defeated Rockefeller in the fall but he nosedived days before the election after the *Arkansas Gazette* revealed that as Speaker of the House he had his wife and three children on the legislative payroll. His eight-year-old daughter was a House clerk making twenty dollars a day. It turned out the week before the election that the three sons of Rep. Bill G. Wells, the Democratic nominee for lieutenant governor, had drawn $5,118 from the state as pages. His four-year-old boy had raked in $88 a week and his more accomplished spawn, who was six, drew $112 a week. That finished Crank and Wells although both men came fairly close. Rockefeller won by fewer than thirty thousand votes.

Had Joe's sense of timing been as acute as it had been two years earlier, he would have run for governor that year. His friend Ted Boswell would not have run, and I have no doubt that Joe would have won the Democratic nomination and defeated Rockefeller.

Election reform was the biggest Special Project. Joe announced early in 1967 that he wanted to overhaul the state's patchwork of election laws to guarantee people a secret ballot and end the confusion that made so much election fraud possible. The legislature adopted a resolution initiating an interim study of the election code, to be conducted in collaboration with the attorney general's office. Modernizing the election code had been an objective, never consummated, of the Election Research Council so I would be returning to that task. For the next nine months, the office received numerous requests from election officials for opinions and advice on voting procedures, which enabled us to stop some of the practices, at least in some places, that Bruce Bennett had sanctioned. That fall we produced a 138-page manual for election officials explaining precisely the duties of everyone from county clerks and sheriffs to election commissions and judges and clerks. In many places, deputy sheriffs would pick up the ballot boxes and election results at the polling places and deliver them to the election commission and county clerk, sometimes the next day. We advised election officials that neither a deputy sheriff nor anyone else but precinct election officials could take possession of election records. Precinct officials had to deliver the returns to the headquarters in person. Before the fall elections we conducted regional seminars for election officials in every part of the state.

On the day before the legislature convened in January 1969, Joe held a Sunday afternoon press conference to release the big election-reform bill that we had been drafting for nine months. It recodified every scrap of election law, changed the dates and timetables for primaries, guaranteed a secret ballot by placing a black patch over the voter's ballot number that could only be removed in case a court ordered it in an election contest, and tightened absentee-ballot procedures in ways we thought would halt their widespread abuse. Endorsements came from everywhere and we expected its passage after a few weeks of deliberation. Joe explained the provisions, rather well I thought, at long sessions of each house. The absentee-ballot section I thought was pivotal. It prohibited the casting of absentee ballots on the day of the election except by mail and required that they be opened and counted at 1:00 p.m. on election day rather than during the night after the polls closed when the ballot thieves waited around tables in the courthouse bowels with registration lists to see how many votes would be needed to carry the day. We were careful to make it appear to be a Democratic Party bill. My

Winthrop Rockefeller

friend Charles D. Matthews, who had served a term in the House thanks to the work of the women of the Throw the Rascals Out campaign, was the state Democratic Party chairman. He called it an important initiative for the Democratic Party. Governor Rockefeller supported the bill but kept his support sub-rosa. Both houses were trouncing his tax-and-spending programs, the heart of his Era of Excellence agenda, by margins of 9 to 1. Anything bearing the yoke of his endorsement was doomed.

The House of Representatives, which had been transformed into a relatively progressive body by the 1966 and 1968 elections, passed the bill virtually intact, seventy to nine. The House Speaker and the majority leader, Hayes C. McClerkin of Texarkana and Ray S. Smith Jr. of Hot Springs, respectively, were progressive reformers within the constraints of the Democratic Party. The state senate, however, remained nearly intact from the Faubus era. It was a Bermuda Triangle for any stray legislative vessel that was chartered for new territory. The election bill had to navigate the Judiciary Committee, where some of the big mules of the Senate did their work. The chairman was Max Howell of Little Rock, who over twenty-five years in the legislature had morphed from a hot-spur reformer to the gatekeeper for the old order. Senator Guy H. "Mutt" Jones of Conway, a bantam lawyer who pinned fresh red bou-tonnières on favored members of the press, lawmakers, and Senate employees each day and often broke out his harmonica from his back-row desk at adjournment, was the cleverest and meanest member of the committee. He made it clear to Joe that he would not stand for the absentee-ballot law to be changed by even a word. Conway County was in his senatorial district and Jones was a legatee of Sheriff Marlin Hawkins's beneficent absentee-voting system.

"That's the horse I rode in on and that's the one I'm going out on," Jones told me when I explained to him why the changes were needed. Joe said that we ought to give up on that one because it offended too many Democrats. I wanted the legislation to permit designated poll watchers inside polling places but Joe took that out, too, after Jones and others objected.

History offers some satisfying irony. Five years later, Senator Jones would be expelled from the Senate after his conviction for tax fraud, and it would be the election to fill his seat where the good people of Conway and Faulkner Counties finally triumphed over the ballot thieves. That story is coming. I was bitterly disappointed that Joe capitulated to Mutt Jones without a fight, but I was naïve then about Jones's ability to make mischief. No one in the legislature would go to his extremes to win a fight. He once wanted the US Army Corps of Engineers to build a highway bridge across the dam on the Arkansas River at Toad Suck to connect Faulkner and Perry Counties, which then was served by a ramshackle ferry. Since the state highway department would not buy the privately run ferry, Jones checked out the agency's two-year appropriation bill near the end of the 1957 leg-islative session and took it home so that the session came to an end with the state highway program unfunded for the next two years. Highway Director Ward Goodman capitulated and Governor Faubus called a special session solely to enact a highway-funding bill. So that Goodman would not renege, Jones amended the bill to require the highway director to buy the ferry for $25,000. As soon as the state owned the ferry, the Army Corps of Engineers built the bridge on the dam to relieve the state of operating

Mutt Jones

an unsafe ferry. We would not have bested Mutt Jones on election reform either.

The Senate adopted fourteen amendments that stripped out nearly every meaningful reform, including the entire section on absentee ballots. The House stood its ground, refusing to concur in the Senate amendments, but in the final hours of the session the two houses reached an accommodation that carved off most of the big changes, including the absentee-ballot provisions, but restored a modicum of reform. We had an act that Joe could claim as a great achievement but each of us knew was humbuggery. That did not keep me from going before the Arkansas League of Women Voters at its fiftieth anniversary dinner two nights after the bill's passage and telling those marvelous women, who had been the greatest champions of election reform, that Act 465 of 1969 was "a progressive step signifying a new day in Arkansas elections." Political wisdom dictates that you always declare a victory if you have a shred of claim.

It would be trite to say that I was disillusioned. The defeat of reform was more a confirmation that an illumination. But I felt some disenchantment with Joe because it had seemed that he was too solicitous of Mutt Jones and the powers in the Senate. In reality, he probably did all that he thought he could do without rupturing his shaky relationship with his party's Old Guard. I could stand uncompromising on principle, but he was the one who put his name on the ballot and his career on the line. Still, I thought I detected a glacial change in Honest Joe, the stalwart warrior for right and principle. He had wanted to go along with the Old Guard strategy of trying to strip Rockefeller or his party of the power to name two of the three election commissioners in each county, those represent-

ing "the majority party." By law, the majority party was the party holding the office of governor. The state election commission, on which the attorney general served, appointed the county election commissioners, including the majority- and minority-party representatives and a third swing member. Democrats devised the strategy of appointing Old Guard Democrats like Faubus's crony Harry W. Parkin to "represent" the Republican Party on the theory that you didn't have to actually *be* a Republican to represent the party's interests. I talked to Charles Matthews, the Democratic Party chairman, about Joe's capitulation and he agreed that the third-member plot was a bad idea. He talked to Joe, who agreed that it would not look good or be the right thing to do. Still, the state election commission appointed Democrats to "represent" the Republicans in a few of the machine counties—notably Conway County—and the Arkansas Supreme Court amazingly upheld the appointments, explaining that there was no reason why a yellow-dog Democrat could not rise above petty partisanship and represent the interests of Republicans in an election as well as a Republican could.

By the summer of 1969 Joe was convinced that his time had come, that he was ready, and that voters were ready for him to lead them. We began to talk strategy for a race in 1970. Rockefeller had promised in 1966 that he would not serve beyond two terms. Breaking faith with voters in that way is overcome with great skill. He also had been mortally weakened by his disastrous efforts to raise state taxes by 50 percent. Any relatively clean Democrat could win. As the highest-ranking Democratic office-holder in state government, Joe considered himself the titular head of the Democratic Party, by default. No one on the scene seemed apt to challenge him seriously. I do not believe that Joe had even heard of Dale Bumpers.

As the 1970 election season approached, the Democratic ballot was filling up after all. McClerkin, the young speaker of the House, would run for governor. So would Bill Wells, the right-wing legislator with a baritone radio voice who had been the Democratic nominee for lieutenant governor in 1968, and three or four other inconsequential figures, including a forty-three-year-old lawyer and hardware merchant with the funny name of Bumpers from Charleston, a town most Arkansans had never heard of much less visited. Orval Faubus, who sported a stylish new wife with a beehive hairdo, said he was thinking about making a comeback. Joe decided that he needed as much of the establishment as he could get on his side, people like the banker Herbert McAdams and Harry Parkin, who had been Faubus's highway commissioner from Central Arkansas. Parkin owned Parkin Printing Co., Inc., which had enjoyed the beneficence of many state printing contracts, including the largest one, to furnish office supplies for all the agencies and institutions of government. Parkin's bid for the general printing contract always listed bid prices for every office item that were much lower than any other printing and office supply house dared to submit until 1968, when Rockefeller's purchasing director figured out why. Nothing was ever purchased under any of the specifications in Parkin's bid but rather under a catchall item at the bottom of the contract that said if an agency needed anything not covered by any of those items it would be sold at the wholesale price plus 15 percent. Nothing mattered in the many pages of bid prices for supplies except the line at the bottom of the last page for miscellaneous purchases. The other bidders never knew that.

One day we drove to the Coachman's Inn on Interstate 30, which was owned by Witt and Jack Stephens, to collaborate with a small delegation of South Arkansas politicos headed by Benny Ryburn Sr., a Monticello automobile dealer who had been Faubus's main man in the southeast. Ryburn's son, Benny Jr., was the county's delegate in the House of Representatives. Joe told me as we were driving to the Coachman's that this was his chance to make inroads into the Stephens network. He figured that to make a serious race for governor he would need the support of businessmen who could bankroll a statewide race. They were the businessmen who gathered every two years for the "put sessions" where commitments were made to finance the campaigns of Faubus and Senators John L. McClellan and J. William Fulbright, if they had serious opponents. Benny Ryburn's group indicated that they were receptive but they had certain expectations of Joe if he were to get the support of the organization. One was that he had to improve his public style, get to be a polished speaker, and learn how to move through crowds with *savoir-faire*. They wanted him to take a charm course from a guy named Roger Reddy, a former broadcast star in the Dallas-Fort Worth market, who would improve Joe's modulation and timing and show him how to use his hands to make a point. Joe was sensitive to the constant jokes about his straitjacket poise and his leaden cadence at a lectern.

"I guess a Boy Scout helping a senior citizen across the street is dull," Joe told one crowd, "and a person who goes down the street breaking out lights is exciting." It was the most colorful remark he ever made.

But he agreed to study under Roger Reddy, and it got into the papers.

The makeover didn't work. A couple of weeks before the primary in the summer of 1970, Doug Smith, a political writer for the *Arkansas Gazette,* wrote in a Sunday election profile that people had been known to fall asleep shaking Joe's hand. Faubus, who thought he was going to be facing Purcell in a runoff in a few days, read the piece and giggled hysterically. He turned to a reporter who was traveling with him and said, "This is the line from this campaign that people will always remember." Actually, that line—and Joe himself—would vanish from people's memories almost overnight after Dale Bumpers's stunning election-night upset.

After the Coachman's session, I told Joe that he shouldn't do it, that he should not contrive to be something that he was not, merely to get the favor of these men. I was sort of plaintive.

"Joe, this is just not you," I said. I thought his strength was that he was different. He was not a slick politician, and people appreciated him for who he was. I was probably naïve about that. Anyway, he ignored my pleas.

Joe told me to be prepared to leave the attorney general's office in the spring of 1970 to run his campaign full time. I thought about it and decided that it was time instead to leave altogether, get out of politics, and go back to the law. Some part of my thinking, I'm sure, was an uneasiness about the prospect of directing a campaign against Winthrop Rockefeller, who, in spite of his failings and the near certainty of his doom, I believed to be the most principled exponent of reform in the arena. As far as I knew, he had never once trimmed his sails to the political winds, to use Orval Faubus's cynical metaphor.

While the personality transplant failed, Joe ran a creditable campaign for governor that rested on his reputation of probity. In a field of eight Democrats, all of whom owned sharper political skills but, except for Faubus, were lesser known, Joe was the one who people were pretty sure they could trust. Polls consistently showed him running a little behind Faubus and well ahead of the rest of the field. Faubus would get all the votes he could get in the preferential primary, and whoever made the runoff with him was almost a certain winner. Voters carried the memory of all the scandals of Faubus's last term in office, and he carried the weight of his divorce from Alta, his wife of thirty-seven years, and marriage to Elizabeth Westmoreland. Beth, as Faubus called her, had come down South to do a clumsy weekly TV show for the Democratic Party in which she attacked Rockefeller with scripts written by Faubus and party officials. At loose ends and needing cash just to pay the mortgage on the mountaintop stone mansion designed by E. Fay Jones, Faubus had taken a job as manager of the Dogpatch USA theme park about thirty-five miles east of his home. He was bored by the pedestrian work of looking after the trickle of tourists who visited the little park, and his affair and then marriage to Beth refurbished his energy and ambition. She persuaded him that his charms and allure with the electorate were undiminished. But he did not count on the scorn of his ex-wife, who had been so self-effacing for all their lives together. The night Faubus announced in a television commercial that he would run again, Alta told the *Arkansas Gazette* in a front-page article that people should consider his promises that evening of a fresh, bold administration to be worthless because, after all, he had broken his pledge to honor her until death did them part. Then Faubus made the mistake of taking Beth on the campaign trail with him. Pretty, tanned, and sporting a taller beehive permanent and shorter skirts than any Arkansas rustic had ever seen, the thirty-year-old bride made Faubus look especially old. She was a traveling spectacle and scandal, and Faubus looked like he sensed it. Traveling with him must have been her idea. He barely acknowledged her presence, as if she might be part of the little press coterie that was following him around the square. His troubled son Farrell, obese and accompanied by a petite miniskirted blonde whom he called Trinket, sometimes joined the entourage, to Faubus's obvious displeasure.

Orval Faubus

Joe developed an uncharacteristic confidence and serenity in the closing couple of weeks and took no risks that could jeopardize his standing. He hardly got his name in the paper again. Dale Bumpers, who started last, kept gaining in the polls and surged in the last week as Joe seemed to drop out of sight. He edged Joe for second place by 4,500 votes and then buried Faubus in the runoff and Rockefeller in the general election.

Few people ever took a political setback harder than Joe Purcell. Henry Woods, the late federal judge, told of a mission that he and another Bumpers adviser, Edward Lester, undertook a day or two after the vote in the first primary was certified. They were trying to get endorsements for Bumpers from the losing Democratic candidates, and Joe obviously was the key. They were prepared to pay off some of Joe's campaign debt, a common practice in those days but later made harder by campaign finance rules. They found Joe lying on a sofa in an office near the capitol.

He had a wet towel on his forehead and he complained about campaign mistakes and betrayals and he suspected fraud in a county or two. Woods had written a short statement endorsing Bumpers that they wanted Joe to sign. The haggling continued until Lester, who had recently suffered a mild heart attack, felt ill and left. Woods continued to importune Joe until he signed the statement. Woods delivered it promptly to the media. Nearly forty years later, Bumpers would recall at a lunch gathering that he and Bob Justice, a campaign aide, drove to the home of one of Joe's assistants to pay his respects and thank him for the endorsement. En route Justice handed him a check for what he remembered was $5,000 made out on his campaign account to Purcell's campaign.

"What's this for?" Bumpers said he asked.

Justice explained that it was in gratitude for Purcell's endorsement and to help pay off his campaign debt. Bumpers said that making such payment would be scandalous and tore the check up.

"Can you imagine what would have happened if it was reported that I had paid Joe Purcell for his endorsement?" Bumpers said. A friend of Woods who was at the table that day told Bumpers that he hated to tell him but Woods had considered the payment an obligation and delivered the check without Bumpers's knowledge.

"I'm sorry I came here today," Bumpers said.

Joe's ambition never subsided. He was elected lieutenant governor in 1974 and he bided his time for three terms. In 1982, his health and faculties failing, he made a final race for governor and came close again, losing this time in a runoff with Bill Clinton, who was staging a comeback after his re-election defeat by Frank White. His family and friends counseled Joe not to run for governor. It was such an improbable scenario for him. He would be running against the two most charismatic young politicians in the South, both

Dale Bumpers

desperate to get back on their career paths after devastating defeats. Jim Guy Tucker, the former attorney general and congressman, had lost a close race for the US Senate in 1978. But Joe came surprisingly close to Clinton in the first primary and a younger, healthier, and better-financed Purcell might have beaten Clinton in the runoff. Like the old Joe, he took a stand on principle and it hurt him. He refused to sign an initiative petition for a constitutional amendment to install a ten-thousand-word utility-regulation scheme into the state constitution because he said it was terrible constitutional law. Clinton signed the petition—the amendment actually was written by Hillary Rodham, his wife, and supporters—and he savaged Joe for not wanting to let people vote on a law that would protect consumers from the utilities. The Arkansas Supreme Court—I was not there yet—tossed it off the ballot the week before the election because voters could not possibly comprehend the madcap amendment.

In the spring of 1970, I do not think I had premonitions of Joe's electoral failures, either in that year's elections or afterward. He seemed bet-

Joe Purcell, Jim Guy Tucker, and Bill Clinton in campaign mode.

ter positioned than anyone else. Faubus clearly had a ceiling above which he could not rise except in the face of a particularly inept candidate, and that ceiling was well below 50 percent in the primaries or the general election. The rest of the Democratic field lacked Joe's familiarity and wholesome image with voters. Rockefeller was beset with so many political problems, most arising from his wearisome stalemate with the legislature and the rest of government, that he was unlikely to prevail against any Democrat except Faubus. But running Joe's campaign and the prospect of working at the top level of the Governor Purcell administration were both looking distinctly unappealing. We were having differences about policy as well as style, and probably with excessive piety I was disturbed about what I believed was his desire to make accommodations with the old order.

While Joe was setting up his campaign that spring, I took my leave and set up a lone law practice in the Tower Building at Little Rock. I thought I could revive something like the Election Research Council and continue the drive to clean up elections while building a private practice. Despite my ambivalent loyalties to the Democratic progressives, Rockefeller's overwhelming defeat that fall (he got fewer than a third of the votes against Bumpers) was disheartening, but Bumpers would prove to be almost as progressive as Rockefeller, whose failed program he adopted and passed *in toto*. Although his own dreams were shattered, Rockefeller continued to support my election-reform efforts. He took the huge defeat as a personal repudiation by the people of Arkansas and slumped into despondency. Two years and a month after leaving office he was dead.

Winthrop Rockefeller

CHAPTER 5

• • • • • • • • • • • •

Petition Parties

"If I was 20 years younger, I would go to Little Rock, and knock your teeth down your throat for your determined attempt to deny me the right to vote for the party of my choice."

—LETTER FROM AN ADMIRER

Soon after leaving the attorney general's office and setting up a solitary office in Little Rock in the spring of 1970, I went to see Robert W. Faulkner, Governor Rockefeller's executive secretary, and proposed that the governor contribute to a new organization called The Election Laws (TEL) Institute, which would monitor the conduct of elections and educate people on the proper and legal ways to hold elections, count votes and maintain voting records. I did not anticipate conducting large-scale investigations of vote fraud like the Election Research Council did in 1964 and 1965. TEL Institute would not have the resources nor would I have the time for it while trying to build a fledgling law practice. My notion was that laws were finally in place to control the wholesale abuse that had marked elections in many counties for a century. Voters had amended the state constitution in 1962 to permit voting machines as a substitute for paper ballots, and the largest counties were beginning to buy the electronic machines that we thought promised greater secrecy and security for the franchise. The permanent-voter-registration system, which was installed by the voters at the general election two years later, had ended the terrible abuses that accompanied the poll-tax system. While I was disappointed that the new election code that we had drafted in the attorney general's office and that the legislature had adopted in

1969 did not fix the source of the most flagrant corruption, the absentee ballot, it did streamline the election process, guarantee the secrecy of a person's vote, and spell out clearly how voting was to be conducted, the duties of election officials, and the penalties for ignoring them. If everyone involved in the electoral process knew what the law required or forbade them to do and the consequences of flouting the law, surely it would deter all but the most desperate vote thief. Widespread public knowledge of the voting laws would be extra insurance against the conniving of solitary vote thieves and political machines. That is what we proposed to accomplish with TEL Institute.

Rockefeller was instantly agreeable and put $20,000 into TEL that year. We incorporated in May and set up a board to govern its work and raise money. Board members mostly were lawyer friends who had supported my work and who I knew were independent and impervious to political pressure: James B. Wallace of North Little Rock, Robert F. Morehead of Pine Bluff, Oliver L. Adams of Rogers, and Rice Van Ausdall of Harrisburg. They also included Henry Ketcher Jr. of North Little Rock, a roofing contractor; Mrs. H. W. Badley of Mountain Home, president of the League of Women Voters of Baxter County; and Sam Hodges of Little Rock, the irreverent owner and publisher of the *Benton Courier.*

Many people and both major political parties would contribute to TEL over the next five years. But the first two years, we struggled day to day with financing while my law practice was maturing slowly. I obtained a bank loan to get us through the first months. But Rockefeller's gifts made our survival possible. Counting small gifts from his estate after his death in 1973, he gave us $90,778 and never asked for or expected the smallest favor for himself or the Republican Party. He merely asked that I do what I could to give people an honest voice in their government that was undiluted by fraud and deception.

For the first two years, TEL Institute tried to carry out my idea of perfecting elections through education. We began to provide local officials opinions on election questions much as I had done as a deputy attorney general for the three previous years, although now those opinions did not carry the stamp of officialdom. I worked with the Pulaski County Election Commission to train election judges and clerks. I began a drive to reapportion the seats on the City Council in North Little Rock, where I lived, to bring representation in the city's hugely disparate wards into rough population parity, as the United States Supreme Court had mandated in *Avery v. Midland County* three years earlier when it expanded the one-man, one-vote doctrine from state legislatures to local jurisdictions. Cities and counties across the state were dragging their feet complying with the mandate. We prepared a timetable for state and local election officials that detailed everything that should be done for the 1972 election season, and published a pamphlet entitled *So You Want to Be A Candidate* that explained to potential candidates for all public offices everything they needed to do to comply with election and campaign laws. When Faulkner County failed, in my opinion, to follow the wishes of people who had voted to substitute electronic voting machines for the paper ballot, I filed a lawsuit in Faulkner County Circuit Court, Russell C. Roberts presiding, to compel the county to buy or lease machines. Tom Eisele warned me that I would have trouble getting a transcript of any proceeding in Roberts' court, and I would need a speedy transcript to get the case to the supreme court after the anticipated unfavorable ruling by the judge. I showed up for a hearing with my own court reporter. Judge Roberts quickly stopped the proceedings and called me to the bench.

"What is that person doing here?" he demanded.

I said she would provide a speedy transcript so a timely appeal could be made to the supreme court. Roberts ordered the reporter to leave the courtroom, and he provided a court reporter, who did supply me with a transcript in sufficient haste. Roberts ruled that the law did indeed require the county to lease or buy machines but that it was not compelled to obtain enough of them to serve the county if county officials thought the cost would be too high. However many machines county officials wanted to buy were all that they were compelled to buy, he said. The supreme court upheld the decision, and the county acquired only five machines for the next election.

The approach of another election season in the spring of 1972 changed the character of TEL Institute's work and plunged me again into an investigation of election fraud. Harry W. Parkin, owner of Parkin Printing and Stationery Co. at Little Rock and a Democratic Party election official, called me to report that he had heard that people who were circulating petitions for the American Party were gathering bogus signatures. We received reports that many signatures were gathered at signature parties in the offices of John F. Wells, owner of General Publishing Co. at

Little Rock and an American Party sympathizer. At traditional signature parties, people would assemble around a table with telephone or poll books or voter-registration lists, pencils and pens with varying shades of ink, and pass petitions around the table.

I would get similar reports from the Republican Party and others in the next several weeks, so on May 19 TEL Institute issued a news release announcing that we would examine all petitions for ballot issues to be sure that signatures were valid. I said that TEL had received inquiries about who bore legal responsibility for signatures on initiative and referendum petitions. I said that TEL Institute would report any discrepancies to prosecuting attorneys.

Petition efforts under the state's initiative and referendum law have always been rife with irregularities, often the result of ignorance but sometimes of criminal wrongdoing. The initiative and referendum laws—Amendment 7 to the Arkansas Constitution and implementing statutes—are very precise about how signatures must be obtained and what constitutes a valid signature. But examining and tallying the names are a cumbersome process, and the casual way that government officials—the secretary of state for state-level acts and amendments—monitor the petitions encourages the sponsors of initiative campaigns to flout the law.

The American Party petitions were of little political consequence. Once the platform for Alabama Governor George C. Wallace, the party in 1972 was no more than a joke. At its national convention, it nominated for president John G. Schmitz, an obscure congressman from Southern California with right-wing sympathies, and for vice president Tom Anderson of Tennessee, the editor of *Farm and Ranch* magazine and a popular speaker at Arkansas functions. Anderson's wry right-wing column, *Straight Talk,* appeared in a few Arkansas newspapers, so he was presumed to have a small following in the state. Schmitz was a leader of the ultra-conservative John Birch Society but his wild rhetoric about Jews, African Americans, and other minorities got him expelled from even that extremist group. His wicked humor got him the attention of the American Party in 1972 ("I have no objection to President Nixon going to China," he said of the president whose home was in his district. "I just object to his coming back.") but Schmitz's rhetoric quickly pushed him beyond the margins.

For the party to qualify its candidates for the ballot in Arkansas, it needed 42,600 signatures of registered Arkansas voters—5 percent of the votes cast for governor in the 1970 general election. If the party had gotten on the ballot, Schmitz and Anderson would not have won enough votes to have any effect on the presidential election in Arkansas, won decisively by Nixon, but in the spring the Republicans at least were a little worried that the election might be close enough that American Party votes could tilt the presidential election to the Democrat, who at that time was expected to be Senator Edmund S. Muskie of Maine. It would turn out to be Senator George S. McGovern of South Dakota, a World War II hero who managed to get characterized in 1972 as a sniveling pacifist and maybe even a socialist. I had no objection to the American Party having its candidates on the Arkansas ballot as long as it won a place lawfully, and the calculations about how they might affect the election's outcome did not concern me. But if their appearance on the ballot was the product of collusion and fraud and of misfeasance by government officials, the public interest required TEL Institute to investigate.

The chairman of the American Party in Arkansas was Walter Carruth, a stolid farmer who lived in the town of Lexa in Phillips County and had run for governor in 1970. Carruth had hoped that year to exploit the popularity of Wallace, who had won a plurality in Arkansas in the 1968 presidential election. Both major-party candidates for governor in 1970, Bumpers and Rockefeller, were liberals who opposed racial segregation, which seemed to create an opening for a solid segregationist, but Carruth received only slightly more than 5 percent of the votes, which disqualified the American Party and forced the collection of petitions to reinstate it for the 1972 election. Carruth brought his American Party petitions to the secretary of state's office in June and early July 1972 and announced that he had more signatures than were needed. Sure enough, Secretary of State Kelly Bryant said his rigorous analysis of the petitions resulted in discounting nearly 6,000 signatures but that it would leave enough valid ones to certify the party. Eventually, he would say that they counted 48,276 signatures and discounted 4,684 of them, leaving 43,592 valid ones. Those were sufficient to certify the American Party as a legitimate political party, he said. Nevertheless, he gave Carruth's people another forty-five days to supplement the signatures and gain insurance against invalid names, which he said the law permitted if the original petitions met the threshold before the analysis of signatures.

One morning soon afterward I went to the capitol and asked

Joseph A. Madey, the attorney for the secretary of state, to let me see the petitions. I had examined only a few and spotted transparent forgeries on nearly every page. Madey returned in a few minutes and in his nervous sputtering manner told me that "the boss" wanted to see me immediately. Madey closed the door to Bryant's office behind us and Bryant began bluntly: "I want to see all your financial records." He said the law empowered him to do that.

"Do you demand to see the records of all nonprofits that come in here to examine official records?" I asked. Bryant said he didn't but that he wanted to establish a precedent. He said he wanted to make mine a test case.

"Fine," I replied, "let's the three of us go downstairs to the capitol press office right now and you demand to see TEL's records. I will refuse, and then we can have our lawsuit."

"L-l-l-let's don't do that," Madey said. I returned to the petitions.

We gathered a team directed by Betsy Branton of Little Rock to examine the petitions and spent three weeks combing them name by name. We counted the signatures three times and never got a total larger than 47,941. None of us was a handwriting expert, but we found 10,000 signatures that were patently bogus. The forgeries were so clumsy that a child could unravel them. The same person or three or four people signing alternately would pen all the names on a petition, or the names of husbands and wives would be in the same handwriting. The law required that people sign for themselves. One person wrote the names of all twenty-five persons on one petition and made no effort to disguise the handwriting. A forger would use pens with different color ink or alternate a pen and pencil to make it appear that different people were signing. TEL would later hire a handwriting expert to examine petitions from a few counties and he concluded that many more signatures were the work of a handful of forgers. When we announced our findings, we pointed out that Carruth's own name appeared six times on petitions. We raised the number later to nine.

A reporter for the *Arkansas Gazette* telephoned Carruth. He said he remembered signing petitions three times but not six. He signed them more than once, he explained, because circulators told him each time that they had lost the earlier petition with his signature. I pointed out that three of his signatures were on petitions that Carruth himself had circulated. At least he was listed on the petitions as the circulator.

Several newspapers called people from their communities whose names were on petitions that we questioned. The *Texarkana Gazette* showed people their signatures on petitions from Miller County. A few said flatly that the signatures were not theirs or, when telephoned, that they had never signed American Party petitions. Others said they had no memory of signing petitions but didn't want to flatly say they were forgeries. One man said he had signed American Party petitions in 1968 but not in 1972.

It became a media war. Carruth accused me of trying to disqualify American Party signatures to help President Nixon's re-election because I knew that Schmitz and Anderson would take votes away from him. Carruth said it also was an attempt to embarrass Secretary of State Kelly Bryant and advance the campaign of Pulaski County clerk Jerome Climer, Bryant's Republican opponent in the general election. He sent a telegram to Bryant asking him to demand that I disclose TEL Institute's financial records. I responded that his telegram was unnecessary because Bryant had already cited the law and demanded TEL's records and that I had invited him to proceed immediately to carry out his threats.

On September 4, Bryant sent ballot worksheets to the printer with the names of the American Party candidates. The next day I filed a lawsuit on behalf of Phyllis Brandon, a Democratic activist, in Pulaski County Circuit Court to enjoin him from certifying them. Bryant had until September 28 to make the certification and order the ballot printing. The attorney general's office, representing the secretary of state, asked Judge Warren Wood to dismiss my suit because the state supreme court, not the circuit court, had jurisdiction under the initiative amendment. Judge Wood concluded that he did have jurisdiction and scheduled a hearing.

I had found a handwriting expert at Memphis to analyze a few dozen petitions that we had found suspicious. Earl E. Davenport was a commercial artist whom the FBI had used as a handwriting expert in a number of federal cases. Davenport examined twenty-seven petitions from Ashley County and seventy-seven petitions from Phillips County, Walter Carruth's home. G. E. Hagood was listed as the circulator of four petitions in Ashley County, R. G. Farmer of four, John Owen of six, Rex Brown of seven, E. L. White of three, and E. L. Farmer of three. Davenport concluded that three people scribbled nearly all the signatures. One person signed 186 names, another 129 names, and another 89 names. Two people signed all the names of the circulators at the bottom of the petitions. One person executed most of the names on thirty-eight petitions in an unlabeled folder. One person signed for six people whose names appeared as the circulators of petitions. Two of the alleged circulators told us they had never circulated a petition. We could not locate any of the other circulators in telephone directories or poll books. E. L. White, who signed as the circulator of three petitions carrying seventy-five signatures, could not be found. Mrs. E. L. White was in the telephone book but she had been a widow for thirty years and said she had not circulated petitions.

Of the questionable petitions from Phillips County, one person wrote twenty-four of the twenty-five names on each of twenty-eight petitions. On four other petitions, one person forged twenty-three of the twenty-five signatures. On all the other petitions, a single signer accounted for from five to eighteen signatures.

Judge Wood ruled that the petitions were insufficient to qualify the American Party and that Bryant had exceeded his authority in giving the sponsors an additional forty-five days to gather insurance signatures. The American Party, which had intervened in the suit, appealed to the Arkansas Supreme Court, which upheld Judge Wood's orders. John Schmitz and Tom Anderson did not make it onto the ballot.

Many American Party aficionados were not very philosophical about the legal disputations, but civility is not a hallmark of fringe movements. A few of them found my telephone number and my address. This letter came from a gentleman from Hot Springs:

> Sir;
>
> If I was 20 years younger, I would go to Little Rock, and knock your teeth down your throat for your determined attempt to deny me the right to vote for the party of my choice.
>
> I have seen many crooked political deals, but none more rotten than the action which keeps the state's majority political party off the ballot, and does not even allow write-ins.
>
> I was brought up to have contempt for politicians. The older I get the more my contempt increases. But still lower tha[n] the politicians are the creatures like you that live by kissing the politician's big fat behinds[.]

Much later in life I would have responded with more grace, but I sent back a curt invitation that my dad would have liked:

"Dear Mr. Pratt: Please do not hide behind your age."

I could understand Mr. Pratt's pique that he was not going to get to vote for the men he wanted to lead the country, but I suspect that in more tranquil moods he reflected that the courts had prevented a criminal artifice from hijacking the election process, and that the rule of law was worth preserving. Still, I found little more contentment in the outcome than he did. While the law was vindicated and the election in the end was undefiled by fraud, no one was going to be held accountable for any of the wrongdoing. The message would be that the rewards of skullduggery were well worth the risks because no one would ever be asked to pay for their sins. Election fraud had been punished very rarely throughout Arkansas history and then only lightly. That culture was not going to change.

When TEL finished its investigation of the American Party petitions, it turned the findings over to prosecuting attorneys. Two decided to do something about it. At Newport, Prosecuting Attorney David Hodges looked at the questionable petitions in Jackson County and said he was pretty sure that irregularities had occurred on a large scale. In August, Hodges subpoenaed several persons who had circulated petitions or else who were listed as circulators. Two told him that they had not had anything to do with petitions. Three circulators turned out to be fictitious, two others had died more than two years earlier, and two men appeared with their attorneys and refused to answer questions. Hodges turned over his findings to the Arkansas State Police Criminal Investigation Division.

Since most prosecutors in districts where we uncovered serious irregularities evinced no interest in going after constituents who seemed to have been engaged somehow in the forgeries, I considered that the prosecuting attorney in Pulaski County, the Sixth Judicial District, might have jurisdiction for any of the fraud. Jim Guy Tucker, the prosecutor, thought his jurisdiction might be extensive because the petitions were filed at the capitol. I gave him our findings but I said I would send detailed information to prosecutors anywhere in the state who requested it. Except for Hodges, none did.

Tucker eventually charged Bob Currie of Little Rock, the former sergeant at arms of the American Party of Arkansas, who had notarized most of the petitions, affirming that he had personally witnessed people signing the petitions as circulators. He clearly had not. Although Currie, an impish fellow who wore his thinning white hair in a crew cut, was regularly seen at his rooming house, at American Party meetings and mingling with friends at his old haunts downtown a few blocks from the courthouse, law enforcement officials could not chase him down to serve papers.

Both Tucker and Hodges left office seven weeks after the election, Tucker to become attorney general and Hodges to return to private practice, and their successors showed no eagerness to pursue the matter any further. Although Bob Currie never seemed to be trying to elude anyone, they never laid their hands on him.

The next June, I found closure, too. In a talk to the Republican Women's Club of Pulaski County, I called it the worst investigation of a criminal viola-

Jim Guy Tucker

tion that a state could possibly conduct. I found it incredible that the secretary of state had approved heavily falsified petitions and even worse that law-enforcement agencies would not try to correct the abuses. "Although our law-enforcement agencies confirmed TEL's findings that thousands of forgeries appeared on the petitions circulated by the American Party of Arkansas before the last general election," I said, "not one person has been convicted."

TEL Institute's board that fall decided to look at ways to mend the democracy other than reforming and enforcing the election laws. Arkansas's elected constitutional officers—governor, attorney general, lieutenant governor, secretary of state, auditor, treasurer, and land commissioner—were paid less than their counterparts in all the other states. The governor was paid $10,000 a year, the attorney general $6,000, the lieutenant governor $2,500, and the other officials $5,000 each. It seemed to us that there had to be some linkage between the paltry compensation and the number and qualifications of people who sought and won the offices. Salaries that compared even modestly to those in the private sector would make leadership appealing to more people. Governor Bumpers had popularized the situation earlier that year by joking at a meeting of the National Governors Conference that the capitol building maid had spotted his monthly check on his desk, mistook it for hers, and quit. He said he could not hold the job without help from a brother and sister who were successful business executives in other states. They helped pay the college tuition of his children.

We concluded that the time was ripe to get rid of the constitutional ceilings on the salaries, a relic of the reactionary post-Reconstruction period. The board resolved to seek adoption of a constitutional amendment removing the salary limits on constitutional officers and state legislators and permitting the compensation to be set by the legislature, perhaps on the recommendations of an independent commission. It proved to be relatively easy. Many organizations endorsed the idea, and at its next session in 1975 the General Assembly referred the amendment to the voters, who ratified it overwhelmingly. Election reform should prove so easy.

Another constitutional relic, this one from the not-too-distant past, proved easier to vanquish. Amendment 51, the voter-registration law ratified in 1964, required women to register to vote using their proper surnames preceded by one of two honorifics, "Miss" or "Mrs." Pulaski County clerk James Jackson was enforcing the law, barring married women from using their maiden names and requiring them to register as "Miss" or "Mrs." rather than Ms. or avoiding any title altogether. I filed a class-action suit in US District Court at Little Rock in October 1974 for three young women lawyers, Pam Walker, Linda Scholle, and Catherine Harris, who had married but for professional reasons kept their maiden names, and Sister Leona Holting, a Catholic nun who wanted to register as Sr. Leona Holting. We argued that Amendment 51 violated the Ninth, Fourteenth, and Nineteenth amendments to the US Constitution because it imposed conditions on women's right to vote that were applicable to one sex only and because it violated their right to privacy by forcing them to make their marital status public record. The state had no compelling interest in making women abide by the conventions of a past day. Judge J. Smith Henley, before whom it was always a pleasure to try any case, said he could see no reason that a woman should not be able to call herself anything she pleased on a registration affidavit, and he permanently enjoined Arkansas county clerks from enforcing that anachronism.

With the help of the League of Women Voters in some parts of the state, TEL Institute tried to keep tabs on the conduct of elections in 1974. The primaries proved to be more uneventful than most, probably owing to the absence of the usual compelling forces that invigorate and unite the vote burglars. Orval Faubus was running yet again for governor, but this time the vaunted organization that had carried him through most of his previous seven elections had vaporized.

Discerning that Faubus had no chance of winning and wanting to be on the inside again after eight years of Rockefeller and Bumpers in the governor's office, Witt Stephens, the president of Arkansas Louisiana Gas Co. and the linchpin of the Old Guard, summoned one of his famous "put" sessions at the Coachman's Inn in downtown Little Rock, where wealthy allies from around the state put up money for the campaign. This time, it was not for Faubus but for the congenial former state representative and US congressman David Pryor, who had exhibited so much grace after his loss in 1972 to their man, Senator John L. McClellan. Witt's epiphany was as much of a shock for Pryor as it was for Faubus, who would forever remain embittered about the betrayal. Pryor's account was that he was lying in a hospital bed recovering from a blood clot that followed a skiing accident in Colorado when Stephens called and asked if he planned to run for governor if Governor Bumpers ran against Senator Fulbright. Pryor said he had not decided but he did not think so. Stephens told him that he owed him one after working so hard to defeat him in the McClellan Senate race and that if Pryor ran for governor, he would do everything he could to get him elected. Even Marlin Hawkins, who had delivered many landslides in Conway County for Faubus, threw in with Pryor.

David Pryor

But for the machine operators, Pryor did not inspire the same level

of urgency as Faubus and McClellan. Governor Bumpers was running against Senator J. William Fulbright, a son of the Old Guard, but everyone in Arkansas who had any scent for politics—everyone but Fulbright, from whom his campaign withheld the dreadful polls—knew that the race was over the day Bumpers announced. Few were willing to expend vain effort for a lost cause, particularly if it was illegal like stealing votes. But local races, especially for county judge and sheriff and for local-option liquor sales, will drive election officials into the back rooms at the courthouse to gin up extra votes and to use other illegal tactics to dissuade or persuade voters.

Before the May Democratic primary, Robert D. May Jr., a twenty-seven-year-old candidate for sheriff in Lee County, called me to complain that deputies of Sheriff Courtney Langston Jr. were threatening people who had bumper stickers and signs for the challenger. He signed an affidavit relating the beating and arrest of a young man who had told Langston he wouldn't vote for him and refused to shake his hand. Langston or his father had been sheriff since 1939 and his word was the law in Lee County. Ralph Hamner went to Marianna and obtained affidavits from several men recounting the intimidation. The state newspapers reported the allegations and Langston's denial that his men were doing anything unlawful. May won narrowly and he wrote me a note crediting TEL Institute and the publicity that it generated for his victory. He would be re-elected eight times.

TEL Institute's work and influence were growing. It received 305 questions and 63 complaints about voting in the spring primaries. Scores of businesses and organizations, including both Republican and Democratic central committees, contributed to the organizations. Thanks to Sam Hodges and the *Benton Courier*, we furnished weekly informational updates along with cartoons to newspapers across the state during the 1974 primary and general election seasons. It occurred to me that no organization in any other state was doing what TEL was doing. The burgeoning Watergate scandal had illuminated all kinds of chicanery in the 1972 national elections, and the country was in a restive, angry mood. TEL Institute could perform the same functions on the national stage. Governor Bumpers, who was elected to the Senate that fall, and the incoming governor, David Pryor, supported the idea. Congressman Wilbur D. Mills had already written letters to the Rockefeller and Ford foundations urging their support of a national TEL and had received favorable letters from them. I went to Washington in early spring 1974 to join his committee staff to work on health-care and election legislation. Ways and Means had a subcommittee working on national election reform. I used the circumstances to scout the prospects of national political support.

Mills was enthusiastic about the idea of giving TEL a national portfolio. It would champion election reforms nationally and in the states, perform the education functions, and serve as a watchdog at elections. Mills had recovered from his quixotic and humiliating chase for the presidential nomination in 1972 and was at the peak of his power as chairman of the

House Ways and Means Committee. He was working with Senator Edward M. Kennedy and President Nixon to fashion a universal health insurance system. He wrote to David Rockefeller and seemed to have a commitment from the Rockefeller Foundation to support a nationwide TEL project. Soon afterward, I received letters from George H. W. Bush and Robert Strauss, chairmen of the Republican and Democratic National Committees, respectively, expressing interest in joining the effort.

Wilbur D. Mills

Back at Little Rock, TEL Institute with my intermittent guidance was busying itself with the Arkansas primaries. We set up a statewide toll-free hot line for people to report election irregularities, and we reported widespread irregularities with absentee balloting, and the purchasing of votes in three counties. I was confident that we would be taking our act to the national stage the next spring.

At two o'clock in the morning of October 7 that dream vanished. Mills was boozing that night at the Silver Slipper nightclub in Washington with a bosomy stripper named Annabella Battistella, with whom he apparently had been having an affair. The park police pulled Mills's car over near the Tidal Basin. The dancer, who used the fetching stage name of Fanne Foxe, "the Argentine Firecracker," tried to run away and vaulted over the rail into the Tidal Basin. Her career took off (she changed her title to "the Tidal Basin Bombshell" and raised her biweekly fee from $3,500 to $15,000), but Mills's sank. He managed re-election in Arkansas's Second District a month later but resigned as chairman of the Ways and Means Committee. Senator Warren Magnuson of Washington, who had gone to the House of Representatives with Mills in 1938, remarked upon reading about the episode that he was losing his two great friends from Arkansas. Senator J. William Fulbright had been defeated in May by Governor Bumpers.

"Bill Fulbright was knocked off by Bumpers, and Wilbur was bumped off by knockers," Magnuson said.

His influence and effectiveness gone, Mills served out the next term in quiet ignominy and devoted the rest of his life to combating alcoholism. Mills had been the key to the national election project. David Rockefeller wrote me that the project should be put on the back burner. I had no choice but to oblige. I returned to Little Rock.

Our old friends up the river in Conway County were giving us plenty to do.

"I just love the ground I walk on."

CHAPTER 6

• • • • • • • • • • • •

Crime and Impunity

"They perceive Arkansas's first problem to be
the establishment of the essential mechanisms
of democratic government."

—V. O. KEY, *SOUTHERN POLITICS*

Nothing oppresses the spirit more than watching firsthand the exercise of absolute power, even when it occurs in the narrow quarters of a rural Arkansas county. In Conway County for more than a dozen years, from my venture into election research until my surrender in 1978, I would encounter the Southern political machine in its most undefiled form. Absolute political power cannot be exercised overnight in a democracy. The climate has to be right. If you are going to do battle with such power it helps to know its genesis and development. My knowledge came glacially.

While I was still laboring in Winthrop Rockefeller's political office in February 1966, I had the first of many authentic experiences with the control that the political boss of the little county had on every institution of government. I drove to Morrilton to see if I could be of some help— a menacing physical presence if nothing else—to G. Thomas Eisele in that gentlemanly lawyer's final struggle to save a local newspaper editor from the depredations of the political machine that had set out to destroy him. Seven years earlier, Gene Wirges had questioned the integrity of a school board election in Conway County in his weekly newspaper, the *Morrilton Democrat*. Then he challenged the conduct of elections generally, and finally the corruption of law enforcement in the county. Sheriff Marlin Hawkins and his lieutenants fought back with the weapons they knew best, violence and intimidation. When that failed, they tried economic coercion. Wirges lost his newspaper in the long ordeal, but he didn't shut up. At last they resorted to the judicial system. They sued him for libel twice, summoned him to the circuit judge's chambers for extrajudicial questioning and rebukes, and had carefully chosen grand juries indict him for slander, conspiracy, and perjury. Local judges, grand juries, and petit juries, uniformly friends of the sheriff and the ruling political order, unfailingly did their duty as the sheriff saw it and delivered civil judgments and criminal verdicts against the editor. Almost as uniformly, the Arkansas Supreme Court did its duty and reversed them for lack of evidence or for flouting elemental rules of procedure and judicial conduct.

On this occasion, Wirges was accused of perjury for having testified in his last libel trial in the same courtroom that he had not written one of many columns in his newspaper that appeared under the byline "Birdtown Birdie," the pseudonym of an anonymous female correspondent. The $200,000 judgment against Wirges for having libeled Sheriff Hawkins's friend, county judge Tom Scott, in the Birdie column had been thrown out, but a grand jury was quickly assembled and this time it indicted the editor for perjury. Despite his testimony that he did not write it and the absence of any evidence that he wrote it, the grand jury concluded that he had, indeed, been the author of the offending Birdie column and had lied about it.

As we headed for Morrilton for the perjury trial that bitterly cold morning, the road made treacherous by freezing rain, Eisele knew for certain what the outcome would be because it was always the outcome in Conway County Circuit Court. Wirges would be found guilty. But, as he had done meticulously in the previous cases, Eisele wanted to perfect the record so that the supreme court would clearly see the errors and the manifest injustice of the proceedings. He did, and it would.

Sheriff Hawkins's good friend and protector, Circuit Judge Wiley Bean, had died after supervising the judicial hazing of the editor for three years, and this trial fell to the lot of Judge Russell C. Roberts of Conway, who had been appointed by Governor Faubus to fill a brief term in a special division of the court and then was elected to succeed Bean. Roberts was, if anything, less conversant with the law and jurisprudence than Bean, and he also was a part of the political alliance. Several years later, a survey by the *Arkansas*

Gazette showed that Roberts's decisions were appealed and overturned far more frequently than those of any other circuit or chancery judge in the state. The day before our trial, Judge Roberts rejected Eisele's motion to quash the indictment on the ground that the grand jury had been prejudiced against Wirges, and he proceeded to seat twelve jurors who acknowledged familiarity if not outright friendship with Hawkins or the allegedly libeled county judge. Eisele moved that the trial be moved to a different county where Wirges could be tried before an impartial jury, but the prosecutor presented twelve

G. Thomas Eisele

friends of the sheriff who said it was their opinion that Wirges could get a fair trial. Eisele then moved to quash the entire panel from which the jury had been chosen because anyone who did not evince a familiarity with the political leaders had been stricken from the panel. When the trial opened the next morning, Eisele made two final pleas to introduce some impartiality to the proceedings.

"There is not a juror sitting there who won't say he's a personal friend of Hawkins or county judge Tom Scott, and yet not one knows Wirges except to see him," Eisele pleaded. When Roberts said the jury would be seated, Eisele moved that Sheriff Hawkins be replaced as the bailiff of the court because of his obvious interest in Wirges's conviction. Before Judge Roberts could deny the motion, Hawkins asked to be relieved as the bailiff. At recesses in the trial, which went far past midnight, I spotted the sheriff escorting jurors into the men's restroom for conferences. I suggested that we should move for a mistrial for what seemed to me to be blatant jury tampering, but Eisele eventually decided that it would be fruitless and probably unnecessary. He was convinced that the complete absence of evidence and the record of prosecutorial and judicial error would secure a reversal when he took the case to the state supreme court.

Here was Hawkins's shocking evidence that Wirges had lied at his libel trial: The prosecuting attorney produced the author of the Birdtown Birdie columns, who testified that Wirges sometimes changed her columns or simply wrote them and that indeed Wirges had written most of the column that supposedly libeled county judge Tom Scott, although Scott had not even been mentioned in the article. Eisele confronted her with the original copy of the column from the newspaper's files and it was in her own handwriting. She said she had copied the column for herself after it appeared in the newspaper and kept it under her bed. Wirges or someone else must have sneaked into her house and stolen it, she said. Eisele then showed her minor typographical changes in the published column that represented Wirges' editing, which seemed to prove that her handwritten version was not copied from the newspaper. She had no explanation for the changes in the published version. The woman testified that she had been married only twice, but Eisele presented evidence of eleven marriages. She said she had never been arrested for a felony offense, but Eisele offered proof of twenty-six arrests in four states for prostitution, lewd conduct, vagrancy, and other morals charges. She explained that she had been drunk for several years and had no memory of long stretches of time. But the jury found her perfectly credible and Wirges untrustworthy. At 3:58 the next morning it rendered the expected guilty verdict. Wirges was sentenced to three years in the penitentiary.

Fourteen months later, the supreme court unanimously reversed the decision because it said there was absolutely no proof that the editor had said anything untrue. For a neophyte lawyer, the decision did not assuage the disillusionment of having witnessed the dedication of a judicial system—judges, prosecutors, grand juries, trial jurors, and officers of the court—to the single-minded service of injustice and the political machine that pursued it. Tom Eisele handled that bizarre trial and all the irregular proceedings before and after it with a tranquility that I could not summon of myself. I think the Conway County ordeals were the underpinnings of Eisele's judicial career. President Richard Nixon appointed him to the federal bench for the Eastern District of Arkansas

in 1970, and lawyers ranked him among the top federal judges in the country in temperament and fairness.

• • •

What intrigued me most about the persecution of the editor in Conway County and the same singleness of purpose in other counties that perpetuated voting crimes year after year was that the attitudes pervaded the community. The ruling political faction and the local governments, including the judicial branch, united behind the cause of maintaining political power at any cost to democratic traditions and the rule of law. The exercise of such power did not seem to disturb many people in the wider civic community, or else they were too jaded or afraid to raise public objections. Whether they were guided by fear or lethargy, I wondered what could cause such cynicism.

In Conway County, the reasons were barely beneath the surface, in the history and handed-down memories of the hardest and most tumultuous time those hills and valleys have endured: the struggle for power after Reconstruction. That strife, which was marked by unmatched levels of voting fraud and quotients of bloodshed that approached war, was recounted in the first chapter.

The names of the men who engineered the great coups of the 1880s—Bentley, Hervey, Gordon—adorned the county's big political offices well into the next century, and the memories or legends of why and how they did it waned only slightly over a century.

Fifty years later, the lessons from those tumultuous elections were not lost on young Marlin Hawkins, a sharecropper's son who set out to build a political machine unrivalled in Conway County or any other. Hawkins was reared in the community of Sunnyside at the foot of Wolverton Mountain in the northern reaches of the county, but by the time he ran for office the first time, in 1940, hardly a family anywhere in the county did not owe him for some real or imagined favor. Hawkins got a job as the county's welfare caseworker in the depths of the Great Depression, when a good half of the twenty-two thousand residents of the county would need some form of assistance for a member of the family. He certified people for welfare, commodities, and disability pensions, and got youngsters work in the Civilian Conservation Corps and older folks jobs in the Works Progress Administration. He cemented himself with the congressman from the Fifth District, Brooks Hays of Russellville, who began to delegate federal patronage to him. People could not easily forget the person to whom they were obliged and not merely because of his friendly and unusually solicitous manner. Hawkins had lost his right eye at the age of eight when a pocketknife he was using to scrape sweetgum resin from a door slipped and lodged in the eye. The eye had to be removed. Rather than make him timid, the disfigurement seemed to impel young Marlin to boundless bonhomie.

In 1939, Hawkins landed a job as a deputy for Sheriff Elmer Thomas, and the next year he ran for circuit clerk and recorder. All the welfare chits from five years of assiduous labor paid off on election day, and he carried every precinct in the county but one. He would write fifty years later that his political organization was fully in place that fall, but in fact it would take another decade to perfect it. As the sheriff's deputy he earned the gratitude of some county bigwigs by silencing a probe of state highway skullduggery until after the 1940 election. A rich farmer whom Governor Carl Bailey had appointed to the state highway commission converted state drainage tiles to use on his Conway County farm and witnesses signed affidavits about it. The delayed exposure didn't save Bailey, who lost the nomination to Homer Adkins, but it earned Hawkins some important political credit.

As the circuit clerk and recorder and then county treasurer, a job he won without opposition, Hawkins expanded his political network by helping GIs returning from the war qualify for benefits, and he began to explore the marvelous opportunities of the absentee ballot. In 1944, he fraudulently filled out some one hundred ballots for J. Bryan Sims, the state comptroller, whom he described as a friend and who was heavily favored to be nominated for governor in the Democratic primary. It turned out to be a futile bit of legerdemain because Sims mysteriously pulled out of the race in the runoff primary and handed the nomination to Ben T. Laney. In his self-published autobiography, *How I Stole Elections*, Hawkins said it was the only time that he actually broke the law and he was always sorry that he did it.

His break came in 1950 when his old patron, Sheriff Thomas, told him that he wanted to switch jobs—Thomas would run for treasurer and Hawkins for sheriff with Marlin doing the legwork for both of them. Hawkins had taken over the Democratic central committee in 1946 and named the Democratic judges and clerks for each election, and that great advantage was waiting to be exercised. (Having the election officials on his side, he would explain in his book, gave him a psychological advantage and assured him that his opponents couldn't steal the election from him.) The sheriff promptly changed his mind and ran again but Hawkins refused to stay in his old job. It was a bitter race, won barely by Hawkins, but charges that he stole the election would stick with him the rest of his days. He would lament that if he had known how nasty the race would be and that his reputation for pristine rectitude would be sullied, he would have backed out and kept the treasurer's job. It was in the grueling sheriff's race that he perfected the absentee-ballot stratagem. Over the years, at picnics and other shindigs, he assiduously collected the names and addresses of people in scores of families around the county who were living out of the county for one reason or another so that, according to his account, he could notify them of approaching elections and his candidacy and send them an application for an absentee ballot.

For three months before the 1950 primary, Marlin's brother Ray went throughout the county, wherever there were Hawkins supporters, building Marlin's absentee-ballot register, getting the names of everyone in every family who might not be around on election day, including relatives working in other states. He carried about five hundred applications for absentee ballots to the county clerk, who soon ran out of the mail ballots. This was Hawkins's account of it: The secretary of the county committee had ordered only three hundred absentee ballots printed, more than were thought necessary based on the absentee ballot count at recent elections. When the order for a fresh supply of ballots went to the printing contractor, the *Morrilton Democrat,* the editor alerted Sheriff Thomas, who in turn alerted the prosecuting attorney, Robert Hays Williams of Russellville. The prosecutor opined that Hawkins had illegally manufactured the ballot applications. Hawkins insisted that he had cleared his methods with Circuit Judge Audrey Strait. Writing forty years later, Hawkins said Sheriff Thomas and his deputies threatened to lock up people who mailed the absentee ballots back and as a result he got to count only about two hundred of his five hundred absentee supporters. Hawkins would also claim that the sheriff and his deputies employed some of the tactics of 1888 to counter his strong support among African Americans at Plumerville, Menifee, and other precincts in the southern part of the county. He said they shot over the roof of Ed Winston, a big supporter at Plumerville, and set off dynamite at the home of E. L. Brewer, a black leader in the Springfield community, who was working for Hawkins.

Whoever's side you were on, elections were a nasty business. By Hawkins's account in *How I Stole Elections,* he and his men waged a courageous fight for truth and justice. Thomas's two sons-in-law withdrew $25,000 from the First State Bank of Morrilton to pass out on election day at the exchange rate of $25 a vote.

Hawkins wrote that his men overheard Thomas's strategy for election night: If Thomas managed to carry the regular precinct votes, when the absentee box was brought over from the county clerk's office before it could be opened it was to be heaved through the window on the second floor of the courthouse because they knew nearly all the absentee votes would be for Marlin. Confederates on the ground would retrieve the box and toss it into the Arkansas River.

But Hawkins won the regular count by fifteen votes after catching the vote tabulator casting Hawkins ballots for Thomas. When Sheriff Thomas's enforcer, a man Marlin called "Big Son," complained that the stale air was stifling him and opened the window near the end of the counting, Hawkins and his friend W. O. "Bus" Hice, the Morrilton chief of police, formed a phalanx in front of the window to block the absentee-box heave. He won by 218 votes. That, again, is Hawkins's version.

Thomas screamed fraud, contested the election briefly, and then ran as an independent in the general election, where both political parties would have judges and clerks. But Hawkins outmaneuvered the sheriff and his allies and seized control of the Republican voting officialdom as well as the Democratic officials. He won by 345 votes. Two months after Hawkins took office, Judge Strait picked sixteen grand jurors, every one a Thomas supporter, Hawkins said, and directed them with the aid of Prosecutor Williams to look into Hawkins's illegal purchase of votes in the election. Hawkins wrote in his book that he was told later that the grand jurors decided not to indict him after a couple of them recalled having taken money from Sheriff Thomas and his men themselves for the purpose of securing votes. Hawkins said one of the jurors reportedly asked, "Are we supposed to indict ourselves?"

The remnants of the old machine, though not Thomas himself, quickly begged for peace. Sheriff Hawkins granted it, and solidarity was restored. In short order, courthouse officialdom along with municipal and school board offices became dependable reflections of Hawkins's friendship. People who could be identified as the sheriff's friends never lost, at least not after the absentee vote was tallied.

• • •

The peace was never violated again until 1957, when Gene Wirges, who had worked at the *Arkansas Gazette* with his father, the legendary crime reporter Joe Wirges, bought the *Morrilton Democrat,* or at least made a down payment on it. I have related watching the end of Wirges's long battle with Hawkins's organization in the venal court of the county, but I had been only vaguely aware of its antecedents, although the Wirges-Hawkins story had been chronicled in the state newspapers, the *Saturday Evening Post, The Atlantic Monthly,* and *The Nation.*

Actually, comity reigned another three years after Wirges's arrival until a few men from Wonderview, a farming community in the valley between Pigeon Roost and Bull Mountains north of Morrilton, came to see the editor. They accused three members of the Wonderview School Board members of financial skullduggery. The three had been backed by the Hawkins machine and the farmers were skeptical of the election results. Wirges investigated and concluded that they were right. He supported the recall of the three board members, and they were recalled by narrow margins at a special election.

Emboldened, Wirges put his newspaper squarely behind a municipal reform movement in Morrilton—a group in town was trying to replace the aldermanic form of government with a city-manager system—and Wirges let it be known that he was going to take on the whole machine and its election chicanery. Hawkins took that personally and threw his organization behind the city fathers. The city-manager proposition was defeated soundly. Wirges and Hawkins argued at the courthouse on election night and the word spread. Hawkins's friends quickly gathered and state troopers were summoned to protect Wirges as he left that night. Hawkins's sidekick, "Bus" Hice, the former police chief and by then the county tax assessor, had to be restrained from assaulting the editor. A few weeks later the burly assessor pummeled Wirges on a Morrilton sidewalk for writing disparagingly about him. If Wirges wrote about him again, Hice said, he would get another thrashing. Sheriff Hawkins warned Wirges that if he continued to write about politics, his safety could not be assured.

A few weeks after the city-manager election, the county held another special election for a vacant seat in the state House of Representatives. Wirges's paper supported a young feed dealer named Houston Mallett, who was trounced by Hawkins's man, Loid Sadler. Wirges was struck by some of the results. In Mallett's home township of Catholic Point, Sadler beat him ninety-three to two. Wirges went to the community and interviewed voters. He quickly found fourteen who would sign affidavits that they had voted for Mallett. But he couldn't prove it because the voter list for the township had vanished and there was no way to determine who had voted. In nearby Austin Township, more votes had been cast than there were qualified voters in the precinct. That voter list disappeared, too. Wirges printed his findings although friends advised him that he was pushing Hawkins too hard and that the mortgage on his paper made him vulnerable. By year's end, a boycott campaign in the business community had slashed his advertising income by a fifth.

Marlin Hawkins

A few days after the paper published the story about Wirges's election findings, a sheriff's deputy posted a notice of sale on the door of the newspaper. Wirges had been tardy in remitting state employment-security taxes. While he was an idealistic and crusading editor, Wirges was a careless businessman, improvident in his investments and inattentive to the recipes for operating a business, like remitting all your taxes and paying the bills on time. This time, he rounded up money to pay the taxes and forestall the auction. Over the next three years, Winthrop Rockefeller and other friends rescued him and his paper when it was about to fall into the clutches of the machine because he had not tended to business.

A grand jury was convened that October to investigate Wirges's charges of voting irregularities. He supplied the grand jury a list of eighty violations of the law and witnesses to them. The grand jury concluded that the irregularities were minor infractions that had long been customary in county elections. The newspaper called it a whitewash.

The grand jury foreman sent him a letter hinting that if his criticisms continued he could wind up in jail.

Friends of the editor, who had organized as the Better Government League, took up his investigation. They obtained the list of people who had obtained absentee ballots and sent them letters. Many were returned undeliverable because there was no such address or because the alleged voter was not at that address. They examined the list of voters at the election and produced the names of some seven hundred people who had voted but were either dead, fictitious, could not be found, or were otherwise unqualified to vote by law. They filed a suit contesting the votes with Circuit Judge Wiley W. Bean, a friend of Hawkins. He dismissed it with the explanation that the proper time to challenge voters was at the polling place. Wirges tried to challenge the election officials by pointing out that county workers had served as election judges and clerks in direct contravention of the state constitution. Attorney General Bruce Bennett's office opined that there was nothing wrong with the practice.

In the 1962 school elections, Wirges had friends run for school-board positions but they lost uniformly. One, Harding A. Byrd, came close to winning a school-board seat in the East End School District. He carried voters who actually showed up at the polls, 200 to 132, but when they opened the absentee box those votes went against him 143 to 9. Thirty-two percent of the voters in the rural community had business out of the county on election day. The Republican state executive committee asked Marion B. Burton, Rockefeller's attorney, to investigate. Burton filed two lawsuits challenging the results of the school elections in the county. Sixty-six ballots were cast although no application had been made for absentee ballots, which made them automatically invalid. Nearly one hundred of the absentee voters proved to have been at home on election day. Wirges reported the lawsuits in the *Morrilton Democrat* and commented about them in his weekly column.

Judge Bean summoned the editor to his courtroom and had him sworn in as a witness although it was not a part of any litigation. Wirges asked why he was there and the judge told him to sit down and answer questions. He proceeded to dress down the editor while Hawkins and his friends smiled. Then the judge let him go. Wirges unearthed more absentee irregularities, such as double voting by residents of Michigan, who voted in the same election in Michigan and Arkansas, in violation of the laws of both states. The prosecuting attorney told him they were misdemeanors and he could do nothing about it. Wirges took them to the Civil Rights Division of the US Justice Department, which said the double voting appeared to be mere stupidity and not worthy of a conspiracy.

About that time, a well-traveled woman in the Birdtown community north of Morrilton began writing a cracker-barrel column about politics. They were crude but Wirges thought them insightful and entertaining. Eulena Stout remained anonymous and Wirges published her scribblings under the pseudonym "Birdtown Birdie." Eventually, Nathan Gordon, the state's lieutenant governor and a friend of Hawkins, filed two libel suits against the paper over Wirges's reporting and commentary and the Birdie column on behalf of the county judge and the county clerk. As lieutenant governor, Gordon had performed a great favor for Hawkins. The sheriff's father-in-law, Monroe Treadwell, had been convicted in the highway scandal of Governor Sid McMath's administration and when Gordon was sitting in one day for Governor Francis Cherry, who was out of state, he issued Treadwell a full pardon.

The libel trials were a burlesque of jurisprudence. Tom Eisele, who represented Wirges at both trials, quickly exhausted his peremptory challenges of jurors in both trials, and the judges seated juries of Hawkins's supporters. At the second trial, the jury foreman was attorney Gordon's business partner. At neither trial did Gordon adduce any evidence that anything Wirges had written was wrong, but Judge Bean said that was irrelevant. "I don't think proof makes any difference on this," he averred. The county judge claimed in the second suit that he had been defamed by suggestions in the Birdie column that he had used county equipment for private improvements. He denied it on the stand but when Eisele showed him photographs of work done on private property, including a road to the county judge's private cabin on Petit Jean Mountain, he acknowledged it but said there were good reasons for doing the private work. Both juries hastily returned judgments against Wirges, $75,000 for the county clerk for having been libeled by Wirges's reporting and the column on the election irregularities, and the county judge $200,000 for having been libeled by one of the Birdie columns.

Eventually, the Arkansas Supreme Court overturned one of the verdicts and Circuit Judge Paul X Williams, who tried the second case when Judge Bean said he was too tired, threw out the second verdict, but in the interim a Little Rock businessman and Wirges's friends had to acquire the newspaper to keep it from been handed to the county judge and county clerk to satisfy the libel judgments. At the libel trial for defaming the county clerk, Gordon called Marion Burton, who had been executive assistant to the state Republican chairman at Little Rock, as a witness to tell who was having him investigate school elections in the county. When Burton refused to answer questions from Judge Bean about his connections with the Republican Party, which were well known, the judge told Sheriff Hawkins to lock him up and forbade him from practicing law in the five counties of the Fifth Judicial District ever again. Burton was freed in a few hours, and the supreme court sternly reprimanded Bean for both jailing and trying to disbar Burton.

Wirges's troubles were only beginning. He continued his investigations into elections, county hiring, and financial irregularities in the sheriff's office, part of the time without a newspaper to publish his findings. He would call a press conference to announce the results of his investigations. After Wirges released his evidence of financial misconduct by the sheriff's office, Judge Bean impaneled a grand jury to look at his evidence. The grand jury cleared Hawkins and instead indicted Wirges for slander. The jurors called him back a couple of days later to ask him more questions. He refused to answer this time and Judge Bean locked him in jail for contempt of court. Once freed, Wirges collaborated with two justices of the peace to have Hawkins arrested for committing fraud in the handling of traffic tickets, based on Wirges's evidence. Judge Bean assembled another grand jury to see whether Wirges should be charged with anarchy, conspiracy, and usurpation of the power of the court. The jurors promptly indicted Wirges and the two JPs on conspiracy charges. After a brief trial, Wirges was found guilty of conspiracy, fined $250, and sentenced to four months in prison. Judge Carl Creekmore of Van Buren, who had taken the case after Judge Bean excused himself, quashed the conspiracy conviction because he said the indictment was fatally defective. Judge Bean impaneled another grand jury, which charged the editor with slandering and conspiring against Hawkins. In case none of that stuck, the grand jury then indicted Wirges for perjuring himself in the second libel trial, the one accusing the Birdtown Birdie author of sullying the reputation of the county judge. As you will remember, the second Birdie libel judgment, a flagrant miscarriage, was set aside by the trial judge, Paul X Williams. That perjury trial in midwinter 1966, which is where we started this story, ended in conviction and a four-year prison sentence for Wirges. The supreme court would correct that miscarriage, too.

Sheriff Hawkins waives off reporter Herbie Byrd of radio station KLRA outside the Arkansas Supreme Court, where Hawkins had taken newspaper editor Gene Wirges (center) for a hearing in 1964. Hawkins had jailed Wirges for refusing to testify before a Conway County grand jury investigating him for conspiring against the sheriff. The hearing was on Wirges's habeas corpus petition. The supreme court ordered the editor's release. *Photo courtesy of the* Arkansas Democrat-Gazette

Wirges and his friends had won every round but they were Pyrrhic victories. He lost his newspaper, which became a somewhat friendly tribune for the machine. One by one, his allies left the county and so eventually did Wirges.

Conway County's peculiar democracy was unscathed. It would prosper for another eight years.

CHAPTER 7

• • • • • • • • • • •

Snoop Sisters

LYSISTRATA. Oh, Calonicé, my heart is on fire. I blush for
     our sex. Men will have it we are tricky and sly.
CALONICÉ. And they are quite right . . .

In the fictional lore of ancient Greece, the seductive Lysistrata persuaded the women of Corinth and Sparta to wean their husbands and lovers from sex until the men stopped making war with the Athenians. Assembling the women in the public treasury, Lysistrata got them to sip wine from a phallic-shaped flask and take an oath not to go to bed with the men until they finally laid down their swords and made peace, which they did, ending the bloody Peloponnesian War and saving Greece. Aristophanes, weary of the war, might have been trying merely to plant the idea when his comedy was performed in Athens for the first time in 411 BC because the women did not, in historical fact, save Greece, as Lysistrata pronounced they had at the end of the play. The Peloponnesian War would last another seven years until the mulish Athenians went too far and induced the collapse of their empire, bringing down the curtain on the Golden Age of Greece. But if the glory of Athens ceased, the myth of Lysistrata and the women who used their guile to achieve what stubborn or timid men would not was only beginning to inspire.

Adolphine Terry, the grande dame of civil society at Little Rock, knew the Lysistrata story when in September 1958, a year into the integration crisis at Central High School, she went to the executive editor of the *Arkansas Gazette,* and declared: "The men have failed. It's time to call out the women." In the parlor of her Greek Revival mansion, she assembled a cadre of strong-willed women, who went to work on the city's cowed leaders and in eight months booted the diehard segregationists from the school board, reopened the city's high schools, and restored the community's sanity.

They never heard of Lysistrata, but up in Conway County Alidene Malone, her daughter, Dixie Drilling, and Katie Read knew about Adolphine Terry and the Women's Emergency Committee. A dozen years after the women of Little Rock began their crusade, it dawned upon Drilling, Malone, Read, and a few of their friends that their situations were parallel. They were quite sure that the local elections were rigged and that it engendered wider corruption in government—they did not know the degree—but the men who were in command of the civic order were either part of the clique or else had taken a *laissez-faire* attitude. If anything were to change, it would be up to the women.

Except for Read, all of the women who ultimately enlisted in the war with the political machine were natives of the county and knew its long history of electoral thrall. For six years they had watched Gene Wirges and his small band of Republican confederates win one legal victory after another over the Hawkins machine but lose the war. Their defeat and exodus from the community were not an inducement for further civic action. Besides, Drilling and most of her friends were Democrats, and the Republican flavor of the newspaperman's expedition diminished their ardor for his cause. Alidene Malone's father and Drilling's grandfather, Joe Bennett, was a friend and supporter of the sheriff, although he would decline Hawkins's invitation to put a muzzle on his spawn. Malone was the mother of the insurgency. Her decision to challenge the Hawkins machine's candidate for a local office in 1972—unsuccessfully, naturally— set in motion the women's mutiny, which would finally dismantle the machine and erect a semblance of democracy.

Drilling and her husband, a Morrilton businessman, were involved in community affairs but mainly those around the Sacred Heart Catholic Church and the Catholic school that their three children attended. Still, they knew that bearding the political machine bore some risks, for Denis Drilling's business if nothing else. But Dixie would become the sparkplug of the movement. Her puckish humor and irrepressible optimism would keep the others, at various times from eight to a dozen women, coming back for another engagement with the establishment.

For Katie Read, it was all new and a little baffling. She and her husband, Ed, had moved to Morrilton in 1964 from Washington State when he became manager of Green Bay Packaging Inc.'s Arkansas Kraft Division, a paper mill near Morrilton. Ed received an early primer on human-resource methodology in Conway County. As with other major employers in the county, hires at the mill were expected to go through the sheriff's office. Hawkins, it will be remembered, had started the elaborate patronage system as a county welfare caseworker during the Great Depression, when he signed up people for commodities and landed hard-luck men jobs with the Civilian Conservation Corps and the Works Progress Administration. When Ed Read got settled in at the mill, the sheriff told him to send a batch of job-application forms and he would see to it that the mill always got good workers. Read said thank you but he would do the hiring himself. It marked the Reads as people who were not going to be team players.

Unlike the other women, Katie was one of the handful of people in the county who had openly supported Wirges and who didn't leave during or after Wirges's fruitless war with the machine. She was suspected of Republicanism, but she and Ed considered themselves Democrats who, like many other progressives at the time, joined the Democrats for Rockefeller movement. The Reads lived on Petit Jean Mountain west of Morrilton when they first moved to the county, later building a home at Saint Elizabeth at the foot of the mountain. One evening when Katie drove home from a meeting in Morrilton, during one of Wirges's confrontations with the constabulary, someone followed her up the mountain and fired a shot through the Read home. She was intense about getting something done and impatient with the fruitless efforts. The morning after the tensest days she would telephone the other women and tell them that she loved them. "Katie was a real spitfire," Malone would recall many years later.

Because their *modus operandi* became searching and copying election records and chasing phantom voters, the women began to call themselves "the Snoop Sisters." Except for Read, there was a bond of kinship and neighborliness among them. Malone and her sisters, Faye Dixon and Joan Paladino, whom they all called "Tex," lived at Plumerville, four miles east of Morrilton down US Highway 64. Helen Gordon and her daughter, Jan Lynch, were their Plumerville neighbors, as was Margie Brown, Helen's cousin by marriage.

The movement can be said to have begun in the Democratic Party primary runoff in August 1970, although the women then did not have in mind that they were confounding Hawkins or undermining the machine. Dale Bumpers ran for governor that summer and sneaked into the runoff with Orval Faubus from a field of eight Democrats. Hawkins intended to deliver the usual landslide for the former governor. In his memoir, Hawkins said Faubus called him and told him that he needed the organization to give him its maximum vote in the runoff to offset Bumpers's big vote in the cities. He was willing to put up whatever sum of money was needed for Hawkins to produce his maximum absentee vote and to hold Bumpers to 150 votes countywide. Hawkins said he told Faubus that he would get a solid vote and that Bumpers would get no more than eight hundred votes.

Helen Gordon was reared in Bumpers's community, and, while she did not know him, she had heard good things about him and wanted to help a good Charleston boy succeed. She, her daughter, Jan, and neighbor Malone threw themselves into the Bumpers campaign. They telephoned Bumpers's campaign headquarters at Little Rock a couple of days after the preferential primary and asked for a load of yard signs, which were delivered on a Continental Trailways bus. They worked far into the night covering the county with Bumpers signs. They planted them in yards and rights of way and plastered them on fences, utility poles, and trees. On his way to work the next morning Hawkins gazed at what seemed to be a full-scale insurrection. Gordon and her daughter had been seen putting up signs. Hawkins called Malone at her beauty shop at Plumerville.

Dale Bumpers

"Gal, can you do anything about your friend Helen?" he asked. "She is causing us a lot of trouble."

Oh, yes, Malone replied, Helen is supporting Bumpers because they grew up together at Charleston and used to be sweethearts. Oh, Hawkins said, he understood the tug of old romance, but they should still know that this was a Faubus county and it was going to stay that way. Actually, Helen Gordon was pretty sure that she had never met Bumpers. The sheriff may never have discovered the fib, but it became clear in a few days that the women's work for Bumpers was not just a neighborly gesture but a serious challenge to the machine.

Hawkins delivered as promised. Faubus carried Conway County 3,960 to 1,020, a victory margin for the former governor far beyond that of any other county in the state except Faubus's home of Madison County and neighboring Newton County down the same Ozarks ridge. Statewide, Bumpers won easily with almost 60 percent of the vote. But for Hawkins and his men, the gauntlet had been thrown. Still, the women were no more than an irritant for the sheriff and his men, but they would prove to be resourceful at that the next five years.

After a drunken Congressman Mills sabotaged his political career by cavorting with the stripper Fanne Foxe at Washington's Tidal Basin on the night on October 9, 1974, his re-election seemed suddenly in peril. Hawkins considered himself the great Ways and Means chairman's vicar in the Arkansas River Valley, and he organized a statewide rally for the embattled congressman outside Little Rock's Camelot Hotel on October 26, ten days before the general election. He promised Mills that he would lead a caravan of five hundred people from Conway County, and he may have delivered that many. The night before the motorized cavalcade was to leave from Morrilton, Malone, Helen Gordon, and their friends worked into the night on a big sign that said "Wilbur Loves Fanne" and erected it alongside Interstate 30 east of town so that the caravan would have to pass it. Hawkins sent his son to dismantle it after the throng had passed. The women had nothing against Mills; they only wanted to rain on Hawkins's parade. Gordon and her daughter, Jan, went to a costume party dressed as Mills and Fanne Foxe. The sheriff knew the Gordons were friends of Ed and Tex Paladino. He called Ed's employer at Dardanelle, Arvac Inc., a family-service agency, and suggested that he be fired for participating in the humiliation of their congressman and patron.

When Malone's brother-in-law, the mayor of Plumerville, chose not to run in 1972, Malone decided to run for the job herself. The sheriff's friend Charles Bean had already announced that he would run. When Malone went to the courthouse to file, Hawkins asked her what she was doing there. He said he could not help her in the race because his organization would be working for Bean and that she should stay out of it. It should have been a decisive victory. Malone's relatives—she had seven siblings, most of them still around the neighborhood—constituted a sizable part of the Plumerville electorate. Shortly before the May primary, Hawkins's deputies instigated a town scandal by arresting Malone's nephew, Mike Stobaugh, who lived across the street from her. The charge was growing marijuana in his back yard, which set the town to gossiping. A few days later Bean won the primary by fourteen votes with the help of the usual big absentee-ballot turnout. The county then dropped the charges against Stobaugh, whose Big Boy tomato plants had looked to the deputies suspiciously like marijuana. The family was sure that Malone had won handily among people who voted legally but figured there was no way to prove it.

Losing an election for an irksome job that she was never sure she even wanted was not a big disappointment, but the impersonal character of the county's storied election thievery vanished forever. For Alidene Malone and her friends, the ballot stuffing that they all had known was endemic was no longer either a topic of merriment or tea-table talk. They had experienced its curse and they would find out how it worked.

More than two years would pass before they had it figured out and seized the chance to do something about it. The opportunity came in a special election to fill a vacancy in the state Senate in January 1975. The women would turn the little election into a maelstrom that lasted a year and embroiled state and federal courts and law enforcement agencies. That year of strife would also be the fulcrum of my life.

• • •

The strife actually had begun with the election of 1970, when Alex G. Streett, an easygoing but fearless young lawyer at Russellville, took on the machine in the eastern part of the Fifth Judicial District and was elected prosecuting attorney. Prosecutors and the judges of criminal courts ought to keep a polite distance to give the public confidence that justice is administered impartially and aboveboard, but Streett and Judge Russell C. Roberts of Conway at the other end of the district took independence to extremes. Soon after Streett's election, they were trying to put each other in jail. Sheriff Hawkins and his confederates in Faulkner County decided that Streett had to be dislodged. If he could not be beaten at the ballot box, they would simply sever his jurisdiction

Mutt Jones

over Conway and Faulkner counties. So in 1973, state Senator Guy "Mutt" Jones, Judge Roberts's friend and Hawkins's ally, introduced a bill that sliced the Fifth Judicial District into two districts. Streett's county of Pope along with Johnson and Yell Counties would continue to form the Fifth District with its own judge, and Conway and Faulkner Counties would form a new district that would elect its own prosecutor. The bill sailed through both houses by big margins and went to the desk of Governor Bumpers. Under immense pressure to sign the bill or at least let it become law without his signature, Bumpers waited until the last day to act upon the bill and vetoed it. The Senate promptly overrode the veto—a simple majority overrides a veto in Arkansas—but the House of Representatives fell four votes short of an override. Streett and Roberts remained locked in combat. Had the override succeeded and Conway and Faulkner Counties gained a prosecutor who was simpatico with the machine and Judge Roberts, which was the virtually certain outcome, this tale would have had a sadly different ending.

Mutt Jones, a five-foot-four-inch bantam who was both the legislature's jester and its finest orator, already had legal problems that control of the local judicial system would not have overcome. He had been

Map of the proposed new
judicial district

cheating on his federal income taxes. Jones hated Republicans and he had been Governor Rockefeller's most persistent tormentor. He was forever convinced that his battles with the Republican administration had won him the enmity of the national Republican administration, and that the federal tax auditors and the US attorney at Little Rock were carrying out a vendetta. His trial on two counts of tax evasion and two counts of perjury began in July 1972 before US District Judge J. Smith Henley, but Henley quickly declared a mistrial after someone—it was never clear who—contacted members of the jury, apparently in an effort to influence the verdict. A second trial began in November and it ended in Jones's conviction on all four counts. In April 1973, US District Judge Oren Harris fined Jones $5,000 and sentenced him to three years probation.

Newspapers across the state ran editorials calling on the Senate to expel Jones, but veteran senators stood beside their colleague and a resolution to expel him failed to get the necessary two-thirds vote. The furor was so intense, however, that several senior members who had voted with Jones telephoned the young senators who led the expulsion effort asking them to try again so that the elder senators would have a chance to change

their votes. The Senate reconvened on August 1 and voted twenty-five to six to expel Jones. He contended that the constitution did not anticipate the Senate's not allowing a senator to complete his term, but the Arkansas Supreme Court unanimously upheld his expulsion.

That set up a special Democratic primary to nominate a senator to finish Jones's term, which Governor Bumpers set for January 2, 1975. The winner would face a Republican in a special election, but it would be a mere formality. Democratic primaries settled nearly everything.

Special elections to fill a legislative vacancy are ordinarily inert affairs that attract little attention and few voters, but the imbroglio over Jones's expulsion from the Senate, the squabble between the prosecutor and circuit judge in the judicial district that embraced the two big counties in the Senate district, and the challenge to the machine riveted the state's attention on the little election. Two former state representatives, Bill Sanson of Enola in Faulkner County, a friend of Hawkins and Judge Roberts, and Dan D. Stephens of Clinton in Van Buren County, who had been Governor Faubus's prison superintendent, filed for the seat. Hawkins quickly made himself director of the Sanson campaign in Conway County, which settled how the election would turn out in that county. He hung a "Bill Sanson for State Senator" sign outside his courthouse office; it would still be there on January 2 and in the runoff on January 16, when people voted down the hall. The third candidate was Stanley Russ of Conway, an insurance man, cattle farmer, and inveterate civic do-gooder. He was involved in every shiny cause in the city of Conway, from the Boy Scouts and the United Way to the deaconry of the First Baptist Church, and he was president of not one but two civic clubs. Russ promised to work to clean up the dirty politics of the three counties in the Senate district and to be a senator of whom everyone could be proud.

The Snoop Sisters decided that Russ was their man and that the special election was the vehicle to test what they had learned about how Hawkins and his men fixed elections. In the two previous primaries, in 1972 and 1974, the women had tried to monitor the voting at a number of precincts around the county for Governor Bumpers, but it proved impossible for them to watch the balloting all day at crucial precincts. They figured out that you had to be vigilant from the moment the polls opened until they were closed and the votes counted and reported, and even then you couldn't be sure about what you saw.

They were no deterrent to the ballot gremlins either year. Hawkins's man in the 1972 governor's race was not Governor Bumpers, who would be the runaway winner in a four-man race, but Q. Byrum Hurst, a Hot Springs state senator who was under investigation for bank fraud (he would be convicted in the US District Court at Kansas City of lending $210,417 from his banks to friends and relatives and converting the proceeds to his own use). Hurst, who barely left town during the campaign, got only 15 percent of the vote in the rest of the state but in Hawkins's bailiwick he trumped the popular governor by a landslide.

Two years later, in 1974, The Election Laws Institute joined with the Arkansas League of Women Voters to monitor the primary voting in counties across the state where suspicions of illegal voting were most prevalent. The result was I discovered that election officials continued the careless practices that had been handed down by generations. The tightened procedures for conducting elections and counting and reporting votes in our election-code revisions of 1969 were widely ignored. My report two weeks after the 1974 primary was that while we suspected sixty-three violations of election laws in the counties that we monitored, most of them were fairly minor and the worst irregularities were in Conway County. Seven voters appeared at one polling place there at 4:30 p.m. on election day only to find that the door to the room where people voted was locked. After they knocked on the door and waited around for ten minutes, an election official unlocked the door and let them in. One of the voters told us that he saw completed ballots scattered across the table where election officials worked. But the women knew the big problem very well from previous elections: the avalanche of absentee ballots. We obtained statements after the '74 primary from four voters who said that one of Hawkins's deputy sheriffs had voted for them on absentee ballots but they did not know for whom he had marked their ballots. Two of them said they had been handed a five-dollar bill in exchange for letting the deputy vote them.

Dixie Drilling dispatched her friends in that election to watch the polls for Bumpers, who was challenging Senator J. William Fulbright. Drilling went to the First Ward polling place in the gymnasium of what had once been Morrilton High School. Election officials had brought ice chests stocked with beer. When the voting closed, the clerks straightened the ballots in stacks on the table and then took a break to shoot baskets and throw back a few beers. At midnight, the ballots had not been counted. It was three o'clock in the morning before the counting was done. Bumpers won the primary overwhelmingly but he lost in Conway County by the margin by which he won in the rest of Arkansas.

• • •

So in January 1975 the women knew what they faced. They worked hard for Russ in the preferential primary, which was held on January 2, although the outcome was foreordained. Sanson received 82 percent of the votes in Conway County, but Russ handily carried the larger Faulkner

County, where he and Sanson lived, and forced a runoff. Stephens carried the light-voting Van Buren County, where he lived, and threw his support to Russ in the runoff. Although he was a friend of Faubus and had been a member of his administration, Stephens was a decent and progressive sort. He had taken over the scandal-ridden prison system at the end of the Faubus administration and instituted a punishment regimen that was somewhat enlightened by the standards of the day. They stopped torturing inmates with an old magneto telephone that was clamped on the genitals of restive prisoners and cranked until the prickly charge rendered them agreeable. Stephens did even better than that. He organized a convict band, which the inmates named The Dandees after Cap'n Dan, as they called him, and they were allowed from time to time to play at functions away from the prison. The popular Stephens's blessing would carry Van Buren County for Russ, which would assure him victory in the runoff if the phantom vote in Conway County could be held to a medium-sized flood.

For nearly four years, Malone, Dixon, Paladino, Gordon, and her daughter, Jan Lynch, had been brewing one scheme after another to thwart the courthouse, but they knew that it had all been unavailing. They had earned the enmity of Hawkins and everyone in his organization, which had created tension in their own lives and for their families without crimping the sheriff's style at all. If anything, the vast pool of absentee voters got larger and the election-day machinations bolder. After their maiden effort for Bumpers in the 1970 primary, the women started meeting for coffee every few days at the Colonial Cafe in Morrilton. Before long, they found they had the company many evenings of two or three sheriff's deputies, who would settle in at a nearby table to eavesdrop. Patrol cars often followed them in the vain hope, the women figured, of catching them in a traffic violation. Deputies would follow Dixon's and Paladino's daughters to the Dairy Queen, stop them, and warn them that they were violating the city's curfew (there was no curfew) and that if they were caught after nine o'clock at night, they would be arrested. The women developed a little paranoia about it. Alidene and Tex, who were sisters, decided that the sheriff had bugged a wreath that hung above the table at the Colonial where they gathered, so to test their theory they concocted a story at the table one evening about a meeting at ten o'clock that night at an old equipment barn on the edge of town. They left and drove out of town and parked behind the barn. In a few minutes, the deputies came down the dusty road to the building. Husbands felt pressure at their jobs. The wives' shenanigans were costing business, they were told.

Tex Paladino was particularly vulnerable. She worked for the city's popular family physician, Dr. Thomas H. Hickey, who attended half the births in the county for forty years. Hickey also was the city's mayor and chief politico and faithful servant of the sheriff. Hickey explained to Paladino once how it worked. Politics is the wheel of the community, he said, and each person is a cog with political leaders like Hawkins and himself at the center directing where everyone should go. The community prospered if everyone worked in unison. Hickey grew increasingly resentful of the women's defiance. Work became intolerable for Paladino and, no doubt, for Hickey but he would not fire her because she could collect unemployment. One day, the doctor took her keys and scattered them around the parking lot. It was the last straw. In April 1974, she quit. Hickey protested her unemployment application but the Arkansas Employment Security Division determined after a hearing that she was eligible. The next spring when Paladino helped me gather affidavits about wrongful voting in the Russ-Sanson runoff, Robert Jackson, a Hawkins deputy, interviewed neighbors and others in Plumerville and sought to have her punished by the Employment Security Division for having drawn unemployment benefits while she earned some money from self-employment. The deputy went to Paladino's house and told her daughter that Judge Russell Roberts had directed him to check on her mother's illegal unemployment compensation. The Employment Security Division sent an agent to her house to assure her that she had done nothing improper and that a county sheriff had nothing to do with enforcement of the employment laws.

About a week before the runoff primary, the Snoop Sisters assembled twenty-one friends and supporters of Russ at Alidene Malone's beauty shop in Plumerville to talk with Russ about how they could assure that there would be an honest count of his votes and that ballot stuffing would be held to a moderately indecent level. Deputy Sheriff John Robert Hawkins pulled up in a patrol car outside when the meeting began and kept the crowd under surveillance. The women told Russ that votes would be stolen in precincts all over the county and that the only way to hold down the fraud would be to man every polling place with knowledgeable and tough poll watchers who would arrive early and stay late. Russ was dubious that things could be so bad. Election judges and clerks were, after all, ordinary people and they all would have to be in cahoots. He was not persuaded that poll watchers were necessary, but he said he would see what he could do. They approached TEL Institute with the proposition, but we had no money to pay poll watchers and we thought the observers needed to be both familiar with the law and armed with a certain degree of authority. I approached the law school at Little Rock about offering senior law students a chance for a day of quasi-legal work for pay. Three friends of Russ, brothers Charles and Robert Nabholz, and Dr. Bob Benafield, a family doctor, put up the money to man the precincts on January 16. They needed twenty to twenty-five but we rounded up a dozen, including a few novice attorneys as well as law students, with the offer of one hundred dollars for each polling place. At that time, a hundred dollars was a tempting induce-ment. Most of the night law students were struggling on GI Bill checks and part-time jobs.

Dixie Drilling and five other women went to Little Rock and met with them and Russ at the Worthen Bank Building the evening before the election. The next morning they reconnoitered before dawn in freez-ing wind around a fire beside Alidene Malone's beauty shop on US Highway 64 in Plumerville. The women gave them instructions about how to handle themselves, handed out copies of an attorney general's opinion about the rights of poll watchers, and gave them letters from Russ authorizing them to observe the voting and counting for him. Drilling had driven 385 miles that day as she and her friends pinpointed all the rural voting sites around the county, and, lacking enough to man each polling place, they dropped the lawyers and students off at precincts where they suspected that hijinks were most likely.

Mark Stodola, who had passed the bar earlier in the year, had taken the day off without the knowledge of the senior partner of the little law firm where he had gone to work. The hundred dollars was nearly a fourth of a month's salary, too fetching, he thought, to pass up for eight or ten hours of standing around. One of the women drove him to a small community building at Birdtown, a hamlet at the foot of Huett Mountain fifteen miles north of the county seat. He got inside the poll room but once the voting started, the election judge asked him what he

Here I'm presenting tokens from the Election Laws Institute to Conway County women for their valor and industriousness in gathering evidence of voting fraud in Conway County. Starting from my left are Joan "Tex" Paladino, Mert O'Brien, Katie Read (back to camera), Alidene Malone, and Helen Gordon. Outside the frame are Dixie Drilling, Jan Lynch, Faye Dixon, and Margie Brown. *Photo courtesy of the* Arkansas Democrat-Gazette

was doing there. Stodola, who would later be prosecuting attorney in Pulaski County and then mayor of Little Rock, showed him the letter from Russ. The judge telephoned Hawkins. A few minutes passed and a patrol car with sirens blaring and lights flashing sped up to the building. Two deputy sheriffs arrested Stodola and stuffed him into the back seat and the car sped back to Morrilton with its siren whining all the way. A deputy told him that he was in deep trouble for interfering with an election and that he was going to be thrown into a cell with three murderers who had been captured recently.

"Oh, hell," Stodola thought, "here goes my job and my law license."

At the courthouse, a representative of Russ argued with the deputies and Hawkins, who eventually agreed that the law allowed poll watchers to be at the polling place but not inside the room where the voting occurred. The deputies would not take Stodola back but by afternoon one of the women had driven him back to Birdtown, too late for any mean-ingful vigilance. The poll watchers' job was to count every person who entered the polling place and then match that with the number of votes recorded and the number on the voting list. Stodola was forced to stand outside in the cold away from the voting but a clerk unlocked his pickup truck and let him sit inside. Having missed a big part of the day, the obser-vance was pointless. Sanson carried Birdtown ninety-seven to fifteen.

Jamie Cox, a senior law student at the University of Arkansas at Little Rock and later a circuit judge, was stationed at the Morrilton City Hall, the First Ward polling place. Armed with the legal opinion and Russ's let-ter, he positioned himself at the door so that he could see the proceedings inside. Deputy Leo Denton arrived shortly and told him that he had to stand at least fifty feet from the entrance of the voting place. Denton paced off what he said was fifty feet and drew an imaginary line with his shoe in the middle of the street. Cross that line, Denton said, and you are going to jail. When the deputy left, Cox walked back to the door of the voting room. Denton arrested him and took him to the courthouse and eventu-ally to the law office of the city's municipal judge, Joe Cambiano. Cambiano looked at the statutes cited in the attorney general's opinion and concluded that Cox could stand six feet from the door to the polling room. The law had once said that "no person" could get within fifty feet of a polling place during election hours but it had been repealed. The cur-rent law forbade anyone from getting closer than six feet from a polling booth, but it made no mention of the door to the room where voting occurred.

Cox returned to City Hall but two deputies soon arrived and said they had complaints that he was harassing voters. Cox said he was talk-ing to no one, and the deputies warned him that if they received one more complaint he would be locked up. Deputy Denton closed the door to the polls in the afternoon because he said it was too cold in the room, so Cox observed nothing else for the rest of the day except a lot of traffic through the rear door of the little building. The day had been a waste. Sanson carried the box 471 to 118, which was one of Russ's better show-ings in the county.

The women took Robert Govar, a senior law student who would later be a career federal prosecutor, to a remote service station that was converted for the day into a polling place. The election judges told Govar that he could not enter the building or they would have him arrested. He wasn't dressed for thirty degrees and found himself shivering uncontrollably. People had piled their Christmas trees beside the service station so he pulled them together in a pile beside the station and lit them. They made a fine blaze. Judges ran out of the station yelling.

"What the hell are you doing? You are going to blow us all up," one of them said. The fuel storage tank was nearby.

Govar said it was either that or freeze to death and he was willing to take his chances. The men were not without humanity. "Put out the damned fire and come on inside," one of them barked at Govar.

Leo Myers, a law student who was assigned to Ward Four, was ordered to stay fifty feet away from the door and he did. Harold Craig, a Little Rock lawyer who joined the poll watchers, tried to stay in the door of the polling room at the courthouse but was twice ordered away. He finally went to Cambiano's office and the municipal judge went to the courthouse and told the officials that Craig could get as close as six feet from the door. But standing outside proved pointless.

Joe Purvis was the kind of man you assigned to watch for skullduggery at an election outpost that had a history of violence and intimidation. Tall, muscular and square jawed with a head of bushy black hair, Purvis owned a set of uncommonly powerful baritone vocal cords, which he would employ into his sixties as the lead singer for a popular rock band, Little Joe and the BKs. On the morning of the election, Tex Paladino and Faye Dixon dropped Purvis off at Menifee, and told him one of them would be back with lunch at noon. Menifee is a predominantly African-American town in the Arkansas River bottomlands east of Morrilton that has at times lived up to the reputation of its namesake, Nimrod P. Menifee. Nimrod was a physician and adventurer who fled Kentucky to escape the vengeance of the friends of a man whom he had slain in a duel to uphold the honor of his sister, who had been aggrieved in some manner. Menifee devoted his life to healing and honorable violence, in about equal measure. He once raised his cane and bludgeoned William E. Woodruff, the founder and editor of the *Arkansas Gazette*, when the editor tried to draw a pistol on him. Menifee died in 1842 in the last of his numerous duels, this one with knives and pistols.

The town's fidelity to the Hawkins machine was unmatched. The voters there, though nearly all African Americans, marched to the sheriff's tune in every race, even if the choice was a racist like Faubus. Purvis had been at the polling place only a few minutes, huddling around the door to absorb some of the warmth, when the election judge told him he had to get far away from the door. Carl Stobaugh, Hawkins's chief deputy, soon arrived in a patrol car with another officer. He told Purvis he had to leave right away. Purvis tried to show the deputies the opinion from Attorney General Jim Guy Tucker about the legal authority of poll watchers.

"Son, I don't give a damn what that opinion says," Stobaugh told him. "You can't be out here. If you want to see your wife tonight you better get out of here. You're not going to see your family for a long, long time. I'll put you under the jail."

Purvis pleaded that he had no way to leave. When Dixon and Paladino arrived with a sandwich, he told them they had to get him out because he could do nothing there. They drove him in the afternoon to the old Morrilton High School gymnasium, where the reception was only a little warmer but the threats at least subtle. A couple of election officials joined him outside the precinct. They thought he should know how much people resented outsiders coming in and messing with their business. Some pretty nasty things had been known to befall meddlers, they said.

Stretching his six-foot-two frame and fixing them with a baleful stare, the way he approached his opponents on the line of scrimmage in the days when he was a tackle for the state champion Hope Bobcats, Purvis raised his left arm to display a scar across his hand and wrist, the harvest of an accident when he worked for a gas pipeline outfit at Hope.

"See that," he said. "I was in Vietnam. I watched my buddies get blown to bits. You know what I learned from that?"

"What?"

"I learned that there was not one swinging dick on earth that I needed to be afraid of," Purvis said. Actually, he never saw duty in Vietnam. He was a flyboy whose four years were spent on United States soil.

One of the men went over to his pickup truck and brought out a bottle of whiskey. He offered Purvis a swig, which Purvis says he declined.

When the polls closed at seven thirty, the election judge produced a quart of Maker's Mark, the premium Kentucky bourbon, and put it on the table with the precinct binders. Everyone started to drink.

"What about counting the votes?" Purvis asked.

"Not until after supper," someone said. One by one they left for dinner and returned, but still the count did not get under way. Purvis figured they were not going to count the votes until the counting from the other counties was well along so they could see how many votes would be needed for Sanson to win. Finally, about nine thirty they started counting the votes. When they finished and announced Sanson's lopsided vote, 471 to 118, they started for the courthouse to turn in the ballots and the count.

"Gentlemen," Purvis said, "I think we may have a bit of a problem here. You've counted twenty-eight more votes than there are names on the list of voters. That looks like you've counted twenty-eight votes from people who didn't come in here today." The clerks looked nervous for the first time.

"I tell you what," one of them said. "We'll just give those twenty-eight votes to your boy Russ and call it even."

"I don't think it works like that," Purvis said. When they reached the county clerk's office at the courthouse, Prosecutor Streett was there and Purvis announced that the precinct had tabulated twenty-eight more votes than there were recorded voters. Streett said he would look into the discrepancy.

Election night at the Conway County Courthouse could be something of a bacchanal, even when only a single race was to be decided and no one from the county was running. A big and boisterous crowd had gathered to celebrate Sanson's victory. Each time that precinct officials came in with their ballot boxes and records, cheers resounded through the hall. The poll workers deposited their election records and then filed into a nearby office for their customary shots of "election whiskey," as they called it. Sheriff Hawkins would come out of his office and hail each group.

"Good job, boys," he would say, and then go back to his office to keep a running total of the vote from the three counties.

But things were not going well on this evening. All the results from Faulkner and Van Buren Counties were reported quickly after the polls closed and they gave Russ a huge lead despite some resourceful vote gathering by the Sanson-Jones-Roberts organization in Faulkner County. Sometime during the day, the county judge's office carried a bundle of absentee ballots over to the clerk's office, which, as I pointed out later, violated election laws. Although Russ won the absentee votes in Faulkner

County by about the same sizable margin as he did the active boxes, every one of the 119 ballots brought over from the county judge was marked for Sanson. But it was going to take a heroic effort by Hawkins's confederates to salvage the election for Sanson. The fat Sanson vote from each Conway County box narrowed the gap. The tabulation from the two absentee boxes helped hugely. Absentee ballots accounted for a whopping 14 percent of the county's votes, and they went for Sanson 652 to 21. When the First Ward dumped its vote at the clerk's office, Russ's margin fell below 1,000 votes, but only two boxes remained. The little Washington box in the Ozark wilderness a few miles north of the county seat and Morrilton's Third Ward finally reported toward midnight but they couldn't get the job done.

Russ won by 402 votes, defeated the Republican nominee in a light election two weeks later and took his seat in the Senate. One of his first acts was to introduce a bill to allow poll watchers inside voting rooms. The bill failed, but two years later, after the federal district court at Little Rock directed poll watchers to keep a vigil over still another Conway County election, the legislature would pass it, though narrowly in the House of Representatives.

It was impossible to say whether the Snoop Sisters' efforts and the labors of the young lawyers and students made the difference in Russ's election. Russ thought their presence and the heightened attention to the county's election conduct got more of his votes counted and discouraged some phantom voting for the machine's candidate. The accident of Joe Purvis's reassignment to the old gymnasium in mid-afternoon proved fortuitous. His discovery of the discrepancy between votes and voters led to one of the biggest election-fraud disputes of the century and shone an intense light on the county government and judiciary that did not serve them well.

Purvis's wife, Susan, took his hundred-dollar poll-watcher pay and bought him a pair of expensive shoes, the most comfortable and durable he ever owned. He claims to have worn them for ten years. A couple of weeks after the election, Purvis was sitting in his criminal-procedure class at the night-law school when a deputy sheriff stopped the lecture to serve him a subpoena requiring his appearance before a hostile grand jury in Conway County. But his perils at the hands of the political establishment and the Fifth District judiciary were to be brief.

Mine were only beginning.

"Do you suppose this means my sphere of influence has been limited, Mutt?"

CHAPTER 8
• • • • • • • • • • •

Court Jesters

"The Democrats decided to quit cheating each other in the primary by absentee ballot and to make it strictly an anti-Republican weapon."

—V. O. KEY, *SOUTHERN POLITICS*

All's Well That Ends Well makes a nice comedy theme but Shakespeare never knew Conway County. After failing to round up enough legal and illegal votes to stop him in the Democratic runoff primary, Marlin Hawkins threw in with Stanley Russ against the Republican candidate in the special election on January 28, 1975, helped elect him by a landslide and went down to Little Rock with half of the Snoop Sisters, though not in the same car, to see Russ take the oath in the Senate for Mutt Jones's old seat. In his maiden remarks to the Senate, Senator Russ tossed a sweet oral bouquet to his former nemesis, who bowed from the gallery. The sheriff had not developed a sudden affection for Russ, or vice versa, but they were both Democrats and Hawkins had always taken pains to showcase his loyalty to the Democratic Party. After Dale Bumpers defeated Orval Faubus for the party's nomination for governor in 1970, Hawkins resisted Faubus's importuning that he throw Conway County's votes to Rockefeller in the general election to help defeat the upstart. He had repulsed Faubus two years earlier when the former governor asked him to align his machine behind George C. Wallace, the American Party presidential candidate, against Vice President Hubert Humphrey, the Democratic candidate.

But Katie Read was having none of the armistice. She had been fighting the machine for more than a decade, and even after it was dismantled and Hawkins dispatched into retirement two years later she would be a persistent scold to their successors. As late as 1992, shortly before she and her husband retired back to Washington, Read lodged a complaint with the prosecuting attorney that the new county judge, an old ally of Sheriff Hawkins, had brought county road crews and equipment out to pave his own driveway. She had pictures.

On January 31, four days before Russ was sworn in, Katie telephoned me at Little Rock. The women, she said, were at wits' end and they were pleading for my help. They were not mollified by Russ's victory. The poll watchers had been helpful in the special primary and their experiences had confirmed the women's suspicion that election fraud was rampant, but the only evidence the women had, and it was shaky at that point, was Joe Purvis's discovery that twenty-eight more people had voted or had votes cast for them in Ward One than were recorded as having shown up at the polling place. They believed that was only the tip of the iceberg but they did not know what they could do to prove it. The 652-to-21 absentee vote against Russ in Conway County, a staggering collective absentee vote and ratio, was prima facie evidence that something was badly amiss. The women were furious with Alex Streett, the prosecuting attorney, because he seemed to manifest a baffling lack of interest in pressing an investigation of the fraud. We agreed that I would meet with them at Plumerville the following Tuesday, the day Russ would take office. Thus began the most harrowing six months of my life.

Alidene Malone, Dixie Drilling, and Read met me at the Security Bank building on US Highway 64, which was the main drag in Plumerville, and a sheriff's car soon angled up to the building to keep a vigil. I knew Katie from my days with Rockefeller's political headquarters and my tagalongs with Tom Eisele in Gene Wirges's court skirmishes to save his newspaper, but I had never met the other women. Despite Katie's assurances and all the newspaper reports of my activities, they were at first suspicious. When I forgot my briefcase at a meeting a few days later, the women plundered it for evidence of my fifth-column malice. But what they lacked and needed I had, which was a working knowledge of election law, a grasp of the legal procedures that could be used to ferret out fraud, and some confidence that the judicial system in the end could actually work for you. That is what I had learned in the Election Research Council investigations in 1964 and our American Party petition battle in 1972, when both trial

Prosecuting attorney Alex Streett (middle) and I share a rare light moment with Sheriff Hawkins. *Photo courtesy of the* Arkansas Democrat-Gazette

and appellate courts held that bogus petitions could not put a political party on the ballot. Still, nothing had prepared me for what was to come—the destruction of records and the extraordinary efforts by law enforcement and the judicial system not to discover the truth, but to hide it.

None of us had any doubt that morning that votes had been stolen on a large scale for many years, and that in spite of the unusual scrutiny by the media and the poll watchers the special state Senate runoff primary had been a perfect replica of the Hawkins election model. If we could get the records of the voting-day activity, including the voter sign-in registers and absentee-ballot applications, with enough manpower we could pin down who had voted or been voted illegally on January 16. The place to start was identifying the twenty-eight people for whom votes had been cast at Ward One but whose names were not on the voting register—Joe Purvis's little midnight discovery. If what appeared to be blatant ballot stuffing had occurred there it probably occurred in other precincts as well but maybe by election officials who were not so slipshod in covering up the fraud as those in the old gymnasium in Ward One.

Gathering that information proved far harder than I imagined. In fact, it would prove impossible because the circuit judge, Russell C. Roberts, took extraordinary steps to impede our investigation, and the county clerk used the delays to destroy most election records. My brief experience with the Conway County Circuit Court in the final episode of the *Morrilton Democrat*'s long battle with Hawkins in the 1960s should have prepared me for what was to come, but there were few days during the next year that did not bring fresh illumination of the perfidies of that corrupt judicial system.

When Joe Purvis announced at the clerk's office on the night of January 16 that the ballot boxes that were being delivered from Ward One contained twenty-eight more ballots than people who had showed up to vote, Prosecutor Streett said he would investigate the discrepancy. Felver A. Rowell Jr., a Morrilton lawyer who was the prosecutor's deputy in the county, asked the sheriff's office to get to the bottom of it. Four days later, Carl Stobaugh, Sheriff Hawkins's chief deputy and nephew, filed his five-page report, in which he said investigators had put in 102 man-hours. Much of the report was a narrative about how cold it was in the old gym that day and about efforts to heat it so that poll workers and voters were not so uncomfortable, circumstances that he suggested might have something to do with any discrepancies. His account of the day at the gym varied considerably from Purvis's. Stobaugh said the election officials repeatedly tried to get Purvis to come inside out of the raw wind but that Purvis refused. Stobaugh wrote that he had been persuaded by election officials that there was no way they could have counted twenty-eight more votes than were cast. By comparing signatures in the voter-affidavit binders with the names on the list of those who voted, he identified twenty-seven people who had voted but whose names were not on the list.

"I have contacted and verified from each that they did vote on January 16," Stobaugh wrote in his report to the prosecutor. (That would prove to be a fabrication.) He concluded that the missing names from the list were "nothing but an honest mistake." Several of the people whose names were missing from the voter list were long-time enemies of Hawkins, he said, which he implied meant that any skullduggery would have been by the sheriff's foes. Stobaugh's report was good enough for Streett, who declared that the investigation had concluded, that the sheriff's office had conducted a thorough investigation and that no laws had been broken.

I was visiting relatives in Missouri and upon my return to Little Rock, Katie Read called to beseech my help. The women thought that Streett had screwed up the investigation. I was a little miffed, too, but I told them that Alex was doing the best he could under the circumstances. He had to invest some confidence in the sheriff's investigator. Streett had been fighting them a long time and he really didn't believe that he would uncover any illegal acts because they were too smart.

The next day, Ralph C. Hamner Jr., a former FBI agent who was my associate at TEL Institute, and I went to the courthouse at Morrilton with Katie and Dixie to re-enact much of Stobaugh's investigation of the twenty-eight missing voters. Hamner was a lanky, easy-going fellow like his father, who pitched for the Chicago White Sox and Chicago Cubs for four years after World War II. The four of us went through the binders of voter-registration affidavits for Ward One and put a small pencil check beside the names of those who signed their affidavit forms in the precinct binders that day but whose names did not appear on the list of voters at the gym, which was evidence of either fraud or a failure to log in the voters at the polling place as the law required. Driving back to Little Rock I began to worry that something would happen to the telltale evidence. I told Hamner that we needed to go back and get photographs, both to preserve evidence for our handwriting expert and in case the forms somehow disappeared. Hamner thought I was overwrought. No one, he said, would dare steal a voter's registration form from the county binders. We pulled in to the *Log Cabin Democrat* newspaper offices at Conway and presented the problem to the paper's editor, John Ward, who had directed Winthrop Rockefeller's public-relations office during my dalliance with Rockefeller's political organization in 1965 and 66. Ward assigned Gary Speed, a young photographer who would later become a leading patent and copyright lawyer, to drive to Morrilton to take the pictures. Speed photographed most of the suspicious affidavit signatures and I sent them to Earl Davenport, the Memphis handwriting expert whom we had employed to examine the fraudulent American Party petitions two and a half years earlier. Prosecutor Streett saw soon enough that Stobaugh's investigation had been a sham and he re-entered the game.

On February 13, I announced our preliminary findings, which received widespread coverage. This is a good place to observe that massive media coverage was the critical factor in the success of the election reforms that took place—that and the perseverance of the little band of women who saw that the moment had come when honest elections might be restored. For the next eighteen months, the *Log Cabin Democrat* at Conway, the statewide newspapers, the *Arkansas Gazette* and the *Arkansas Democrat,* the Morrilton papers, the *Morrilton Democrat* and the *Petit Jean Country Headlight,* and the two press services, United Press International and Associated Press, marked the sparrow's fall in Conway County. Television and radio stations at Little Rock gave the dispute heavy coverage. I do not recall a long-running story outside Little Rock ever receiving such sustained attention again.

The handwriting expert examined the voter-affidavit signatures of eleven of the twenty-seven people cited by Stobaugh as having voted that day but who were absent from the voter list. He said the January 16 signatures were different from most previous signatures on the affidavits, suggesting that they were forgeries. Four signatures were misspelled. John Bernard Maus Jr. and his wife, Mary Joyce, were shown as having signed in the binders that day, but when we contacted them they said they had not been there or voted. Maus and his friend Charles L. Ormond had flown on election day to Moline, Illinois, on one of the tractor maker's customer fly-ins to see farm equipment in action. Mary Maus was shown as also having voted absentee that day so someone had voted her fraudulently not once but twice. One man had not voted for the previous ten years and was purged from the rolls. We also noted that the names of most people on the lists of voters compiled by the workers at polling places were numbered consecutively but quite a few were not, which suggested that the poll lists had been redone to insert names of people who had not shown up that day to vote. Someone had voted for them.

Streett issued fifteen subpoenas to Ward One election officials, to people whose signatures were on their affidavits but whom we suspected of not voting, and to Deputy Stobaugh, and the county clerk, Jack Bland.

The next morning, Dixie Drilling telephoned me. She had ventured down to the courthouse in Morrilton after ten o'clock the previous evening and saw the lights burning in the clerk's office. I told her to get down to the clerk's office quickly and microfilm the voter-registration binders for Ward One and then for the other boxes. She called me back and said Bland told her that she could not see the binders because the affidavits of some voters were missing. I called Streett and we agreed to meet at Morrilton at 1:30 p.m. He and I went to the courthouse to check the binders but Sheriff Hawkins headed us off. He told us that Judge Roberts had impaneled his own grand jury to look into the election and that it would assemble the following Monday morning at nine o'clock—one hour before Streett was to begin taking sworn statements from the fifteen people he had subpoenaed. The grand jury would take the investigation out of the prosecutor's hands and put it behind closed doors under the control of Roberts and the sheriff. Streett said he had never heard of a grand jury anywhere being called without the knowledge of the prosecuting attorney. Prosecutors ordinarily instigate grand-jury investigations.

When Streett and I walked down the hall to the clerk's office to examine the Ward One binders, Bland accused the women and me of stealing affidavits from the binders, which he noted was a felony. He demanded to know where they were. I was glad then that Gary Speed had photographed many of them because his photographs of the signatures would supply compelling evidence of why affidavits had gone missing. I asked Bland which ones were missing and he replied that we would have to find out for ourselves. Streett demanded that he be allowed to examine the binders and Bland turned them over. Katie, Dixie, and a friend, Charles Ormond, began to microfilm them.

It turned out that the two missing affidavits belonged to John Bernard Maus Jr. (misspelled as

"Election irregularities in MY county? Why doesn't someone tell me about these things?"

"Mass" in the January 16 signature, as Gary Speed's photographs showed) and a man named Donald Watters, whose forged signature also had been misspelled. Word at the courthouse was that Dixie, Katie, and I were to be indicted by the grand jury for stealing affidavits from binders. Pressed months later in the proceedings for his evidence of our theft of the affidavits, Bland insisted that he had never really accused us and that he had only been having some good-natured sport with us that Friday.

Then Streett discovered that the sheriff's office had not served the fifteen subpoenas that he had issued two days earlier, which had given Judge Roberts time to organize a grand jury and head off the investigation. We related all the day's events to the media, and I said Judge Roberts's grand jury was an attempt to whitewash the widespread fraud in the special election and the sheriff's phony investigation. As befitting an officer of the court, Prosecutor Streett was, as always, more judicious in his criticism of the judge and the sheriff. We noted that Roberts was the cousin of Bill Sanson, who had lost the disputed election to Russ. The judge would insist that having a relative in the fight did not create a conflict of interest for him, and he refused repeatedly to step down so that an impartial judge would oversee the proceedings. A quick study of the list of Roberts's grand jurors in the sheriff's office that day showed that fourteen of the twenty-five were either federal, state or county employees associated with Hawkins, eight of them had served on the infamous grand juries of 1961 and 1964 that indicted Gene Wirges five times or else served on the juries that convicted him, and ten lived in the Center Ridge community where Hawkins was reared, twenty miles north of Morrilton. One was the foreman of the 1964 grand jury that falsely indicted Wirges for perjury, and one was an uncle of Carl Stobaugh, who had conducted the bogus investigation of Ward One voting and who was subpoenaed to testify.

Suddenly, I had to contemplate the prospect of being convicted of a felony and disbarred. Facts and proof, as I had seen a decade earlier, would not be much help to me in the trial court. I announced that Katie Read, Dixie Drilling, and I were ready to take a polygraph test about the missing affidavits, to be administered by an independent law-enforcement authority such as the state police, and I invited Hawkins, Stobaugh, Bland and his wife (a deputy in his office), and the six Ward One officials to do the same. Thus began a battle that wended back and forth for more than a year between Judge Roberts's grand jury, his court, the Arkansas Supreme Court, and the US District Court for the Eastern District of Arkansas.

The motions, rulings, appeals, remands, and all the other pleadings in such a political feud gone litigious are too tedious and too monotonous to recount so long after the fact, but they open a window on the quaint habits and notions of people who found themselves in the crucible of community struggles.

Before Roberts could swear in his grand jurors on Monday morning, the seventeenth of February, Streett moved to quash the grand jury on the elementary grounds that the judge was related to one of the two central figures in the election dispute and because the judge had no authority to impanel a grand jury without complying with a 1969 law requiring the use of a jury wheel in selecting the jurors. Roberts had simply discharged the old grand jury and ordered the sheriff to choose twenty-five jurors. Roberts said he was not going to grant the motion but he refused to make a formal ruling that would permit Streett to appeal to the supreme court. Sure enough, when a deputy prosecutor went to the supreme court at Little Rock that afternoon four justices who assembled to hear his appeal refused to review the matter without a record of Judge Roberts's denial orders and a formal notice of the appeal to the judge so that he could be present for the court's review. Back in Morrilton the next morning, Roberts finally relented and issued a formal denial of Streett's motion to quash the jury. Meantime, the grand jury said it would not allow Streett to be in the grand jury room but only Rowell, the deputy prosecutor from Conway County. Streett said he was entitled by law to be in the room and that he would stay.

The jurors subpoenaed the same fifteen witnesses that Streett had subpoenaed plus Joe Purvis and me. A deputy served Purvis that evening while he was in his criminal-law class at the night-law school in Little Rock. The sheriff's office said I had evaded efforts to serve the subpoena although I had spent the day in the Faulkner County Courthouse examining election records and in my office at Little Rock. No one attempted to serve me. I read about the subpoenas in the morning papers, talked to Katie Read by phone and decided to appear before the grand jury voluntarily. I had been concerned that the grand-jury appearance would effectively silence me because if I tried to defend myself or tell what happened in the grand-jury room, I could be indicted. But David A. Stewart of Danville, one of Streett's deputy prosecutors, telephoned the office of Attorney General Jim Guy Tucker Monday and received an oral opinion in the afternoon that people who appeared before a grand jury were

"Well, is our little ol' Grand Jury ready?"

not automatically bound by law to maintain silence about the matters they discussed with the jurymen. (The proceedings before Judge Roberts were good early training for young Stewart, who would thirty years later, after a stint as judge himself, become executive director of the Arkansas Judicial Discipline and Disability Commission, which monitors the ethical behavior of Arkansas judges.)

I drove to Morrilton and parked a block from the courthouse. When I approached it, my heart fairly pounding and my palms sweating, Katie Read stood on the steps with twenty other women. They applauded and followed me through the courthouse. I felt marvelously invigorated as I headed to the court. I was ushered into the grand jury room. The jury foreman instructed Streett to leave while they questioned me, but Streett said he had to be there. The jurors conferred a few minutes and then said they would delay questioning me until later. They asked if I would return without a subpoena. I said I would and the foreman apologized for inconveniencing me. At loggerheads over Streett's insistence that he be in grand-jury proceedings, the jurors finally recessed until March 10. There was no rush because Streett's investigation—and ours—had been stymied.

Having obtained Judge Roberts's formal denial of Streett's motions to disqualify himself because of his kinship with Sanson and to quash the grand jury because it was named for the previous year, we went back to the supreme court. The justices were not impressed with the disqualification argument because the judge's cousin, Bill Sanson, having lost the election, was not directly involved in the grand jury's investigation of the election's conduct, at least as far as anyone knew. The justices and the attorneys became cross within minutes. Chief Justice Carleton Harris scolded both Streett and Nathan Gordon, who represented Judge Roberts, for making political speeches rather than sticking to the record.

Gordon was nearly always the Hawkins organization's counsel, whether it was in the pursuit of Gene Wirges, defending Hawkins and other county officials or representing Judge Roberts. Broad-shouldered and muscular, Gordon was as combative in the courtroom as he had been in uniform, particularly if I was involved. A native of Morrilton and a descendant of a Confederate war hero who commanded a private militia in Conway County during the post-Reconstruction wars with Republicans and blacks, Nathan Gordon was a real war hero. He won the Medal of Honor in 1944 for steering a Navy patrol plane to rescue fifteen airmen whose crafts had been shot down by Japanese shore batteries off the Bismarck archipelago in the southwestern Pacific. Although he was under constant fire, Lieutenant Gordon dropped his bulky plane into the sea repeatedly to rescue the men. It was one of the most dramatic rescues of the war. Gordon was elected lieutenant governor the year after the Japanese surrendered and he was re-elected nine times without a challenge.

Somehow, more than anyone, I seemed to irk Gordon. He mocked Alex Streett but he literally sputtered when he talked about me. He grabbed a copy of the *Arkansas Gazette* and waved it in front of the justices. He said Tom Glaze was trying the good people of Conway County in the newspapers and he figured that Judge Roberts must have impaneled the grand jury just to keep him (me) from convicting good people in the press.

"The only thing they don't like about the grand jury," Gordon said, "is that Tom Glaze won't be able to write a story about it accusing everybody of forgery." The chief justice admonished him, "Oh, Mr. Gordon, let's don't get into all that."

The justices wound up ordering Judge Roberts to hear Streett's evidence that the grand jury was improperly formed because it was the previous year's jury panel. As we were leaving the courtroom, Gordon chased me down. Red-faced and barely able to restrain himself he said he resented my throwing his wife's name around in the papers as if she had done something criminal. He demanded to know why I was doing that. I pointed out again that his wife, Virginia Frances, had voted in Ward One but her name was not on the list of people who had voted that was kept at the polling place.

"She did not vote," he declared. "She was sick all day."

"Nathan, you are a son of a bitch," I said and walked away. I wrote him a letter a few days later apologizing for the remark and saying that I had come to understand his anger.

The little exchange proved to be crucial in building our case for election fraud, but neither Gordon nor his wife was complicit in the scheme. I mentioned Gordon's remark about his wife's not voting to Sylvia Spencer, the state capitol reporter for United Press International, who had covered the hearing. She walked over to the capitol pressroom and telephoned Virginia Gordon, who also was steaming about her name getting into the papers. She said she had not voted that day and she also mentioned that the wife of Edward Gordon, Nathan's brother and law partner, also had not voted that day because she was tending to her sick mother at the hospital. Edward Gordon's wife confirmed that, too. Her signature on her voter affidavit for January 16 was misspelled.

Someone had forged the signatures of both women on their registration affidavits and had cast ballots for them. That was prima facie evidence of fraud. Deputy Stobaugh's investigation report had strangely omitted the Gordon wives from the list of people who had signed their registration affidavits for that day but whose names were not on the official voter list. Another innocent slip-up would have been Deputy Stobaugh's explanation.

The investigation and the prospect of extensive and heated litigation seemed to be more than I could undertake, even with Hamner's part-time help. I went to see Edward L. Wright Sr., the managing partner of the state's largest law firm, Wright, Lindsey, Jennings, Lester, and Shults, and asked if he could lend a lawyer for some pro-bono assistance. He said our work was important and he related his firm's dismal experience trying cases in that judicial district. If opposing counsel lived in the district, the Wright firm's clients automatically lost. My future father-in-law, Sam Laser, a legendary defense attorney, would tell me years later that in dozens of cases in that district he never won, although he nearly always won on appeal. Wright assigned Pat Goss, one of the firm's newest attorneys, to help. Richard H. Mays, a contemporary of mine, shared a suite of law offices in the Worthen Bank Building with me and he offered to help any time that I needed him, which turned out to be often the next two years. Mays had been an all-state end for the El Dorado Wildcats and went to the University of Arkansas on a football scholarship, but he gave up sports and transferred to the University of Oklahoma as I was arriving in Fayetteville in 1956. Mays would become one of the leading environmental lawyers in the region. Handsome and courtly, a magnet for young women, Mays was tough but diplomatic and careful, a nice antidote to my rashness in those days.

My short brush with the grand jury convinced me that I was going to be indicted, for perjury if not for theft and maybe both. I had been there when the same court and essentially the same people convicted Gene Wirges of perjury after the truth of his words had been firmly established by evidence. Bland said I had taken the voter affidavits, and my saying otherwise was all the evidence of perjury that would be needed. I told Streett that we had to put them on the defensive and quickly. Three days later, Mays and Goss filed suit in federal district court at Little Rock for ten Conway County women, including the Snoop Sisters, to dissolve the grand jury. The suit contended that Roberts's juries systematically excluded women, blacks, young people, the poor, and people whose political philosophies differed from the philosophy of county officials and the handpicked jury commissioners. Two African

Americans who were known to be friendly to Hawkins were on the grand jury or on the list of alternates, but no woman had ever served on a grand jury in Conway County. A federal judge by then, G. Thomas Eisele disqualified himself from presiding over the case because he had represented Wirges in his legal battles with the Hawkins organization and Judge Roberts. The case fell to Judge Oren Harris of El Dorado, who had sentenced Mutt Jones two years earlier for tax evasion but had announced at the sentencing that he believed that the federal charges against Jones, a fellow Democrat, had been politically motivated. It was Jones's conviction and sentencing that created the Senate vacancy and led to the current predicament. Judge Harris's assignment gave me some concern, but the next week he ordered the grand jury to cease until he decided the women's case.

No one could have doubted the outcome of the suit. A month earlier—five days, in fact, after the little runoff primary—the US Supreme Court had ruled flatly that women could not be systematically excluded from jury service. It had said long ago that juries could not exclude blacks.

Although the trial before Judge Harris lacked suspense it offered fetching theater.

Floyd Bradshaw, sixty-nine, one of Hawkins's jury commissioners, testified that he had always believed that if women were on a jury there shouldn't be very many because "I always thought the men ought to run things myself."

Mays, the women's lead attorney, asked him why and this exchange followed:

"Well, the Bible tells you that he's the man of the house. If the man ain't the boss over his family, he ain't nothing no how."

"Well, are you saying then that you felt that there ought not to be very many women?"

"That's the way I felt about it. I ain't a-talking about the other boys or the other jury commissioners. I ain't saying what they . . ."

"I understand. That's your personal opinion."

"Yeah. But I even put some women on it, myself."

"But generally you felt there ought to be more men than women."

"Yeah, I was always taught that, you know."

Judge Harris ruminated over this ponderous evidence for thirteen days and then abolished the grand jury because women had been system-atically excluded in violation of the Sixth and Fourteenth Amendments. In a deadpan understatement the judge added: "The recurrent appearance of numerous members of the present grand jury panel upon previous grand jury panels causes the court to conclude that the frequent selection of these persons to serve on the grand jury in Conway County resulted from more than mere coincidence." He seemed to warn Judge Roberts and his friends that if they reconstituted the grand jury it would have to be impartial and not a band of brethren who harkened only to the master's voice.

The ruling ended Judge Roberts's diversion, but the machine's uni-fied determination to thwart the election investigation at any cost had already begun to dissolve. When the state supreme court and the federal district court first issued their preliminary orders stalling the grand jury, Katie Read, Dixie Drilling, Helen Gordon, and others returned to the county clerk's office to examine and copy election records. The county clerk and his deputy, his wife, told the women and the prosecutor that the precinct binders carrying voters' registration affidavits could not be viewed or copied on the orders of Judge Roberts. The judge said he had issued no such order. Streett advised the clerk that the voting records were subject to the Freedom of Information Act and he could not bar anyone from examining or copying them. Finally, Streett subpoenaed Bland, the county clerk, to appear at the deputy prosecutor's law office in Morrilton with the binders for Ward One. Bland didn't appear but telephoned Streett and said all the binders would be available thereafter in the clerk's office for anyone to copy. Streett requested help from the state police in the investigation and got it.

The women ferreted out more irregularities, such as double voting in five of the county's sixteen precincts, and interviewed people whose voting records were suspicious. The misdeeds were sometimes perverse. An election judge cast a ballot for Calvin Johnson, a well-known Repub-lican, in the Democratic primary without his knowledge and presumably for his enemies. One woman who went to vote said she was asked if she also would like to vote for her husband, who was in a nursing home. She did and cast a ballot for him, which was illegal. Another said she automat-ically received absentee ballots for every election without applying for them. She had already voted absentee in the Senate race but on January

16 she was telephoned by two precinct officials and told that she needed to go vote again in person, which she did. An elderly couple voted absentee but both voted again in person on election day, he after receiving ten dollars and she after a taxicab arrived at her house to take her to the polls.

Prosecutor Streett moved quickly on the forgeries in Ward One that Joe Purvis had turned up on election night. He charged one of the election officials with forging signatures on voter affidavits—she admitted one forgery when investigators interviewed her but denied the rest—and the other five officials with aiding and abetting the felonies. The charges would have to be tried before Judge Roberts and a jury that he and Sheriff Hawkins would select, which gave us little hope for a conviction. It would take ten months to get Judge Roberts off the bench and bring the case to trial.

Meantime, all of us—the women, Streett, and our TEL Institute volunteers—began to appreciate the predicament that we had created, particularly for the women who had to live in the aroused community. The weekly *Petit Jean Country Headlight,* the old and predominant newspaper in the county and a staunch ally of Hawkins, assailed us regularly. The editor, Clifton L. Wells, son of another nemesis of mine at Little Rock, publisher John Wells, wrote that the investigation and the election-fraud accusations were a giant publicity stunt hatched to enrich my "one-man institute" and me. I was manipulating a group of "possibly misguided or grudge-bearing women."

What had formerly been simple rudeness when the women had ineffectually badgered the machine turned into harassment, almost daily. The women, their husbands, and their children received threatening telephone calls. Faye Dixon's daughter, Ricki, was driving home in her mother's car after getting off work one evening. A sheriff's patrol car tailed her down the road, then pulled alongside her and forced her car into the ditch. Several husbands were told that their jobs were in jeopardy if the wives continued to try to embarrass the county and its leaders. The sheriff's office began investigating Tex Paladino for collecting unemployment benefits illegally, although the Arkansas Employment Security Division said she had done nothing wrong and that the sheriff had no authority under federal or state law to conduct such an investigation. The women felt particularly vulnerable in their isolation because neither law enforcement nor the local courts were likely to afford them any protection or justice and, in fact, were their likeliest antagonists. It was easy for all of us to develop some paranoia. One evening when I went to the Ranch House Restaurant at Plumerville, where we sometimes rendezvoused, a man walked over to the table and said, "I figured I'd find you here." I asked him how he knew. He said he had heard a police radio report that said I was headed for the Ranch House to meet some of the women.

If the United States opened an investigation, we thought, it would provide a warning to the miscreants and a patina of protection for the women. I found two federal statutes that would allow the US Justice Department to proceed and both carried heavy punishment for those who violated the law. One made it a criminal offense punishable by ten years in prison and/or a $10,000 fine to engage in a conspiracy to deny a person's rights and privileges. The US Supreme Court had ruled that the law applied to ballot-box stuffing in a congressional election but it had been silent about whether the law could be used in a state election. The Fourth US Circuit Court of Appeals had extended the law to state and local elections. Arkansas was not in the Fourth Circuit's jurisdiction but it was a precedent that the Justice Department could use. The other federal statute made it a crime punishable by a $1,000 fine and/or a year in prison to interfere with a person's vote in any primary, special or general election.

Streett and I asked the Federal Bureau of Investigation at Little Rock to look into the Conway County election. The agent said he would send some of our evidence to the Justice Department in Washington to see if federal agencies had jurisdiction. On April 4, we went to see US Attorney W. H. "Sonny" Dillahunty. We told him that the situation was dangerous and that the women who had stuck their necks out to fight the fraud were in some peril. I thought Dillahunty had been a pretty diligent prosecutor. His office had prosecuted Senator Jones for tax fraud, which had led to this imbroglio. Dillahunty told us that he had followed the business in Conway County and was inclined to investigate the voting but he would do it on his own terms. He did not want to be seen as collaborating with Tom Glaze and Alex Streett. Dillahunty was believed to be in line for a federal judgeship for the eastern district of Arkansas—President Ford had elevated Judge J. Smith Henley to the Eighth US Circuit Court of Appeals at St. Louis—and everyone was waiting on Ford to nominate Dillahunty for the vacancy. In four months, Dillahunty would be bitterly disappointed. Senators J. William Fulbright and John L. McClellan instead settled on a chancery judge from Jonesboro, Terry Lee Shell, and Ford would appoint him in the late summer. But in March, the Conway County investigation seemed like it would be an ornament on Dillahunty's résumé. The administration in Washington, after all, was Republican and all the scoundrels in the Conway County dispute were Democrats.

Two weeks later, federal marshals marched into the county clerk's office at Morrilton to seize all the records of the runoff primary, including the ballots and stubs. Bland did not have many records. He had burned them. Although state law required all election records to be kept for six months in case there was an election contest, Bland said he had burned all the ballots except those in Ward One because he said he needed the boxes for school elections. The marshals took what records they could find, which included the registration binders for each precinct, and the ballots of a school election. A federal grand jury was impaneled and Dillahunty said the Conway County election was one matter that it would consider. The grand jury handed down indictments on April 29 but none involved the election.

By mid-summer it was clear that the federal investigation was over. Word leaked that Dillahunty had been passed over for the judgeship. I tended not to be circumspect in my public comments. The papers carried my speculation that the US attorney had lost interest in the election fraud when he was passed over for the judgeship. Dillahunty and I were not on cordial terms after that. Finally, on October 30, he let it be known that he had ended the federal investigation. It was announced by a Justice Department press officer in Washington. His statement said that there was "a total lack of evidence that any fraudulent ballots had actually been cast" in the special election. I said the excuse for closing the investigation was "the most asinine, most inaccurate statement I have ever heard." We had supplied them affidavits of people who had been voted without their permission and evidence of illegal voting in five precincts and via the absentee box.

"It is totally blind to the facts," I said. He would soon be embarrassed by developments, but that day Dillahunty described my remarks as "scurrilous." Bobby Fussell, the assistant US attorney and future federal bankruptcy magistrate, who had prosecuted Senator Jones nearly two years earlier, telephoned me to complain that I had unfairly criticized his boss. He insisted that the election fraud was purely a state matter outside federal jurisdiction and that this was primarily why Dillahunty had not pursued it.

Streett had stepped back after Dillahunty opened the federal investigation, and when we surmised that the feds were not going to make a serious investigation, Streett resumed the probe in Conway County and expanded it to Faulkner County, where we knew that there had been irregularities in the heavy absentee voting. He asked the state police Criminal Investigation Division to help, and troopers Ken McFerran, Buddy Young, and Doug Stephens got affidavits from the people whose voting in Ward One in Morrilton seemed to be at odds with either the voter list or their signed registration cards. A few confirmed that they had not voted that day and that their signatures had been forged. Others, supporters of Hawkins, insisted that they had voted and that the signatures were theirs even if their names were misspelled or looked different from previous signatures. But we had lost months while the US attorney dallied, and so many election records had been destroyed that the investigation was hamstrung. Judge Roberts threw up one roadblock after another in both counties.

None of us had any confidence that the prosecution of the Ward One election officials would bear fruit, especially if they were tried in front of Judge Roberts and a handpicked jury of the faithful. Streett moved repeatedly for Judge Roberts to disqualify himself because of his kinships and political associations with people involved in the case. Not only was he second cousin to Sanson, the losing candidate, but the defense counsel for the election officials was Nathan Gordon, who also was Roberts's personal attorney. Roberts refused to recuse and Streett again went to the state supreme court. The court ruled that Roberts could preside, but this time three of the seven justices dissented. Chief Justice Harris and Justices George Rose Smith and J. Fred Jones said Roberts was bound to step down to avoid the heavy appearance of partiality, but the majority saw no conflict whatsoever.

We worried about what would happen to the remaining election records, including the Ward One ballots and records, when the federal marshals relinquished custody. Streett asked Judge Roberts not to let them be returned to the county clerk but rather to the state police because he feared that Bland would burn them as he had the other election records. Roberts ordered the county to have the election returns stored in a bank vault once federal authorities returned them. That would impede the investigation, but it didn't much matter as long as no one got a chance to destroy the Ward One records, where we had already established clear-cut evidence of fraud.

When we turned seriously to Faulkner County's election, the stakes went up. It was Judge Roberts's and Sanson's home. The county was in some ways a twin of its western neighbor but the political machine did not have a single patriarch, or at least he was not so identifiable as Marlin Hawkins. Judge Roberts and his close friend Mutt Jones were the most prominent. The courthouse and the local bar were part of the informal fraternity, but Francis Donovan and his son, Tom, who was Streett's deputy prosecutor for Faulkner County, were not part of it. Francis had been the Faulkner deputy but he dared to run against Roberts on the premise that the judge's coziness with some of the bar and political insiders was bad for justice, particularly the criminal justice system where crimes were plea-bargained away. Roberts refused thereafter to permit Francis Donovan to be a deputy prosecutor. The law at that time gave circuit judges a veto on deputy prosecutors. The young Donovan recounted his father's story that after he lost the judicial election, Judge Roberts called him to the bench during a trial that fall and said, "You know, Francis, I almost had you killed this summer." Donovan said his father never thought it was a joke.

Macabre jokes were a specialty. During the legal battles in Morrilton, Sheriff Hawkins spotted Tom Donovan in the courthouse one day and asked him about his fourteen-year-old girlfriend.

"What fourteen-year-old girlfriend?" Donovan asked.

"The one I'm going to tell people about," the sheriff replied with a grin.

Tom had gotten an accounting degree and then passed the bar at the same time as Judge Roberts's son, Russell "Jack" Roberts, but, shy and uncombative, he shunned trial law for a quiet business law practice in North Little Rock reading abstracts and doing tax work. But when Streett called Donovan and asked him to move to Conway and be his deputy, Tom thought it would be exciting and he wanted to go back to Conway. Apparently euphoric about Jack's accomplishment in passing the bar Judge

Roberts consented to having Tom, his son's contemporary and acquaintance, be the county's deputy. Donovan moved to Conway and began his trial and prosecutorial practice in time for the big imbroglio over expelling and replacing the disgraced Mutt Jones in the Senate. Judge Roberts's tolerance for the spawn of his enemy soon turned to enmity.

Streett had telephoned Donovan the first of January 1975 and asked him to come to Morrilton to help the women set up a poll-watcher system for the Senate runoff primary. Donovan arranged CB radios and military authentication codes for some of the young lawyers and law students. Streett got an opinion from the attorney general saying that poll watchers could observe the voting and the counting and they passed it out to the poll watchers. At Dixie's house in Morrilton and then at his office in Conway, Donovan took calls from the distressed poll watchers who had been turned away from the polls and warned that they would be arrested if they hung around the polls. He told them that they had a lawful right to be there but that he could not advise them to get arrested.

Donovan joined the women and me in the post-election investigation at Morrilton. Streett's Conway County deputy, Felver Rowell, was a friend of Hawkins and his heart was not in the hunt. For economic as well as social reasons, Rowell could not be seen as actively helping Streett in what was locally regarded as a vendetta against the sheriff and his people. Donovan came to rival Streett and me as public enemies at the courthouse. For years it seemed that every time he traversed the county a sheriff's patrol car picked him up in the neighborhood of Menifee or Plumerville and trailed him to Morrilton or to Blackwell on the Pope County line. He took care to observe the speed limit. He would many years later admit to having succumbed to a little paranoia.

In Faulkner County, the foreboding would prove to be justified. They were after him. Prowling through the absentee voting records for the primary, we began to find irregularities. We were particularly suspicions of the 119 absentee votes in an envelope that was delivered from the county judge's office to the clerk on election day, all of which were cast for Bill Sanson. We obtained affidavits from people who affirmed that, contrary to the absentee records, they had not asked for absentee ballots and had not voted. On May 1, Streett asked Judge Roberts to order the county treasurer, custodian of the absentee-ballot stubs, to turn over the records to the county clerk, Leaster Merritt, so that we could examine them. Judge

Roberts swung into action. He granted Streett's motion to open the stub box and remove the absentee-voter statements, but, without a motion by anyone, he also impounded all the county's records for the Jan. 16 election. He said Streett, Donovan, I, and anyone else could examine election records only in his presence. Then he told Sheriff Joe S. Martin to select twenty-five people for a grand jury to inquire into the special election and other matters that he might want it to study—he mentioned bootlegging in Conway. It was unprecedented for a judge to create a grand jury on his own volition and to have the sheriff instead of jury commissioners choose the jurors. It was unheard of because it was illegal.

I was subpoenaed to testify at the grand jury, about what I did not know, but the jurors never got around to questioning me. In fact, they never got around to investigating the election seriously, although they eventually indicted the county clerk for some questionable absentee ballots. Roberts hinted at what he was up to when he addressed the grand jurors. He told them that if for any reason they decided to investigate Streett and Donovan they could bar the prosecutors from the jury room and appoint their own special prosecutor. They chose to do just that and named John T. "Tom" Tatum of Danville, who had lost his job as deputy prosecutor in Yell County when Streett was elected. Tatum soon stepped aside and the grand jury employed Floyd Lofton of Little Rock as a special prosecutor.

William R. Wilson Jr. of Little Rock filed a lawsuit in federal district court at Little Rock to halt the grand jury. He represented the Conway mayor, Jim Hoggard, who was part of the rival political faction and who figured he was going to be indicted in some connection with bootlegging. I filed an intervention for four Faulkner County taxpayers asking that the grand jury be dissolved because it was illegally formed. Streett, meantime, asked the Arkansas Supreme Court to quash the grand jury on the same premise. Federal Judge Warren K. Urbom of Nebraska, who had been assigned the case because the Arkansas federal judges disqualified themselves, temporarily halted the grand jury until he could determine jurisdiction.

Ultimately, the Arkansas Supreme Court would nullify the grand jury because a sheriff could not appoint a grand jury even if he had been ordered to do so by a circuit judge, but not before the grand jury had indicted Streett and Donovan for misfeasance and malfeasance. The charge carried no particulars about what they had done or not done, but Roberts had said they were not prosecuting cases in a timely manner. Criminal cases had piled up in Judge Roberts's court and he and Streett had carried on a public dispute for three years about who was to blame for so many cases being dismissed because they had not been tried in a timely way. Streett said the judge wouldn't fix trial dates and Roberts said he found Streett and Donovan unprepared for trial. Streett had once accused Roberts of charging fees to defendants to suspend or dismiss charges against them. A month after those indictments, the grand jury indicted Donovan again, this time for smoking marijuana. Streett remarked that the second indictment had the same substance as the first ones. The grand jury indicted Hoggard for taking bribes to protect bootleggers. I said the indictments were all intended to divert our investigation of vote stealing in the Senate primary. Not content, the rogue grand jury also indicted the Faulkner County county clerk, Leaster Merritt, for fraud in the handling of a number of absentee ballots, including a batch that he took to residents of a nursing home.

Leaster Merritt afforded everyone a lesson on the cost of violating the first imperative of a political machine, unswerving loyalty. Merritt had been on the Roberts-Jones team, but after Jones's conviction for tax fraud he consulted with Streett, who advised him that the law required him to remove a convicted felon from the voter rolls. Jones discovered in 1975 that he was no longer eligible to vote or to run for office. The Arkansas Supreme Court had suspended his law privileges for a year. Jones and Judge Roberts still controlled the Faulkner County Election Commission, and the commission ordered Merritt to put Jones back on the voter rolls. He refused. The commission went to court and a special circuit judge, the irascible Melvin Mayfield of El Dorado, later my colleague on the Arkansas Court of Appeals, said the Election Commission was right and that the clerk had to restore Jones's voting privilege. Merritt, flashing an independence and stubbornness no one knew he possessed, appealed to the supreme court, which ruled that he—and not the Election Commission and Judge Mayfield—was right, and that the law required him to cancel Jones's voting rights.

Meantime, Merritt was paying a price for his rebelliousness. When the Roberts grand jury indicted him, Sheriff Martin arrested him and he had to make bail.

When the Arkansas Supreme Court demolished the grand jury because Roberts and Martin had constituted it illegally, it nullified all the jury's indictments. A special circuit judge appointed by the supreme court impaneled a new grand jury, this one formed according to the law, and the Jones-Roberts organization could get no indictments against either Streett or his deputy, Tom Donovan, or Mayor Hoggard or Merritt. The judge called Streett and asked him to appoint two jury commissioners, who would be matched by two commissioners named by Mutt Jones. Streett protested that neither he nor Jones should be choosing the jury commissioners but the judge told him that if he did not appoint two, Jones would appoint all four. They picked a grand jury, which listened apparently to the same testimony as the first one and announced that there were no grounds to indict anyone.

But the Jones organization was determined not to let poor Merritt escape the consequences of his disloyalty. An example had to be made. Three dozen Democrats friendly to Jones and Roberts formed the Committee for Honest Elections to look into the way Merritt had handled his election duties in the January 1975 special election to fill Jones's Senate seat. Several members of the quashed grand jury who were on the committee signed affidavits accusing Merritt of mishandling absentee ballots for residents of nursing homes—it was some of the evidence that we had gathered in our investigation of voting fraud in the special Senate election—and in mid-January 1976 two justices of the peace who supported Jones, Roberts, and Bill Sanson, their losing Senate candidate, lodged warrants with the sheriff for Merritt's arrest for election fraud. The sheriff promptly jailed Merritt again although he soon released the clerk on his own recognizance. It took two months for the courts to quash those charges, too, not because Merritt hadn't mishandled the nursing-home ballots but because a sheriff had no authority to arrest and charge someone on the say-so of a JP. Months of headlines about the clerk's arrests and charges of ballot fraud seemed likely to torpedo his political career—he had served ten years—but remarkably he was nominated again in the primaries that spring and re-elected. Matters did not go nearly so well for Mutt Jones's organization.

By the end of winter in March 1976, more than a year after the little special state Senate primary, the people of Conway and Faulkner Counties—indeed of the whole state—who had tried to follow these bewildering developments could not have known what to think of the whole circus, even to sort out the ever-shifting cast. Although they may not have expected or liked the precise outcomes of all their conniving (the appellate courts quashed every initiative), Sheriff Hawkins, Judge Roberts, and their confederates got their interests served by the delays, distractions, and utter confusion. Their political organizations had survived more or less intact going into a fresh round of elections in 1976, although with an aroused public skepticism even in their own ranks.

After Roberts finally relinquished the case in December 1975 and allowed Judge Van Taylor of Dardanelle to be assigned to it, five of the six

Ward One election officials in Conway County pled guilty to reduced charges of forging voter signatures on registration affidavits or else drinking at the polls in the special Senate primary—all misdemeanors. Streett dropped charges against the sixth worker. The two women who admitted forging signatures paid $1,000 fines and Streett agreed not to prosecute them for other election crimes. To me, the punishment seemed to be far less than what would be required to deter future chicanery, but none of us really had expected a jury in Conway County to convict any of them. Neither the election officials nor Nathan Gordon, the election officials' attorney, wanted to take a chance on the whims of a new jury that might be objective. I was furious with Alex for reducing the charges to misdemeanors and allowing them to plead guilty without a trial and without suffering a meaningful penalty. So were the women. But he was convinced that he could not get a conviction from a Conway County jury that was almost certain to be sympathetic and that the guilty pleas would send a powerful message to the community and the state that elections in Conway County were indeed corrupt. It did seem to be an awakening but I and the women who had worked so hard to gather evidence of fraud were disappointed that all of it would not be spilled on the court records for the people of Conway County and the state to see. I think Alex also felt a twinge of sympathy for the ordinary folks who would have borne the disgrace and penalties for carrying out the schemes of political bosses, who would have gone unpunished and perhaps even unsullied.

Soon afterward Streett charged Jack Bland, the Conway County county clerk who had destroyed the election records after the primary, with a felony. If Bland had been convicted the law prescribed from one to five years in prison and a fine of up to $5,000. The case bounced around for two years and the supreme court finally assigned Circuit Judge Taylor to try the case. Streett met with Bland and his attorney before a pre-trial hearing that was scheduled in January 1978. Bland offered to resign from office if Streett would drop the charges against him. The Snoop Sisters and I still wanted to see Bland tried and the evidence laid out for all to see, but Alex said he thought that the important thing was to get Bland out of the clerk's office before the next election because he was convinced that the county clerk facilitated much of the fraud. Alex *nolle prossed* the charges, Bland resigned, and Governor Pryor appointed Ray Wood in February to finish Bland's term as county clerk.

Sure enough, the 1978 primaries and general election were Conway County's cleanest in memory.

Despite all the minor victories in the courts, I was dismayed that so little punishment had been meted out for so much fraud. At the time, I doubted the deterrence value of the plea-bargained admissions of guilt and the light punishment. I could not permit myself then to believe that a new day had dawned.

CHAPTER 9

• • • • • • • • • • •

Independence Day

"As long as I have the energy, I hope I can continue to 'steal elections.'"

—MARLIN HAWKINS, *HOW I STOLE ELECTIONS*

Nineteen hundred seventy-six was a very good year. It was the bicentennial of American independence, and the country and our little state were caught up in a wave of nostalgia and patriotism. For a year before the culminating Fourth of July celebration and for months afterward, the country, every state, and thousands of cities heralded the anniversary of the Declaration of Independence with fireworks, wagon trains, speeches, and every novel event that local bicentennial committees could imagine and stage. The euphoria and the endless recitation of the stirring words of the Declaration of Independence seemed to bring the country out of the national funk that followed those deeply divisive and embittering episodes, Watergate and the Vietnam War. It helped engender an era of good feeling in Arkansas, too. The state emerged from a prolonged recession and it would be another two years before the oil shocks and inflation would send the economy reeling and the nation and Arkansas back into gloom. Governor David Pryor named my old friend and boss Joe Purcell, by then the lieutenant governor, to chair the commission that planned the 200th-anniversary celebrations in Arkansas. It occurred to me that Pryor chose Purcell because he was sure that Joe, celebrated for his somnolent stage presence and wooden oratory, would not be upstaging him or anyone else. But I'm sure that Pryor picked him because he knew that Joe would consider it the most important task in the world and would work at it with the same seriousness and doggedness that he approached the most inane task, which he did.

The bicentennial was a faint motif all spring and summer as we went about the business of trying to ensure that people got honest and fair elections in counties with a history of election rigging. While we were trying in the spring to get the Democratic Central Committee in Conway County to appoint election officials who would give an honest accounting of the voters' preferences in the May and June primaries, Joe's bicentennial wagon train made its way down old US Highway 64 from Fort Smith and stopped at Morrilton for some local festivities. An express rider delivered a scroll that proclaimed that the state was renewing its commitment to the principles of the Declaration of Independence and the Bill of Rights. Oh, if only that had been true! The bicentennial nostalgia evoked conflicting feelings—a cynicism that here in Arkansas we were demonstrably falling short of ensuring everyone an equal voice in the democracy, and on the other hand an abiding sense that we were indeed engaged in a patriotic effort to renew the founding principles by trying to protect people's right to vote and to have everyone's vote counted fairly and undiluted by fraud.

It would perhaps not be coincidence that 1976 would be the year that two of the most notorious counties, Conway and Searcy, managed with great effort to have reasonably honest elections for the first time in many years. They were in both instances the products of aroused citizenry—the Snoop Sisters and a growing band of supporters in Conway County, and a handful of determined citizens in Searcy County fifty miles to the north. In the end, in both counties it required the intervention of the United States District Court.

The women who had worked so hard to unmask the deceit and intimidation in Conway County's elections were determined that all the labor they had put in before and after the 1975 runoff election, all the anger and heartache that it had engendered, and all the evidence of fraud that they had assembled would not be wasted. They wanted to make the 1976 party primaries a test of the progress that had been made both in the education of the voters and in making ballot thievery too dangerous for Sheriff Hawkins and his friends to risk. Although we would have preferred to press forward with a trial of the year-old charges of fraud against the six judges and clerks in Morrilton's Ward One, we agreed with Alex that the first admissions of illegal voting that the plea bargain produced might be a wake-up call to voters who had always believed Hawkins's regular assertions that elections were scrupulously honest and that all the allegations year after year were merely Republican politics and schemes to generate legal fees for me and TEL Institute.

Three weeks before the first Democratic primary on May 25, Alex filed charges against fifteen other officials who had conducted the 1975 runoff primary in two Morrilton wards and three rural precincts. Using evidence gathered by the Snoop Sisters and the state police, he filed charges accusing them of arranging illegal ballots for a number of people, typically by having them vote twice, by absentee and in person at the precincts. He filed charges against four other persons accusing them of buying votes in the runoff. Those cases would never go to trial either, and the *Petit Jean Country Headlight* and the election officials' attorney accused Streett and me of manufacturing the charges to influence the approaching election. I did hope that the charges would keep the pressure on county officials and the scores of precinct judges and clerks who would conduct the voting, and I am sure that was on Alex's mind, too. I hoped that it would not be lost on election workers in other counties around Arkansas that there might be consequences for the individuals who played even subordinate roles in election cheating.

We set out in March to make the playing field in the May and June primaries as level as we could make it. Faye Dixon, one of the three actual sisters among the Snoop Sisters, decided to throw herself under the wheels by running for county clerk, the office that runs elections and, specifically, handles absentee ballots. Jack Bland, though his trial for election fraud kept getting delayed (he would resign from the clerk's office two years later in exchange for the charges being dropped), would still be supervising the 1976 elections. The County Democratic Committee set the filing fee for county offices so high that it discouraged long-shot candidates who were not in the courthouse's favor. I filed a lawsuit in the US Court for the Eastern District of Arkansas asking that Faye's name be placed on the ballot without her having paid the fee because the $1,025 required for the clerk and the fees for other county offices were set high to prevent people from running for public office. Exorbitant filing fees violated the equal-protection clause of the Fourteenth Amendment. Judge Terry L. Shell granted the request and her name went on the ballot.

A larger problem was installing precinct judges and clerks who would follow the law or else create conditions under which the election workers would monitor one another. The county Democratic committee would meet on April 19 to designate the six workers at each precinct. I assembled a group at the Arkansas Power and Light Co. building in Little Rock to talk about strategy, and we came up with a plan. When the Democratic committee assembled and nominated the slate of judges and clerks for Austin Township, the first precinct on the list, we had one ally on the committee, who voted against the slate, and he was prepared to dissent on the slate for each precinct. Alex arose and advised the committee that Arkansas law provided that a minority could name two of a precinct's six election officials. He read the statute. Panic ensued. Hawkins huddled with the chairman, who promptly recessed the meeting for a few hours. When the committee reassembled, it was soon clear that we had underestimated the sheriff's adroitness again. The chairman called for another vote on the Austin township workers, and this time four committee members instead of one voted no. Hawkins had persuaded three other central committee members to join the lone dissenter. Then the three Hawkins plants outvoted the honest dissenter and picked the two minority representatives for each precinct, who were, of course, Hawkins allies. There would be no independent monitoring inside the polling place on election day. Then, in another flagrant violation of the law, the committee chairman assigned ballot positions for the 115 candidates who filed for offices in the county, a much larger turnout of candidates than normal. The law required that the candidates draw for ballot position. Current officeholders were given the top line on the ballot for each office, which conveys a small advantage, and people we liked to call the reform candidates got the bottom position.

Four days later, I filed a lawsuit asking the federal district court to stop the illegal election practices in Conway County, which flouted the plaintiffs' rights to due process and equal protection of the laws. It named the county clerk and an array of Democratic election officials as defendants. My friend Richard Mays and Oscar Fendler, a brilliant and acerbic lawyer at Blytheville who had some familiarity with the Conway County political culture from Gene Wirges's legal battles with the machine, were my co-counsel. Fifty-three residents of Conway County, including the Snoop Sisters, were the plaintiffs along with seven other

Sheriff Marlin Hawkins could command the attention of political bigwigs. Here, he gets major political figures to join him on the steps of the Conway County Courthouse to publicize his drive to register young people to vote in 1971, after ratification of the twenty-sixth amendment to the Constitution, which lowered the voting age to eighteen. Mainly, the event promoted Marlin. From left are Sheriff Hawkins; Senator John L. McClellan; Congressman Wilbur D. Mills; former attorney general Joe Purcell, who was chairman of the Arkansas Democratic Party; my future nemesis Walter Carruth, chairman of the American Party; and Congressman David H. Pryor, who would run against Senator McClellan the next year. *Photo courtesy of the* Arkansas Democrat-Gazette

people from around the state, including several members of the TEL Institute board of directors like Hank Haines, the editor and publisher of the *Blytheville Courier News*. They were to represent all the voters of the state, whom we maintained had an interest in having an honest vote count in the county. Fraud in Conway County would dilute their own votes in the statewide races that would be on the same ballot with county offices. The suit sought to stop the fraudulent election practices that we had identified in the 1975 runoff election and others that were already occurring in the preparation for the 1976 election. We asked the judge to issue injunctions against the violations and to prevent election officials from interfering with poll watchers inside the polling places as they had in the January 1975 primary. We were prepared to finally put on the considerable evidence of fraud in the runoff election that the women and the state police had accumulated. Judge Shell scheduled a hearing for April 30 on my motion for a temporary injunction.

I subpoenaed forty-five witnesses, mostly people who had ballots cast for them without their knowledge, people who were paid cash or whiskey for their votes, people who had voted both in person and absentee in the same election, and five troopers from the Criminal Investigation Division of the state police, who had collected evidence from the Snoop Sisters' investigation. One reluctant witness would be the wife of the former lieutenant governor and attorney for the county officials named in the suit. She was not eager but she had admitted that her signature had been forged on the registration affidavit at Ward One. I really looked forward to Nathan Gordon's cross-examination of his wife.

The reaction at the courthouse was immediate and surprising. The county officials did not want a federal trial or even an injunction hearing and they were willing to make some big concessions to avoid them. We worked out a compromise with the machine's ubiquitous attorneys at the law firm of Gordon and Gordon. They would agree to Judge Shell's ordering them not to violate election laws in the primaries as long as they could stipulate in the decree that they were not admitting any past violations of the law. They would agree to court-supervised poll watchers who would monitor the voting and ballot counting inside every polling place, one poll watcher for the plaintiffs and one for the defendants in each precinct. Again, the order would stipulate that it was not to be a precedent for future election cases and that the county was not agreeing that the law actually permitted poll watchers inside polling places. Hawkins and the other county officials had contended steadfastly that the law did not authorize poll watchers to go inside where they could watch as voters cast their ballots and poll officials went about their work. The order would apply to 1976 elections alone. For our part, we consented to letting the election officials appointed by the Democratic county committee serve at both primaries in spite of our belief that the slates violated the law's promise of minority representation in each precinct. We drafted the consent order and Judge Shell signed it the day before the injunction hearing was to be held.

While we looked forward to laying our evidence of vote tampering before the court and the state, we figured that the poll watchers and the stern court order, which was to be given to every county officer and precinct official, would discourage most of the cheating, perhaps all but the absentee-ballot manipulation. We hoped a little education would stem the absentee fraud. I drafted a letter from The Election Laws Institute to people across the country who regularly cast absentee ballots in Conway County and those who had applied for absentee ballots within a few days of the election. It explained who could cast absentee ballots legally and the procedures required by law to cast an absentee ballot, and it mentioned the penalties for violating the law: a $1,000 fine and up to a year in jail for casting an illegal absentee ballot, and from one to five years in prison if a person voted absentee and cast a second ballot at the polls. I also explained that it was illegal for a county official or anyone else to include with absentee-ballot materials sent to voters any campaign materials or anything that attempted to influence how the person should vote, which had been standard practice for many years.

Clifton Wells at the *Petit Jean Country Headlight* editorialized every week. He accused me of seeking to intimidate voters. Of the court-ordered poll watchers, the paper said Tom Glaze would not stop until he was able to get his hands inside the ballot boxes.

Whether it was from the pressures generated by the investigations or internal quarrels, or both, the machine was showing signs of decomposition. Ordinarily, the sheriff's slate ran unopposed in the Democratic primaries but this time the sheriff's men, both incumbents and fresh candidates for county offices, got one or two opponents. Two old-time Hawkins men were running against his slate. Hawkins found himself opposed by his old friend and enforcer, W. O. "Bus" Hice. When he was the Morrilton chief of police and later county tax assessor, Hice had been Hawkins's staunch ally in the battles with Gene Wirges, once having flattened the editor on a Morrilton sidewalk for writing an unflattering article about him. Hice had retired four months into his term as tax assessor the year before and his son took his place for the remainder of the term, but Hice went to the sheriff in the spring of 1976 and said he didn't like retirement and wanted to get his old job as assessor back. Hawkins told him that he had already picked T. J. Mahan to run for assessor and he was sticking to it. Seeing that he would have to run without the sheriff's support anyway, Hice decided to run against Hawkins. After all, his background had been law enforcement. Few people took Hice seriously, but this was not going to be like the lock-step primaries of the previous quarter-century.

• • •

Reporters converged on Morrilton for the primaries and speculated on the end of the state's most famous political machine. Seventeen law students and more than fifty local people were assigned poll watcher duties. They were armed with copies of Judge Shell's order and wore badges with gold stars and red, white, and blue ribbons. The badges read "Federal Court Poll Watcher." They were linked by sixteen citizen-band radios or telephone to the reform headquarters in the home of Denis and Dixie Drilling and their four small children in Morrilton. Tom Donovan, the deputy prosecutor from Faulkner County, set up the CB radio system and arranged military authentication codes for the radio operators. The poll watchers were to keep in touch with Dixie and Alex Streett about irregularities or difficulties at the polling sites. There were a few, but not grave ones. A poll watcher at Overcup radioed that an election judge was passing out campaign materials for Hawkins's candidates to people as they came in to vote. Streett and I drove to Overcup and told the fellow that he was violating the law. In the Springfield community, a man tried to vote but was told that the records showed that he had already voted absentee. He said he had not even applied for an absentee ballot and insisted on voting. He was allowed to vote and his bogus absentee ballot was disallowed. We got reports and subsequently affidavits of attempts to buy votes with cash and half-pint bottles of untaxed liquor. Poll watchers at one site saw election officials watching people mark their ballots and making notes about the votes. Robert Dittrich, a first-year law student who was stationed at Menifee, spotted the chief election judge going to voters to instruct them on how to mark their ballots and actually marking ballots for them. He told the judge that he could not do that and that he could only assist a voter who asked for help. When the judge persisted, Dittrich, a very large man, physically restrained him. Sheriff Hawkins and his two sons drove up in a police car within minutes and asked Dittrich what the hell he was doing.

"I'm enforcing the law," Dittrich said. That seemed to suffice.

Still, when the polls closed that evening I pronounced it the cleanest election that Conway County had seen in a generation.

No one dared hope for a thorough repudiation of the machine, but the election came closer than most of us expected. Hawkins beat Hice handily but not by the margin to which he was accustomed, and his closest confederate, county clerk Bland, defeated Faye Dixon by a considerably smaller margin. Bland would resign the next spring to avoid a trial for destroying evidence of election fraud in the 1975 runoff. County judge Tom Scott, who had run the county in tandem with Hawkins since 1959, was forced into a runoff and then defeated two weeks later. Hawkins candidates for county surveyor, treasurer, and assessor were defeated. Hawkins had run one of his deputies for treasurer. The husbands of two of the Snoop Sisters and another ally were elected in the first primary to the new streamlined county legislative body, the Quorum Court, and others were elected two weeks later. Hawkins would be sheriff again but a big majority of the new Quorum Court, which would have strong legislative powers under Amendment 55 to the constitution, would not be rubberstamps. Several of Hawkins's slate in the statewide races lost in Conway County. Voters had nearly always followed Hawkins's recommendations in every race.

Although the absentee vote in the first primary was still abnormal compared with most counties, it fell about a third from the absentee vote in the runoff for the state Senate the year before. But it was as lopsided as ever. Hawkins carried the absentees 380 to 45.

Late in the evening of the runoff primary, when nearly all the returns were posted and the magnitude of the victory in the two elections was clear, I left the courthouse and drove to Denis and Dixie Drilling's house, which was the command center for the reformers. The surrounding blocks were packed with cars and the Drilling home was filled with celebrants. There was a sense of liberation and relief in the exultation. People who had never evinced the slightest sympathy for the women were there telling Dixie that the elections were a rebirth for the community. The Snoop Sisters were no longer pariahs. I told Dixie that I wished that Rockefeller were still alive to see what had happened in the community that had so frustrated him.

Surrounded by unfriendly faces in the courthouse and on the Quorum Court, Hawkins carried on after his re-election but announced in 1978 that he was tired and would not run again. His nephew and chief deputy, Carl Stobaugh, ran for the job, but Hawkins mourned in his autobiography, *How I Stole Elections,* written by Dr. C. Fred Williams, that Stobaugh spurned his help, including his absentee-ballot system, and tossed him and his friends aside for the Republicans. Stobaugh told him that he wanted to win the office and run it in his own way. The memoir ends with recriminations against friends, relatives, and political allies who betrayed him, from Orval Faubus to David Pryor and Bill Clinton. He recounted that he had turned to hard liquor and prescription drugs in his last years at the courthouse and that the pain of separation from the courthouse and from politics made him dependent upon them. He related regretfully that his family and friends had to put him into a treatment center. He said a self-help spiritual program there cured him. Hawkins died in 1995.

Three days after Christmas 1991, Bobbie Bengston cleared out her attic on Kentucky Street on Morrilton's east end so that insulation could be sprayed between the rafters. She found a paper grocery sack closed by tape, on which was written "Tuesday, July 30, 1968 Ward #1 Box #1 & 2 voter ballots cast in the Democratic Elect." It would provide an illuminating postscript to our and Hawkins's saga.

The Bengstons had bought the little frame house in 1985 from Cecil Jackson, one of Hawkins's longtime deputies, who died soon afterward. County records showed that Jackson lived there in 1968 and that he was sheriff for Ward One, box one, and his wife was an election clerk for Ward One, box two. The grocery sack contained 200 marked ballots for the 1968 Democratic primary. Of the 200 ballots, 122 were initialed by two poll officials and still had the stubs attached. All but two were marked for all the same candidates up and down the ballot. The "X" marked by each name was uniform across all 122 ballots. The other 78 ballots were marked in a variety of ways and the Xs were different, suggesting that these ballots were actually cast at the polling place that day. The stubs had been detached, as they were supposed to be, and presumably deposited in the stub box. The other 122 were obviously stuffed ballots. But they were all counted on election night.

The *Petit Jean Country Headlight,* by then a remarkably different paper than the one that castigated Gene Wirges, the women, Alex, and me so regularly in the 1960s and '70s, reported the grocery sack's discovery and figured out what it meant. The big race in 1968 had been for prosecuting attorney between Jeff Mobley and Robert E. "Doc" Irwin, both of

Russellville. Mobley was friendly with Hawkins and was on the sheriff's slate. Mobley carried Conway County by the usual landslide but he won the five counties of the district by a total of only twenty votes. Irwin had asked for a recount of eleven boxes, including the two boxes in Ward One. A recount would have turned up the 122 illegal ballots and Irwin would have won because all 122 of the bogus ballots were marked and counted for Mobley. (Alex Streett defeated Mobley in the next election, in 1970.)

Sixteen of the twenty-three members of the Conway County Democratic Committee assembled to certify the primary results that July 1968 and refused the recount. They adopted a statement saying that they had "the utmost faith in the honesty and integrity of the election officials" and that the request for a recount cast aspersions upon the reputations of the people who conducted the election in those polling places. Irwin explained to the paper in 1991 that he had agreed to not formally contest the election in exchange for a promise from the county officials that they would support him in the next election. They violated the agreement and laughed about it, he said.

The *Headlight* article said its reporter had talked to a longtime insider with the Hawkins machine who agreed to talk about how elections were stolen on condition that the paper not reveal his identity. He called it "a fool-proof scheme so long as the election officials did not squeal on each other."

According to this source, extra ballots would be printed and election officials would meet in the courtroom at the courthouse two nights before the election to prepare the extra ballots. He said that through experience in voting patterns, it could be determined how many extra ballots would be needed for each box in the city of Morrilton.

At the voting precincts, a pre-arranged number of legitimate ballots would be allowed to be cast. Then cardboard separators would be placed in the ballot and stub boxes to separate these votes from any cast later. At about 3 or 3:30 p.m., the doors to the polls would be closed briefly while the legitimate ballots above the cardboard separators would be removed and replaced by the previously marked extra ballots.

Officials in rural areas did not bother with such sophistication in switching ballots, the source said.

"Hundreds of people knew about the procedure," he said.

This went on until 1976, when what he called "the first honest election" in Conway County was held and incumbent county judge Tom Scott, even with the strong support of Hawkins, was beaten by David Trafford in a runoff vote of 4,262 to 3,139.

• • •

All of us indulged the belief that the 1976 primaries ended election thievery in Conway County, an impression left by the Morrilton paper's extraordinary story about the purloined ballots. Although I would be involved in another venue, it would not be my last experience with ballot cheats in Conway County.

CHAPTER 10

· · · · · · · · · · · ·

A Penny for Your Vote

"A bumper of good liquor
Will end a contest quicker
Than justice, judge, or vicar"

—RICHARD BRINSLEY SHERIDAN

Sometimes election fraud is not a secret enterprise but a transparent way of life, undertaken with the willing participation of parties and factions. Votes are bartered for cash, whiskey or favors, and practically everyone willfully enters into the competition and accepts the outcome with the philosophical cheer of the losing bidders on a government printing contract. In the 1976 primaries alone, we found evidence of vote buying in Conway, Madison, Stone, and Marion Counties, but the system had developed in its most pristine form in Searcy County, a poor but picturesque bailiwick in the Ozark Plateau of northwest Arkansas best known for the gorgeous river that traverses it, the Buffalo National River. It was the perfect embodiment of a certain strain of mountain political culture, intense and often violent, and I would get to know it only peripherally but far better than I would have preferred.

Discerning readers of President Bill Clinton's autobiography, *My Life*, could get a sense of what it was like. Clinton writes of his first foray into Arkansas politics, his unsuccessful race for the US House of Representatives in 1974. Carl Whillock, a former administrative assistant to the late J. W. Trimble, who had lost the House seat to John Paul Hammerschmidt eight years earlier, squired young Clinton around the most remote of the twenty-one counties of the Third District that spring to hook him up with the movers and shakers who could help him in the Democratic primary against three opponents and against Hammerschmidt in the fall if he won the party nomination. Whillock in the book *The Clintons of Arkansas* and Clinton in *My Life* tell about arriving after nine o'clock at night at the home of Will Goggin, the county Democratic chairman, who was then in his 80s, outside the hamlet of St. Joe.

Few places in Arkansas were poorer than St. Joe or more fertile ground for populist fervor. Some thirty years earlier, one of Goggin's neighbors, a poor hillside farmer named Joe Johnson—the father of eight children—became the first person ever arrested and convicted of flag desecration in Arkansas when he went to the Searcy County Courthouse at Marshall to get commodities for his starving children. Word had got around that Johnson was a Jehovah's Witness, an unpopular sect that believed saluting the flag violated the biblical injunction against worshiping graven images. The county welfare director told Johnson that he could not get any foodstuff until he saluted the flag in the cramped office. In a short speech quoting the Bible, Johnson allowed his hand to brush the flag, a flagrant desecration according to a state law passed at the end of World War I. The farmer was jailed for the offense, and the next year, soon after Pearl Harbor, the Arkansas Supreme Court put aside the First Amendment and ruled that Johnson got exactly what he deserved.

Will Goggin was a populist who developed an ardor for the Democratic Party in the crucible of that bleak time and place.

Whillock had told Clinton that if Goggin supported him he would easily carry Searcy County in the primaries. Goggin had gone to bed but let them in and listened to Clinton make his pitch about how he could beat Hammerschmidt. Sure enough, Goggin was infatuated with the young law professor and promised to support him.

"When he said he'd be for me," Clinton wrote, "I knew it meant a lot of votes, as you'll see."

Clinton discreetly didn't tell the whole story, but Whillock did, privately. Goggin told Clinton that he would be on the slate for the primaries and the general election if he was the nominee, and he suggested that Clinton contribute to the fund that would elect the candidates. He explained that small payments would be required for some votes. Clinton was reluctant to participate in the scheme, but Whillock negotiated an understanding that the Third District race would be exempt from the vote-buying arrangement even though Clinton would still get the chairman's nod. Clinton did recount in the autobiography that when he was forced into a runoff with state Senator W. E. "Gene" Rainwater of Fort Smith in the May primary he learned that Goggin was going to open only one polling place in the whole county for the runoff, which Clinton thought would discourage voting and hurt his chances of winning. Clinton telephoned Goggin, who told him not to worry, "you'll get whatever votes we cast." Clinton carried the county against Rainwater 177 to 10. After his loss to Hammerschmidt that fall, Clinton called Goggin to thank him for supporting him, and the old cattle farmer told him: "I know you think I rigged that runoff vote for you but I didn't. Actually, you won 177 to 9. I gave Rainwater another vote because I couldn't stand to see anyone not in double figures."

Here is the way the system worked: Agents for the parties, factions or individual candidates haggled with voters who needed an extra incentive to participate in the democratic process. A pint of moonshine or bonded whiskey might be the price, or the cash bidding might go as high as a hundred dollars or, according to rumor, sometimes higher, although typically the price would be five to twenty dollars per vote. Inside the polling place, the voter would cast his ballot under the watchful eye of a poll official, who would give him the token of the day—let's say, a kernel of corn for a Republican vote or a button for a Democratic vote—and the tokens would be redeemed outside the polling place at the agreed-upon price.

No one could be sure when the system was set up but it was believed to have predated World War II. The Great Depression sounds like the right circumstance. People like Joe Johnson, who was desperate for the smallest kind of assistance, were prevalent in the hills, although Johnson sounds like he might have had the stubborn principle to resist selling his vote. The story was that sometime after the war there were complaints about the vote bartering and the FBI sent agents to the county to investigate. An FBI official was supposed to have explained later that agents abandoned the investigation because they figured that if they locked up one person they would have to lock up half the county.

Searcy County was especially suitable for vote marketing in general elections because it was one of three or four Arkansas counties that had always been competitive. The fall elections predictably turned upon a few hundred votes. Until the 1990s, everything south of Searcy County was reliably Democratic, but Searcy County had tilted slightly toward Republicans since Reconstruction. Democrats with a good marketing effort and a good war chest could win on occasion.

The county's Republican leanings and its unusual volume of strife around elections are not hard to trace. The hardscrabble farmers around Marshall, who did not own slaves, were never keen on secession, and during the Civil War the county was a hotbed of insurgency. Men were captured, taken to Little Rock, and forced into Confederate service. Many deserted and returned to the county and then joined Union regiments in Missouri. Searcy County men eventually made up most of six Union companies. The returning Union veterans took control of the county after the war and the Republican Party clung tenuously and intermittently to office for the next 150 years although populist stirrings outside the party during the Depression made the Democrats more competitive—that and the fact that the Democratic Party's perpetual majority status in Arkansas gave Democrats in the county the right to appoint most election officials in each precinct. Election judges and clerks were the most important people in Searcy County.

The bitterness of civil war and Reconstruction barely subsided over the next century. Extreme poverty, illegal whiskey, ancient feuds, and the power of even minor political offices were a volatile mixture. The *Arkansas Gazette* wrote that no fewer than six county sheriffs had been gunned down. My foray into the county that summer to try to correct electoral abuses would get me involved to my ultimate dismay in the last political murder.

• ٩ •

A few weeks after the 1976 Democratic runoff in Conway County, I received a call from Rex Elliott of Marshall, who said he was active on the Searcy County Republican Committee. He had followed the Conway County battles in the newspapers and he thought election conduct in his county merited as much attention as Conway County's. He wondered if TEL Institute could undertake the same legal action at Marshall that produced stunning results in Morrilton. He described the vote-buying system and admitted that he and the Republican leadership as well as Democrats had bribed voters for years. They were tired of it and Rex thought most people wanted to have honest elections as long as everyone else was made to live by the rules, too. He gave me the names of a number of people who would tell about the vote buying and participate in a lawsuit if I would bring one like the Conway County suit. I drove up to Marshall to meet him and his wife, Fern, and the people who were ready to blow the lid off the vote-buying scheme.

Rex was an unlikely maverick. He was a friendly, easy-going bear of a man, six-foot-four and 275 pounds, who was developing an ample belly after giving up his twenty-five-year career as a long-haul truck driver and taking up the sedentary life of radio. He and Fern had a band in the '50s that performed country and western and gospel music around the country. Rex played guitar and bass and sang. Sometimes he played with Wayne Raney, the harmonica legend from Wolf Bayou north of Heber Springs. Raney performed on XERF, the big Clear Channel station at Del Rio, Texas, as Wayne Raney and the Delmore Brothers and popularized *A Fast Train Through Arkansas* and *The Del Rio Boogie*. Raney was impressed with Elliott's rich-timbred voice and gift for easy gab and kept telling him to get into radio because he had known far less talented men who made it big. Elliott took his advice. He converted the garage that housed his trucks into a radio station, of which he was the owner, manager and chief on-air voice. He also got into politics, although without much personal success. He lost two races for sheriff.

Rex's friends did not seem as disquieted by the fraud as he was, or else they were distrustful of a young Little Rock lawyer who wanted them to put down on paper how they had for years violated the law. None of them would own up to ever paying for a vote or taking money or whiskey for their votes or knowing anyone who did. I told Rex that it was pointless to file a voting-fraud suit if no one was willing to testify that they had brokered votes because I was quite sure that no one on the other side, whom we would name in the suit, would admit it. Without a proffer of proof, no judge was going to entertain the complaint or our petition for a restraining order. A few days later, Rex showed up at my office in Little Rock with two longtime Republican election workers, John Eaton and Olas Taylor, who were willing to tell their stories for the record. I got a court reporter and we recorded the depositions of all three men. Rex supplied a list of dozens of people whom he personally had paid for their votes during the years he was running for sheriff, or running the vote-buying operation for the Republicans: people who distributed cash to voters for him, election judges and clerks who had voted people inside the polling place, or observed the voting and distributed the tokens. He identified Republican candidates and workers and their Democratic counterparts who pooled money for the bribes and distributed the payoffs to voters.

Taylor, who had served a couple of terms as the county treasurer in the late 1950s, and Eaton gave similar accounts. They told not only about vote buying but all sorts of illegal acts. Although the voting age was then twenty-one, Eaton said he started voting when he was sixteen and that later, when he became an election judge, he and the other officials allowed anyone who showed up to vote whether they were of age, had a poll tax or, later, had even registered to vote. All the ballots were tossed into the ballot box and counted. It didn't matter. No one ever double-checked the registration affidavits to see if the people who signed at the polls matched the number of votes cast. No one, Democrat or Republican, ever blew the whistle on the other side.

Rex said that the Republican candidates typically would raise $20,000 to $30,000 among them to pay voters and the Democrats usually raised about the same amount. The candidates of a party would get together before the election and pool their money, usually $5,000 from the candidates for sheriff and county judge and smaller amounts for other offices. Someone would handle the cash and be responsible for the distribution to voters on election day or the day before. The evening before the election they would make the rounds of homes of people who regularly sold their votes to close the deal, although much of the bargaining took place on election day. In party primaries and in school elections, there were different methods but the bartering took place in nearly all elections. Rex estimated that a third of the votes in a typical general election were bought.

Rex described how it went.

> Q: How do you make sure that that person votes your list?
> A: We've got a man on the inside. We have to have a judge inside. Of course, the judges are usually about the same ones, just like the same guys that handle the money [and] the same people sell out year to year. The man inside will have different codes. One time it might be a grain of corn that he gives the man, and when he brings back this yellow grain of corn, for instance, we know the man voted right because our judge probably got to mark his ballot

or he stood and looked over his shoulder. That way we sure didn't want to spend money for a vote we didn't get. Sometimes if the other side gets wise to this and they go to giving out grains of corn we will change and give out maybe a penny, a new penny, or just different codes that we used to know that the man voted right. Some cases, when you take them to the door, you walk close enough that you can see inside the polling place and see how they vote, to see if the judges are getting to mark their ballot or looking over their shoulder. Sometimes, the [election] judge will nod his head back at you that they voted right.

Q: Who designates the judge inside the polling place?

A: Most usually the candidates and the chairman of the party. They get together and try to decide who is the best for all concerned because sometimes you get a judge that may not be for one on that ticket. You've got to be careful when you are buying votes. You want to let every man's money get what he pays for.

Eaton described the haggling with voters over the price for voting for the Republican candidates. The price tended to go up during the day of the election.

They will come to you or they will say, "How much you'uns paying? You tell them and they will say, "Well, the other side is paying more." Or they will say, "That's not enough, I'll wait until it gets higher." You are standing out there bidding them off all day like you are buying cattle.

The most he ever paid for a vote, Eaton said, was seventy-five dollars, although it was typical for a person to demand one hundred dollars for his and his wife's votes. Eaton served as an election judge several times and usually marked the ballots for people who had sold their votes, although a few people insisted on marking their own ballots because they did not want others to know that they had sold their vote.

He named his own sister Geneva, who had married a Republican politician, a former sheriff, as one of the craftiest vote manipulators in the county. She was a judge for every election in the box at Bear Creek, about a dozen miles southwest of Marshall on State Route 27. Bear Creek was the biggest box in the county.

You can't . . . I don't care who or where, you can put her right in the election down here in Little Rock if you are voting ballots, and I'll guarantee you she can mark more ballots and pull more crooked stuff than anybody you've got down here.

One old-timer thought the vote buying got started in the Depression because people needed a few dollars to buy shoes for their kids. A man always had a need for a few easy dollars. Elmer Gregory, who lived on a rural route near St. Joe, said he and a hunting buddy noticed a walkie-talkie set on sale for $39.95 at a store in Marshall, and they figured it would come in handy in the deer woods. They had no particular interest in the election but they went to the St. Joe box on election day and haggled with the vote buyers until the price got to forty dollars. They took the forty dollars, voted Republican, and bought the walkie-talkie set.

Whether you were a Democrat or a Republican, the key to the system was a clutch of judges and clerks in every precinct who were dependable and resourceful. When a candidate put his money into the pool to buy votes, he deserved the assurance that people whose votes he had bought actually voted for him. Thus if a man came in to vote for the Republican slate but identified one of the candidates as someone he disliked and didn't want to vote for, the judge marking the ballot for him would mark all the races except that one and then distract the man in conversation, mark it for the candidate who had paid, rip off the stub, and deposit the ballot and stub while the voter wasn't watching. So it was important, Eaton said, to have the right judges and clerks for your side in each box so that you got all the votes for your side, legal or illegal, that were possible or at least that you had paid for. He said you had to be ready to beat down the other side, sometimes literally, if there were protests:

> Well, if you get a precinct set up just right you pretty well run it. The other candidates can sit there and object but still that don't do them no good. I know I went down to Leslie one night to watch the vote count down there. Well, they was pulling some stuff off down there and I had a pistol on me and I just pulled it out and I backed them all up against the wall until help got down there to help me with it. If you've got the right people in there they will try, the other side, but if they don't have enough strength they will try to argue against it but it don't make any difference, you go ahead and run it the way you want to. If you are not hooked up that way, you do the best you can do.

Rex brought along a petition signed by fifty "voters and businessmen of Searcy County" saying they were dissatisfied with illegal-voting practices in the county and wanted them stopped. "These voting practices include the buying and selling of votes, the gathering of candidates around polling places, and the casting of ballots other than one's own," it said. "We feel the time has come to end this type of activity and return to the lawful casting of votes and set the local political scene back upon the right path." A few days later, he brought affidavits from several people recounting efforts to buy their votes or observing payments to voters.

Armed with all that evidence, I announced at a press conference in Little Rock that I would file a federal lawsuit to stop the vote buying and other illegal practices, and direct poll watchers to monitor the general election inside every precinct in the county. I filed the suit in mid-September, six weeks before the election, and the case was assigned to Judge Terry Shell, who had issued the decree in the Conway County election suit in the spring. The plaintiffs were eighty-eight residents of Searcy County and six TEL Institute supporters from around the state, including the redoubtable Blytheville newspaperman Hank Haines. The suit listed a number of illegal election practices, including the sale of votes for cash and whiskey, and contended that they violated the equal-protection rights of all voters in Searcy County and the rest of Arkansas because people were entitled to have their own votes counted and not diluted by fraudulent ballots. I asked for a speedy hearing, an order forbidding the practices in the general election, and the assignment of poll watchers inside every box in the county. The suit named the three county election commissioners—Will Goggin, another Democrat, and the Republican commissioner—and the county clerk, who was the voter registrar and supervisor and custodian of absentee votes.

Judge Shell scheduled a hearing for September 28, and I had subpoenas issued for the four defendants and a number of others who we believed were involved in the vote buying for both parties. They all showed up, sullen and nervous, at the United States Courthouse at Little Rock that morning with their attorneys, Gail O. Matthews and J. D. Patterson of Little Rock. Gail called to me in the hallway outside the courtroom. He said we needed to get some things worked out. It's a little late, I said, because we're going to trial in a few minutes.

"There's not going to be a trial," Matthews said.

Everyone in Searcy County, he said, knew that the vote buying and the other practices were normal occurrences and had been going on, as far as anyone knew, since before any of them were born. But they were not going to get on the stand and admit they had committed felonies or lie about it. So he had advised all of them to take the Fifth Amendment against self-incrimination. Everyone, he said, was amenable to just stopping the whole mess. I notified Judge Shell that we had compromised the case, and we drafted a consent decree, which the judge signed that afternoon. They would admit the corruption but they wanted the order to say that while they knew about them, they did not personally participate in any of the illegal acts. The decree ordered an end to all the illegalities, directed the county to require all the judges and clerks for the November election to attend a seminar that I would conduct on how to administer an election and to properly count and record votes, and ordered county officials to allow poll watchers from outside the county to observe the election from inside every polling place. Copies of the order were to be given to every candidate for office and every election official in the county.

Although I was apprehensive, the seminar for judges and clerks and other election officials in a courtroom at Marshall actually went well. I thought many seemed resentful but a number of the officials asked good questions. I explained exactly what the law required them to do in each polling place and in the clerk's office, and I emphasized the penalties for violating the law, especially any effort to influence a person's vote with cash, intoxicating spirits or other favors or participating in any way in such a scheme. Forty poll watchers, mostly students at the University of Arkansas at Little Rock School of Law, watched the voting and counting that day. I had gotten myself into a situation that might be perceived as a conflict of interest, so I excused myself as the attorney in the lawsuit the week before the election and Jack Lavey, a Little Rock labor and employment lawyer, supervised the poll-watching operation. He and Walter Davidson, another Little Rock lawyer who was president of Common Cause, would handle the suit for the next two years.

Republicans had swept the Democrats from power in the 1974 election and they won this one by big margins. They obviously realized that they enjoyed a natural advantage even without the dissemination of cash and whiskey, which accounted for the sudden interest of so many of them in clean elections. TEL Institute petitioned Judge Shell in 1977 and 1978 to order poll watchers for school elections, primaries, and the general election, and he did. A final consent decree in 1979 directed the county to keep elections free of taint in the future. Rex Elliott continued his campaign to clean up the elections. He heard about a county that had bought new voting machines and was casting off its old ones. Rex and a friend pooled their money and bought a half-dozen used machines, and brought them back to Marshall. Parts of the county cast their ballots on voting machines for the first time in 1978.

I was never so naïve as to believe that they were always or ever simon-pure or that the sheer physical danger of electioneering ever subsided. In a school election in September 1977 watched over by our poll watchers, an election judge parked outside the school at St. Joe where the election was held. Robert Dittrich, a law student at Little Rock who would later become prosecuting attorney for life in southeast Arkansas, asked why the school was closed for the day. It was closed, the election judge told him, so that in the event of gunplay no children would get in the way. When the election official returned to her car alongside Dittrich after the vote counting, two of her tires had been slashed. When she pulled a pistol from her glove compartment and marched across the school lot and back into the school, Dittrich figured that his work was done and headed down US Highway 65 for home.

• • •

Judge Shell's decree and the '76 election regrettably did not foreclose my further education on the Byzantine politics and electioneering in those hills.

In the late evening of February 9, nearly nine months before the election, Billy Joe Holder, a six-term Democratic sheriff who had lost to the Republican Loren Reeves in 1974, was watching television while his wife, June, sat across the living room crocheting. Someone put a shotgun barrel against the window screen, aimed between the potted plants on the windowsill, and shot Holder in the head. The big redhead, who had been the nation's youngest sheriff when he was first elected in 1950, died en route to the hospital. Someone had cut the telephone wire to the Holder house, and to call the state police his wife had to use a police radio in Holder's car. He had gotten a job as an agent of the Arkansas

Alcoholic Beverage Control Board after his defeat. June wouldn't let Sheriff Reeves in the house when he came the next day.

Nearly five months later, the police arrested Robert A. Baysinger, a local bootlegger, his wife, Nina, and two other men, Charles Dye and Norman Keith Sutterfield, and charged them with involvement in Holder's murder. Baysinger supposedly hired Sutterfield to kill Holder because Holder had arrested his wife for bootlegging, and the others were accomplices to the murder. Baysinger would be tried, convicted, and sentenced to life in prison without parole, but the Arkansas Supreme Court reversed his conviction because of the misuse of a recorded admission of his involvement. He was tried again and acquitted. Charges against the alleged triggerman, Sutterfield, were dropped because he produced witnesses who said they drank beer with him in Missouri the evening of the shooting, and charges were dropped against the other two as well. Except for Baysinger's short time in prison after his original conviction, no one was ever punished for Holder's murder.

Sheriff Reeves was an instant suspect after the murder and spent the summer and fall loudly protesting the whisper campaign against him by the Democrats, especially my old friend and law school classmate Kenneth R. Smith, who had been the prosecuting attorney for the Fourteenth Circuit since 1973. My first venture into election sleuthing had been in the summer of 1964, when I went to Yellville to investigate a whiskey-for-votes scam in Smith's race for state representative.

Two weeks before the '76 election, in which Reeves was running for re-election, the prosecutor charged Reeves with being an accessory to the murder of his political enemy and hindering the prosecution of the murderers. Reeves said it was all politics aimed at defeating him in the election. Voters must have believed him because they re-elected him 2,263 to 1,392, a much bigger margin than his victory over Holder two years earlier. Holder's embittered wife ran against the Republican county clerk and she, too, was beaten badly. There was no sympathy for a widow in that county, but there had been rumors, encouraged by Sheriff Reeves, that she was the real culprit in her husband's death.

Reeves asked me to defend him, and although I had little real experience as a criminal lawyer, I agreed. I figured that I would need help and associated Richard Mays, who had little more experience than I had, as co-counsel. It was a good thing. When I collapsed during the trial, from the heat, tension, exhaustion or something, Richard was able to take over for a day. I made it back for the closing arguments.

Sheriff Reeves, as I would discover, did not have the most endearing alibis, but the state did not have any direct evidence linking him with his political enemy's murder. The previous fall, Baysinger had told Reeves that he wanted to kill Holder for arresting his wife and he wondered if Reeves would like to invest in putting his old political foe out of his way for good. Weeks before Holder's murder, Baysinger met Sheriff Reeves on the bank of the Buffalo River at the US Highway 65 bridge north of Marshall and asked if he had thought any more about their earlier conversation. Reeves would later tell the FBI and juries at two trials that Baysinger had asked him that day for $2,000 to "take care of it" but that he had refused and told Baysinger that he shouldn't kill Holder. For four and a half months after Holder's murder, the sheriff told no one about the conversations although the state police and FBI questioned him extensively. He told the investigators that Baysinger was a hunting buddy and wouldn't kill any-body. Reeves finally told them about the conversations and agreed to col-laborate in taping a conversation with Baysinger in the parking lot of the Sunset Cafe at US Highway 65 and State Route 27 at Marshall, in which Baysinger told the sheriff that he had hired a Conway man, Sutterfield, to kill Holder. On the stand, Reeves said he had kept silent because Baysinger had told him the day after the murder that he had "damned sure better keep my mouth shut" or the bootlegger would sell his pickup truck to get enough money to hire someone to kill him, too.

"I said I wouldn't say nothing," the sheriff testified. We told the jury in our closing argument that he had good reason to be terrified because while the six-foot-four sheriff was a big and powerful man, he was no match for an assassin's rifle.

Throughout all the trials, politics and whiskey were unifying threads. The prosecution insinuated that despite his victory, Reeves was so embittered by the 1974 election that he tried to block Holder's hiring as an Alcoholic Beverage Control agent. They tried to prove that Reeves had set up a phony raid on Baysinger's still to stymie Holder and that Sheriff Reeves had agreed to let the moonshiners operate undisturbed in exchange for their support against Holder. The sheriff denied it all. He did admit that he had bought three gallons of moonshine in 1974 to bribe people to vote for him rather than Holder but insisted that he had made no promise not to arrest them after he got elected. For a Searcy County jury, that kind of alibi was sufficient.

Aside from the circumstantial evidence of Reeves's enmity for Holder and his association with Baysinger, the state's case was weak. I had a vague feeling starting from the *voir dire* of prospective jurors that the evidence was not going to make much difference either way. Community feelings were going to decide it. Most people were convinced, if they wanted to be, that the charges against the sheriff were politically motivated, perhaps because everything in Searcy County was politically motivated. One of the state's star witnesses was FBI agent Jack Knox, who would investigate the sheriff off and on for another five years. On cross-examination, Knox insisted that the charges had nothing to do with the approaching election in the sheriff's race. Mays then asked him if he had not confided to the local Farrah Fawcett look-alike, with whom he had struck up a warm friendship, that the charges had been timed to influence the election. The young woman, who must have reminded the FBI man of Jill Munroe, Fawcett's role in the then-popular TV series *Charlie's Angels,* was in the courtroom. The agent hung his head and muttered something. The judge asked him to speak up.

"Yes," he said.

The jury acquitted the sheriff on the murder charges but could not reach a verdict on whether he had impeded the investigation. He was tried again for hindering the investigation and the second jury acquitted him, too.

The violence didn't end with the acquittals. A few months later, someone fired a shotgun at Baysinger as he was on the highway near Harriet. Someone parked a pickup truck with explosives in the carport of Sutterfield's father at Big Flat.

As for Sheriff Reeves, he kept winning and getting charged with felonies until 1982. Richard Mays defended him in 1978 on federal charges of bagging and selling marijuana that his deputies had confiscated in raids. FBI agents sent a man wired with a hidden microphone to the sheriff's office to buy marijuana, and they tried to use the tape at his trial by reference. Richard finally asked the judge to make them play the tape for the jury. Reeves was seated at his desk and the crackling police radio made his conversation with the informant unintelligible. The jury acquitted him. Reeves was the prime suspect in a state police and FBI investigation of the death of a teenager whose body was found in a car that had wrecked and burned on a county road a few miles north of Marshall in November 1979, but no charges were ever filed.

"The FBI likes to look at me," the sheriff told a reporter for the *Arkansas Gazette.*

The FBI, the federal Drug Enforcement Administration, and the state police nailed him again in 1982, and this time he and a deputy sheriff were convicted in US District Court at Fort Smith of distributing marijuana. Reeves was sentenced to five years in prison. A local marijuana grower testified that between 1978 and 1980 he had given Reeves $2,000 not to raid his marijuana patch. In a sting operation orchestrated by federal and state officers, the man went to the sheriff's office six weeks before the general election in 1982 and gave Reeves $200 for his re-election campaign and then met the sheriff and the deputy on a dirt road on a mountain called the Devil's Backbone east of town, where he gave them $2,500 in marked bills for five pounds of marijuana. A San Antonio barrister replaced Mays as Reeves's attorney for this trial, and the jury did not buy his theory that the sheriff and his deputy were engaged in a "reverse sting" operation where they hoped eventually to catch a Harrison businessman named Carr selling marijuana. The trial followed the general election by two months. This time the sheriff lost.

Clean elections aren't guaranteed to produce clean government or even very desirable results. They can only give the public the satisfaction of knowing that the wishes of people who cared enough to vote were reflected with the maximum possible accuracy. The people of Searcy County got reasonably honest elections in 1976 and 1978 and they were happy about it, but I would not warrant that votes were never sold again.

Searcy County ended my active engagement—though not my interest—in election reform. The leadership of The Election Laws Institute passed to someone else in the fall of 1976, although I would participate in some litigation for another two years. By 1980, the organization was effectively defunct.

Whether it was general malaise after years of election strife or sheer exhaustion, I decided I had to move on—earn a living, if nothing else. I think it came to me finally when I sprawled on a desk in the judge's chambers in the courthouse at Marshall after collapsing during Reeves's murder trial, from hypertension, it turned out. Aside from the Conway

County and Searcy County legal battles, we had investigated fraud or irregularities in fifteen other counties that year, distributed seven thousand election calendars, pamphlets, and advisories on elections, and conducted seminars for election officials and poll watchers. I had filed a suit in Crawford County over voting irregularities in the primaries, and our investigation eventually led to charges against sixteen persons for crossover or double voting in the Republican and Democratic primaries. Fourteen pled guilty to misdemeanors and their $500 fines were suspended. I had spent considerable time in Stone County, on Searcy County's eastern border, investigating the exchange of liquor and cash for votes in the county judge's race in the Democratic primaries. A criminal investigator for the state police and I produced affidavits from voters alleging the offer or purchase of liquor or money for votes by the candidates themselves and five of their agents in the May primary. We gave them to Prosecutor Leroy Blankenship at Batesville, but neither he nor a grand jury produced charges.

My inability to handle the stress of the work and the financial hardships had taken a toll on my family. I needed a career adjustment.

CHAPTER 11

· · · · · · · · · · · ·

Judicial Remedy

"These judges are an awfully overworked set of fellows. They come down to their office about ten in the morning, leave at noon, come back at two and leave at four. Judge, you must be worked to death to stand such a constant strain. Upon what meat do you feed, Judge Wood, that you are enabled to do such heavy work?"

—GOVERNOR JEFF DAVIS, CAMPAIGN OF 1904

While a dozen years of strife over election rascality and my perpetual anger over the refusal of every branch of government to deal firmly with the vote stealing finally drove me from the battle, I found my ardor for politics not diminished but sharpened. Every politician with and for whom I had worked, which included earnest reformers like Rockefeller, Purcell, Bumpers, Pryor, and Mills, along with judges and prosecutors, sooner or later exposed feet of clay. My disillusionment was always bitter. It would be a long time before I could acknowledge a verity of democratic government, which was that good men and women could make imperfect judgments and yield to the mean realities of politics and popular opinion without being unprincipled or betraying the public trust. Anyway, no sooner had I surrendered the reins of The Election Laws Institute and the clean-election movement than I decided that if I couldn't support someone else with unreserved abandon I ought to run myself. I had never before, at least after high school, wanted or intended to run for office, but I did not suffer from insufficient vanity.

In the many years since then, I have often reflected upon a fatuous little event from my days in the attorney general's office with Joe Purcell. Someone told me about an uncanny fortuneteller who lived in a small house off Wright Avenue in Little Rock. Although she refused to be interviewed, the *Gazette* carried a story about her. Her name was Rosie Gray and she read tarot cards. On a caprice one day I looked her up. She was in the back room at a small table. I gave her five dollars. She shuffled and studied the cards and told me that I was a lawyer, had four children and would have another, and she furnished some details about my father's future work on engines in Missouri. She said I would work simultaneously in Little Rock and Washington, DC, that I would be divorced, that I would marry a redheaded girl and be very happy, and that I would be elected a judge.

For how long? I asked.

"A long time," she said.

All of that was either true or would become true.

The legislature soon enacted a law taxing fortunetellers at the rate of one hundred dollars a week, which I presume put Rosie and others like her out of business. A Fort Smith woman sued in federal court in 1975 contending that the law was unconstitutional because it violated a fortuneteller's free-speech, association, and equal-protection rights. A three-judge panel ruled that the state had a perfect right to tax fortunetellers out of existence, although other jurisdictions have been more sympathetic to the First and Fourteenth Amendment rights of practicing occultists. I suppose that if the issue had come before the state appellate courts afterward I would have recused owing to my own experience. The fortuneteller law may have been punishment for Rosie's trying to inflict me on the judicial establishment, though I suspect religious impulses were behind it. I offer no defense of fortunetellers, but I have always marveled at Rosie Gray's studied or lucky guesses at my situation and my future. They say that many people are particularly susceptible to suggestion, so it may be that she shaped rather than forecast my conduct, but I do not think so. In the years afterward, I could not repair the marriage that my single-mindedness and angst about all things had damaged, and Susan and I divorced in 1974. In 1978, I got into politics and judging for real and then married Phyllis Laser, a redheaded businesswoman who mastered my temperament and gave me my fifth precious child, fulfilling the last of Rosie's predictions.

Dr. Joel Anderson, who was chairman of the Pulaski County Republican Committee and later chancellor of the University of Arkansas at Little Rock, telephoned me in the early spring of 1978 and asked me to run for Congress—on the Republican ticket, of course. Jim Guy Tucker, who had succeeded Mills as the Second District representative the year before, announced that he was running for the US Senate (he would be beaten by Governor Pryor), so the open seat gave Republicans a chance in a district that had been reliably Democratic since Reconstruction. Anderson believed they could generate enough financial backing for me to make a competitive race. The Republican Party in Pulaski County was still a Rockefeller enclave led by people of moderate to liberal leanings like Anderson, William T. Kelley, and Bob K. Scott. Elsewhere, the party was already hardly distinguishable from the hard-eyed conservatives who had ascended to power in most other Southern states after the passage of the civil rights laws in the 1960s by a Democratic president and Congress. In spite of my affection for Rockefeller, I felt more affinity for the Democratic Party, and I also had no interest in being a lawmaker, state or federal. Compromise was not in the nature of any of Slick Glaze's spawn. Although I thought then that compromise signaled a shortage of principle and courage, I would eventually realize that it was the secret art of great lawmakers. I called Anderson the next week and told him I couldn't be the candidate. Ed Bethune, a former prosecutor at Searcy, eventually filed as the Republican and defeated state Rep. Doug Brandon of Little Rock, the Democratic nominee. Bethune, who was a better candidate than I, might have had a long career in the US House of Representatives but he foolishly let party bigwigs in Washington convince him in 1984 that he could beat Senator Pryor, his good friend and collaborator, whom he had just said he would never oppose. Pryor thrashed him.

The legislature in 1977 had created a new division of chancery court in Pulaski County and I decided to run for the new judgeship, which Steele Hays was filling by a temporary appointment. So did three other lawyers—Ruby Hurley, Ben D. Rowland, and Harlan Weber. It would be the beginning of a charmed political career; lucky may be a better word for it. The chancery race would be the only tough election that I would ever have.

Ruby Hurley, a fine lawyer who had years of domestic trial experience, was clearly the best-credentialed candidate, but people were not electing women to judicial offices or to much of anything. A dozen years of headlines, pictures, and editorials from the voting-fraud battles gave me more name recognition than the others. Weber would later serve on the bench, but his political instincts often failed him. We appeared one evening before Fathers for Equal Rights, an organization of angry divorced men who thought the legal system unfairly favored women in divorce and custody proceedings. I was divorced and I would not marry for another two years. Weber proclaimed that he was the only family man in the race. That room was probably the only venue in Arkansas where that appeal would not resonate. I'm sure I got every vote there. The *Gazette* endorsed me, which was a sizable advantage in local and judicial races where most people weren't likely to be familiar with candidates. But the decisive development was an editorial cartoon by George Fisher in the *Gazette* that arrayed me against the unflattering caricatures of my enemies in the Conway, Faulkner, and Searcy county election battles.

Ruby Hurley led all of us in the Democratic preferential primary but she fell well short of a majority. I beat Rowland for the second spot by a thousand votes. Ruby's lead was big enough, 33 percent to my 26 percent, and her relationships with Weber and Rowland were good enough that she took her victory in the runoff two weeks later for granted and campaigned very little. I had learned better in my one foray into politics, as a senior at Joplin High School. I ran for president of the student body assuming that everyone would want to honor me for my head-butting fierceness on the football, basketball, and baseball teams. When I started asking students to vote for me I had a humiliating catharsis. While everyone in school knew me, I knew almost no one except my teammates. Fred English knew everyone in school and called them by their names. The school politely never announced by how much English beat me, but I am quite sure that it wasn't close. I would never again take people for granted. Ruby had old and deep roots in the community and that, no doubt, persuaded her that she would have a huge advantage against an interloper in a runoff, where voting traditionally is much lighter because most races have been decided in the first election and casual voters stay at home. But a heated runoff campaign for the US Senate between Governor Pryor and Congressman Tucker produced a surge of new voters all over the state, more than four thousand of

them in the chancery race. The gender-advantaged male candidate for judge got 53.5 percent of the vote.

Anyone could have been pardoned for doubting that I had the necessary "judicial temperament," that overused term that the American Bar Association defines as "compassion, decisiveness, open-mindedness, sensitivity, courtesy, patience, freedom from bias and commitment to equal justice." Patience had never been my long suit, and there must have been questions among lawyers about my sensitivity and open-mindedness. It took time and adjustment but I believe I eventually fulfilled all those qualities in fair measure. One or two of my colleagues on the appellate courts on which I would serve, recalling my occasional churlishness and brusqueness, may respectfully dissent. To hell with them.

I was sworn in January 1, 1979, but it would be a few months before I became a judge for real. I was trying a case in which a mother was seeking to regain custody of her three-year-old daughter from foster parents. Grif Stockley of the Pulaski County Legal Aid Bureau represented the mother, who had been subpoenaed along with the beautiful little blonde girl. The hearing was contentious and Stockley was a zealous advocate. He argued and argued with my rulings and told me I was just dead wrong. I was on the verge of holding him in contempt. I called a recess and had the chamber to myself. My hands were trembling. I thought to myself: I'm a judge now and not an advocate. If I'm going to be an impartial arbiter I have to listen patiently to everyone, even lawyers who are as contentious as I was, and indulge their zealousness. When the hearing resumed I felt great relief. That moment came back to me hundreds of times at choleric moments in the courtroom and in conferences the next thirty years. I always felt a little obliged to Stockley, who was a young lawyer then and who would spend his life as a tribune for the poor and mistreated and as a chronicler of Arkansas's terrible history of racial repression.

Chancery work with its agenda of family issues was the perfect antidote to the quarrelsome and heavily political work in which I had been engaged the first fifteen years of my legal career. The repressed softer impulses of my nature became ascendant. Nowhere do you have a better chance to help individuals and families work through their personal distress. We started a pre-divorce workshop where family psychologists like Pat Youngdahl helped people work through the conflicts that arise in every divorce and that often leave lasting imprints on children.

A fresh opportunity presented itself two years later. Amendment 58 to the constitution, which was ratified by the voters in 1978, created an intermediate appellate court under the supreme court. The first judges were appointed in 1979, and in 1980 voters were to elect replacements for the appointed judges. I decided to run for the Court of Appeals position for the Central Arkansas district comprising Pulaski and Perry Counties. W. H. "Sonny" Dillahunty, the former United States attorney for the Eastern District, filed, too. We were not on good terms. I had excoriated him publicly in 1975 when he refused to press an investigation of vote fraud in the runoff election for Mutt Jones's Senate seat. He said there was no evidence of wrongdoing. The election judges and clerks in Conway County, the ones we wanted him to investigate, eventually pled guilty to illegally manipulating votes. But if Dillahunty nursed a grudge, he didn't show it. He had little to say about me in the primary and, in fact, he did little to get elected. He manifested almost no interest in the election and seemed to have put his name on the ballot on the chance that I would screw up or the voters would pick him because they remembered some of the high-profile cases he had prosecuted. His campaign manager was Sam Perroni, who had pledged his support to me early but who called after his old boss filed and asked to be relieved of his obligation. I worked hard but rarely saw Dillahunty in the three-month campaign. The vote was not close. I had to run again in 1984 for the full term but no one ran against me. Judges are privileged politicians. Once elected, a judge almost never gets an opponent. You get to put your name on the ballot as "Judge" or "Justice," which carries a huge advantage.

• • •

When Justice George Rose Smith retired in 1986 after thirty-nine years on the supreme court, it seemed to be the perfect time to fulfill my ambition to serve on the state's highest court. I filed early for the seat and I was again fortunate in my opponent. R. David Lewis, a Little Rock personal injury lawyer, filed but made only a *pro forma* race. Lewis had gotten himself associated with the movement to legalize marijuana, which might have hurt his election chances if the issue had been raised. He seemed to be even less engaged than Dillahunty had been. At the only forum we shared in the statewide campaign, at the Mount Nebo Chicken Fry near Dardanelle, he came over as we prepared to clamber onto the truck bed to talk.

"Do you like to do these things?" he asked.

"I love 'em," I lied.

"I don't," he said. "I can't stand them."

I didn't see him again and I encountered little evidence that he made any effort to win. I heard that former Justice Conley Byrd and Justice John I. Purtle talked him into running, but I don't know that to be true. Purtle and I would serve together, uneasily, on the Court for four years.

Lewis's anemic race and defeat proved to be a lucky break for him. He developed a good trial practice and won some big personal-injury judgments the next twenty years.

I felt particularly exuberant about being elected to the seat held by the dour George Rose Smith, the most esteemed and longest-serving judge in Arkansas history. Smith's crisp opinions, laconic and delivered in perfect prose, were the gold standard for opinion writing. There were two camps of supreme court justices—those who tried to write with Smith's economy and clarity and those who knew they couldn't so strove for the opposite. His last official act was to swear me in.

"George," I said when we finished, "I feel privileged to be taking your place, but I don't think I can ever fill your shoes."

"I know, Tom," he said mirthlessly. "I know."

Appellate judging may not always be the most rewarding labor that a lawyer can undertake, but it is the most pacifying. In trial work you may win a heartwarming victory that seals justice for a deserving client, but you also represent people who you know should not win but who expect your maximum though insincere effort. As a supreme court justice you owe everyone in every case exactly the same, your singular determination to discover what the accumulated law deems to be right in this circumstance. You put aside your philosophical sympathies and your instincts about the lawyers in the case and the nature of everyone's work and try to reach what the federal or state constitution, statutes, or precedents say is the proper resolution of the dispute before you. It is seldom easy because the law is conflicting or vague and the facts are not always established. If the constitution and statutes do not produce a fair remedy, all you can do is say so and suggest that lawmakers or the voters change the law to bring about surer justice in the future. If you think you've done your best to isolate the truth of the law, you go home every day a satisfied man, sometimes a little disappointed that you have not persuaded the other judges of your unfailing insight. For the next twenty-two years I retired in the evenings with the certain feeling that my labors had been worthwhile. I loved nearly every day.

Over time, I became convinced that nearly all the appellate judges and those on the trial courts strove for the same independence and impartiality and that the great judicial reform movement of the late twentieth century, which was to end the election of judges, was misguided. I had

spent much of my early years in the law dealing with judges who decidedly were not independent. Judge Russell C. Roberts, who came close to locking me up in the Conway and Faulkner county voting-fraud battles, was the poster child for a corrupt judicial selection system. If Roberts and two or three others with whom we dealt in the ballot-thievery cases in the '60s and '70s were representative, we badly needed a merit-selection system. Federal judges with lifetime appointments were the ones who came to the rescue. So when the Constitutional Convention of 1970 explored the idea of converting to a merit system similar to the Missouri plan, where judges are appointed by the governor from a list of able lawyers supplied by an independent panel, it sounded like a worthy reform, especially since my old professor, Dr. Robert A. Leflar, the chairman of the convention, seemed to favor it.

But my own experience as a chancellor and then an appellate judge convinced me that despite its imperfections, the elective system was more apt to supply justice or at least do no worse. Judges who depend upon the periodic whims of voters are supposed to be prone to render the most popular decision rather than the just one and to be swayed by the prevalence of campaign money from powerful interests that have a stake in the orders of courts. But only rarely did I detect political calculations in the judgment of my colleagues on the two appellate courts and almost never did they prevail. The politics of getting a federal appointment and confirmation by the United States Senate seemed to me to be more insidious than the occasional referendum by the voters.

It would be hard to find a more politically charged issue than the regulation of the private, consensual sexual activity of homosexuals. State agencies, the legislature, and Arkansas voters through initiated acts and constitutional amendments sought to make such conduct illegal and to punish those who engaged in it. While a member of the state Senate, Vic Snyder, subsequently the congressman from central Arkansas, tried repeatedly to repeal the state's sodomy law, but he could not get even one senator to make a motion to report the bill from the committee so that senators could vote on it. But in a string of decisions starting in 2001 with *Jegley v. Picado,* Arkansas courts struck down state laws and regulations regulating private consensual sexual activity. Judge David Bogard, a superb circuit judge in Pulaski County, held the Arkansas sodomy law to be a violation of individual privacy and of equal-protection and due-process laws.

When the case reached the Arkansas Supreme Court the next year, we upheld Bogard's decision five to two in a particularly forceful order written by Justice Annabelle Clinton Imber. The two dissenters, my colleagues Ray Thornton and Chief Justice William H. "Dub" Arnold, didn't insist upon upholding the law but rather said the issue was not ripe for the courts to decide because the law was not being enforced. And how did the justices of the United States Supreme Court, with their lifetime appointments based upon merit, handle the same issue? In 1986, the justices in a five-to-four decision in the infamous *Bowers v. Hardwick* case ruled that laws that criminalized oral and anal sex between consenting adults of the same gender were legitimate state policies. It would not be until a year after the elected Arkansas courts shunned that precedent and invalidated the Arkansas sodomy law that the US Supreme Court, in *Lawrence v. Texas,* finally recognized a constitutional protection of the privacy of homosexuals. Even then, the court split six to three, with the court's conservative faction sticking with the Bowers doctrine. Mr. Dooley's famous jibe "No matter whether th' constitution follows th' flag or not, th' supreme court follows th' iliction returns" was not aimed at an elected state court.*

Yes, I know that the Arkansas Supreme Court has also quailed before public opinion from time to time, particularly in the old days when segregation was the unchallenged orthodoxy of the land. Its most embarrassing slip came in 1967, just as I was arriving down the hall in the Justice Building to work for Attorney General Joe Purcell. Susan Epperson, a biology teacher at Little Rock Central High School, sued the state because an initiated act passed by Arkansas voters in 1928 made it a criminal undertaking for her to tell her students about evolution. The school's new biology textbook for the 1965–66 school year carried a chapter discussing Charles Darwin and evolutionary theory. Before his defeat in 1966, my old nemesis, Bruce Bennett, the attorney general, ardently defended the law in the trial before Judge Murray O. Reed. Reed—an elected judge, mind you—held that the law "tends to hinder the quest for knowledge, restrict the freedom to learn and restrain the freedom to teach."

Epperson arrived at the Arkansas Supreme Court in 1967 and the justices in conference first split four to three in favor of reversing Reed and upholding the anti-evolution law. George Rose Smith and Justices Lyle Brown and J. Fred Jones were the dissenters, and Brown wrote a courageous opinion for them. Chief Justice Carleton Harris, in an aberration to a sterling career, feared a firestorm around the court and insisted that

---

*Mr. Dooley, a South Side Chicago bar-keep and keen observer of American politics, was the satirical creation of Chicago newspaperman Finley Peter Dunne. Dunne's sketches, which began running in the late 1800s, provided commentary on both local and national events using dialogue that often drew on ethnic stereotypes of the time, including the heavy Irish-immigrant brogue of Dooley. —E.D.

the justices show a united front. For a year he would not release the decision and importuned his colleagues to abandon their dissents. Smith and Jones eventually went along on the condition that the strongly worded defense of the law in Justice John A. Fogleman's majority opinion be scrapped and that the court issue a simple per-curiam order reversing Judge Reed. The order consisted of two sentences, which upheld the law but did not offer any reasoning. Brown was adamant that his dissent be recorded. The US Supreme Court in 1968 unanimously overturned the state supreme court and rebuked it for its cravenness. None of the Arkansas justices ever discussed the case publicly, although their law clerks talked furtively about the ordeal. The *Epperson* decision was its lowest moment and cast a pall over the court for years.

George Rose Smith

Judges who were worried about political repercussions, either their election or an infuriated legislature, would not declare the state's methods of financing public education unconstitutional and direct the government to fix it, as the court did in 1983 and as we did again in *Lake View School District v. Huckabee,* not once but repeatedly. *Lake View* was the most important case before the supreme court in my twenty-two years, and also the most satisfying.

The state constitution, written and ratified in 1874, directed the state to provide a "general, suitable and efficient" education for all children, and elsewhere it required that education to be equally accessible to every child. In the fifteen-year course of the lawsuit, eighteen justices, including special appointments, pondered the issues. Although there were occasional dissents from individual justices, including me, on the precise course of action, there was unanimity that the state had not lived up to its obligation to provide a suitable and equal learning program to Arkansas children and

that it absolutely had to do so. Although we were careful never to specify how the state should meet its responsibility, the legislature and the governor concluded that the only practical ways were to raise taxes, overhaul the way school funds were divided among districts, assure that the schools always enjoyed priority in the distribution of state revenues, and consolidate the state's smallest and most inefficient school districts. As I think all of us expected, there were charges that a high-handed court had usurped the constitutional prerogatives of the legislative branch and that it had ordered higher taxes upon the people of Arkansas. A few legislators talked about reprisals against the court through its appropriations.

The legislature's supremacy in all fiscal matters, including the compensation and staffing of judges, may be the largest impairment of the courts' independence, not the occasional reckoning from voters, but that is one of the checks in our constitutional balance of power. I would not claim that we were always oblivious of the threat of repercussions from that quarter, but I cannot recall an instance where the supreme court pulled its punches because it feared what the popular branches of government might do.

A test came in September 1997, when I received intimations that the attorney ad litem program for children was being corrupted by a handful of state legislators and their cronies. Since becoming a chancellor I had been interested in the provision of legal counsel for children in divorce and custody proceedings. They are often pawns in the rivalry of parting mates, and decisions are made without the children's best interests being considered. The state set up a $3 million program crafted by state Senator Nick Wilson of Pocahontas to appoint attorneys for children. It would be administered by the Administrative Office of the Courts, which was under the supreme court's supervision. It appeared that Senator Wilson and others had set up scams to split the money among themselves and a few lawyer friends. Children might get some benefits in the process but it had turned into an enrichment scheme for the politicians.

Phyllis and I had been on a vacation cruise and when I returned my old friend from the attorney general days, Bob Smith, called and asked, "What are y'all going to do about the ad litem thing?"

"What ad litem thing?" I asked.

Several chancellors who dealt with family issues, including his brother, Judge Vann Smith, had become suspicious that a few lawyers were ripping off the ad litem program. One lawyer was getting paid $750,000 when the county had been spending no more than $20,000 on representation of children. I did a little investigating and asked the justices to assemble. I presented my suspicions and the evidence that I had gleaned. The ad litem law had been amended so that the $3 million would be parceled out in grants without competitive bidding to a few of Senator Wilson's lawyer friends. One disbursement to the lawyers had been made as soon as the fiscal year began in July. What should we do? I asked.

Two of my colleagues, Donald Corbin and Ray Thornton, both of whom had been legislators at the state or federal levels, thought we should be wary of stepping into a criminal matter involving the legislative branch. Corbin, who had served with Senator Wilson in the legislature, said Wilson had a long memory and was vindictive. The supreme court could reap consequences for meddling with legislators, he said. My temper got the best of me, again, before anyone else could speak.

"I don't give a damn what you do," I barked. I said I was going to Prosecuting Attorney Larry Jegley with the evidence and that I might call a press conference, too. For heaven's sake, don't do that, someone said. All of us agreed to issue an order directing the Administrative Office of the Courts to investigate the program and take whatever steps were needed. All seven of us signed it. Then I went to see Jegley at the Pulaski County Courthouse. Jegley said the investigation would take more manpower than he had and he conferred with the United States attorney, Paula Casey, who eventually took over the case.

The FBI and the state police became involved and Casey went after Wilson and friends aggressively. A federal grand jury returned a 133-count indictment against Wilson; three other senators, Mike Todd, Mike Bearden, and Steve Bell; and others. Bell was acquitted. Several pleaded guilty and agreed to restitution. Wilson was sentenced to seventy months in prison and fined $1.3 million.

• • •

Judges are bound by honor to enter upon the bench without an agenda to achieve anything except impartial justice, but it was always in the back of my mind that on the supreme court I might be presented the chance to change the way that the state judiciary treated election misconduct. With rare exceptions across the state's history, courts had been as reluctant as the executive branch to deal firmly with voting fraud even when the laws plainly gave them the option and maybe the clear duty. In election cases as in political disputes, courts tended to find ways to settle the issue on procedural grounds so that they did not have to resolve the harder human issues that were involved in ballot theft. I suspect that it was because election officials were usually stalwart men and women of the community, and prosecutors and judges found it abhorrent to stamp the imprimatur of criminal guilt on citizens for conduct that was widely considered to be acceptable or at least the way that people got things done at the political level. I thought the *laissez-faire* attitude toward election fraud, especially by the courts, ensured that nothing would change.

I did not have long to wait. Soon after I took the oath, the perfect case arrived from—where else?—Conway County. Studying the pleadings, I had a sick feeling. Our great victory in the 1976 elections, achieved with federal court intervention, had not changed the culture in that forlorn county. This time, my old nemesis Marlin Hawkins was not masterminding the shenanigans but among the innocents, or at least the group that was outfoxed. Conway County had voted liquor in during the 1930s, soon after the ratification of the Twenty-first Amendment, which repealed prohibition. Periodically, the anti-liquor forces in the county would mount a challenge and there would be a nasty local-option liquor election, in which the wets, with Hawkins's resourceful help, would always thrash the drys. By the 1980s, his son John Robert owned a flourishing liquor store at Morrilton, so Hawkins had a fresh incentive to revive the old machine. The trouble was that he didn't control the election machinery any more. A hostile faction did, and the preachers, their flocks, and the strange bedfellows that seem to come together in dry campaigns were as dedicated to winning at all costs as Hawkins had been in his heyday.

The liquor question was on the general-election ballot in 1986, and when the vote was certified the drys had won by thirty-three votes. Sixteen days later, the wets formally contested the election, alleging massive fraud. They asked the court to throw out the election, which would leave liquor sales legal. They had the goods, too. They presented evidence that people had voted twice. Nonresident voters and people who were not registered to vote at all were voted by someone other than the voter. The same ballots would be marked by pencil for all other races but by pen on the liquor issue or vice versa, which suggested that election workers or someone else had altered ballots on a large scale. Ballot boxes contained more ballots than people who were on the voter list. The marks in wet boxes were frequently erased and the votes counted as dry. A dead person voted. Electioneering was carried on inside polling places, in violation of the law. The irregularities went on from there.

The circuit judge ruled for the wets and set aside the election. The drys appealed to the supreme court on several procedural grounds, mainly that the election contest was lodged too late, sixteen days after the vote was certified rather than within ten days, as an old law regulating wet-dry elections had required. The modern election code that the legislature enacted in 1969, which I had largely written as a deputy attorney general, allowed twenty days for election contests to be filed. When we were considering the appeal, Felver Rowell of Morrilton, who was an attorney for one side, came to see me in my chambers to talk about the case, which was the way judicial business was conducted in Conway County. I ordered him to leave my office. Anything he had to say had to be to the whole court.

To my amazement, five of my colleagues voted to reverse the trial judge and dismiss the election contest because it had been filed too late. The court would not have to deal with the questions of fraud. My strenuous, and I thought cogent, arguments that the purposely sweeping code of 1969 had changed the law for liquor and every other form of election failed to win over but one judge, Steele Hays. Even my great friend Darrell Hickman, a crusty country judge who loved to flout the economic powers, concurred with the majority, although he thought I was right that the legislature and I had intended for the code to change the ten-day law. That was academic, he wrote. The great George Rose Smith had written a contrary opinion for the court two years earlier, and Hickman wrote simply, "I go with precedent."

The majority opinion, written by Justice Robert H. Dudley, a former prosecutor, argued that since the 1969 code said all conflicting laws were repealed but didn't specifically repeal the old liquor law, it was still in effect. My dissent rather hotly declared that the majority could not have reached a more illogical conclusion. To challenge any one of the results of a dozen or more issues on the ballot would require action within twenty days of certification but only one issue, liquor sales, within ten days. What was the sense of that?

There was none, of course. The court, as it usually had done in such matters, had taken the easy course.

Reading my dissent now, it seems a trifle emphatic even for me. "I am astounded," it began and then grew more agitated. I said the majority opinion was dead wrong in almost every particular and that it damaged the state's election laws and made it harder than ever for good citizens to confront the corruption of their elections. As for the paragon Justice Smith, I wrote that he would have sided with me if he had the benefit of the arguments. I ended by calling on the attorney general and the prosecuting attorney to get to the bottom of the fraud allegations and resolve them. They didn't.

The wets moved for a rehearing, a procedure that asks the court to acknowledge its errors and change its ruling. We argued it again, fruitlessly, except this time Justice Purtle filed a brief opinion, which said that my dissenting opinion had been "a little rough" even by his standards but that he understood why I was so angry. He agreed with me that the comprehensive 1969 law intended to replace the old liquor-election law and its ten-day deadline, but since the supreme court only two years earlier had not caught it he thought we should just stick to the erroneous precedent and ask the legislature to make the law perfectly clear so that in the future there would be no doubt.

Another election had been stolen and the thieves had got away with it, with the artful assent of the highest court.

I was as despondent as I had been after any of the setbacks in the investigations by the Election Research Council and The Election Laws Institute. I also imagined that the intensity of my disagreement permanently strained relations with one or two of my colleagues.

The court got another chance eleven years later and this time made the best of it. Back when we modernized the election code and took it to the legislature in 1969, Joe Purcell capitulated to Senator Jones and removed the tightened restrictions on absentee voting. Jones threatened to block the whole bill if the absentee reforms were in it. He had been elected under the lax procedures of the old absentee system, he told me, and he intended to go out under it. In 1995, the legislature finally imposed strict requirements for qualifying for an absentee ballot and spelled out precisely how absentee applications and the ballots themselves had to be handled, which were supposed to make it harder to stuff absentee boxes.

The first test came in a special election for municipal judge in Camden in March 1999. The election forced a runoff between two lawyers who apparently wanted the job very badly. The race was tight, so both men set out to make maximum use of absentee ballots, which probably would swing the election. Nearly 15 percent of the votes in the runoff were absentee votes, cast by people who supposedly could not vote in person because they were sick, were disabled or were going to be out of town on election day. Tim Womack was declared the winner by seven votes, but without a heavy absentee vote he would have lost by nearly four hundred votes. Shortly before the election, Phillip Foster, the other candidate, complained to the Ouachita County Circuit Court that the county clerk was not following the law on absentee-ballot applications and asked the court to order her to comply. The court issued the order the day before the runoff, but the judge reserved a ruling on whether to throw out all the absentee ballots that had not been cast according to the law.

The case turned into an election contest and both sides produced evidence that hundreds of the absentee ballots were cast by people who did not qualify to vote absentee (one was dead) or by someone other than the voter, or else the procedures for handling the ballots were so flagrantly ignored that it was impossible to say who actually cast the ballots. The judge sorted through all the ballots that could be traced and invalidated 518 of them, all but one having been counted for Womack. He overturned the certified result and declared Foster the winner.

Womack appealed to the supreme court. He argued that the votes of people who genuinely wanted to vote should not be cast out for mere technical failures. Unanimously, we said the law had to be followed to the letter although Justice Robert L. Brown said in a nonbinding concurring opinion that the only way to correct "this electoral rat's nest" was to throw out all absentee ballots, which would produce the same result.

The technicalities of law, we said, are not mere inconveniences but are vital to assuring the sanctity of the ballot and they cannot be put aside. We adopted some of the trial judge's ringing declarations as our own:

> The laws dealing with absentee voting have a very obvious purpose, and they cannot be ignored by the unscrupulous campaign worker, the County Clerk's office, or the Secretary of State. . . . [I]t is this court's hope that the next election will see every voter go to the polls in person on election day, vote early, or cast a valid absentee ballot which expresses the choice of the voter, not some vote hustler; that those charged with enforcing the election rules will do so; that those intent on abusing the rules will know that they will not succeed, and that there is a price to pay for those trying.

What a trumpet call! If that had been the governing doctrine for the previous 150 years, I thought, how different things might have been.

Alas, the trumpet call did not sound far across the countryside. Six years later we would receive another case from east Arkansas where a primary election for state senator was rife with illegal voting, including hundreds of fraudulent absentee ballots. The politician who seemed to be the primary beneficiary of the fraud kept the ill-gotten seat for the full term of four years although the state's highest court repeatedly ordered local officials and the local trial court to glean the truth about the disputed votes, and to see that the legitimate wishes of the voters in the district were heeded. I retired in September 2008 with the case still floundering and justice still at bay. The case would prove as frustrating as any that confounded me in the years of jousting with political machines, election officials, and the courts as a private attorney. I'm still angry that justice has not been done in this case.

Three men ran for the Senate seat from District 16, which embraced all or parts of Crittenden, Lee, St. Francis, and Phillips Counties. State Rep. Arnell Willis of Helena and Jack Crumbly, a school administrator who lived at Widener in St. Francis County, made the runoff, which was held June 13, 2006. Crumbly was declared the winner by seventy-eight votes, but Willis contested the result and challenged hundreds of ballots cast in St. Francis County, where friends of Crumbly were in charge of the election. Willis produced more than enough ballots that were undeniably fraudulent to overcome Crumbly's seventy-eight-vote lead if he could show that they had been counted for Crumbly, which was hard to do. Even if he could not prove that all the illegal votes or most of them had been counted illegally for Crumbly, it should have been sufficient to void the election, vacate the office, and hold a new election. But it never happened.

Willis had to try his case before Circuit Judge L. T. Simes of Marianna, who was as determined as Crumbly's attorneys to protect Crumbly's seat. The attorneys raised objections about the proper jurisdiction of the case and about Willis's ability to keep identifying more and more illegal ballots. The judge would dismiss Willis's suit, Willis would appeal to the supreme court, and we would overturn Judge Simes's rulings, unanimously, and return the case with directions that he take evidence on all the disputed ballots and arrive at the truthful result.

In our third and last order in the case, on November 15, 2007, we reversed Judge Simes's dismissal of the suit and pointed out that even though unnumbered ballots could not be traced, the court could require people who voted illegally or who cast ballots illegally for others to testify about how they voted. Secrecy of the ballot is a protection for legal voters, not illegal voters, we said. In a concurring opinion, I said Judge Simes should not be allowed to preside at the trial because he had shown that he couldn't or wouldn't do it expeditiously.

In a rush of euphoria that now seems naïve, I wrote that our decision promised a new day for Arkansas voters.

Although this case has been a long time getting here, this court has shown its will to decide this election-contest case on its merits rather than dismissing it on the questionable procedural issues offered by the appellees, Crumbly, and the St. Francis County Election Commission. The winners are the voters of Arkansas, because they now can be assured that, in future elections, illegal and fraudulent voters can be purged from election results that are proved to be questionable.

That may prove to be true one day in the future, but it was not true for Arnell Willis and the voters in District 16 because the third and final order of the court was never acted on.

Judge Simes did step aside for the trial—he was subsequently suspended from office for unethical conduct in other matters—and John Lineberger of Rogers, a retired circuit judge, was appointed as a special judge. In December 2007 before the trial was to start, Crumbly's attorneys raised another issue. The courts could have nothing to do with the election fraud, they said, because the state constitution made the Senate and the House of Representatives the sole judges of the qualifications, returns, and election of their members. Of course, this question had long since been settled when the state legislature itself ceded its jurisdiction to the judicial branch by giving the courts authority to decide all election contests in Act 465 of 1969, my pride and joy.

In the face of this clear directive, Judge Lineberger ruled on February 4, 2008, that only the Senate could determine who won the District 16 election and dismissed Willis's complaint. The case never returned to the supreme court for a ruling on the correctness of Judge Lineberger or our own previous judgments, and our orders in the case were never carried out. The effect of Judge Lineberger's order is that the Senate and House of Representatives—not necessarily the electorate— get to decide who their members will be.

So despite having no jurisdiction in the matter, the Senate quickly made a show of conducting its own evidentiary hearing on the election, by then nearly two years into Crumbly's term. The Senate State Agencies and Governmental Affairs Committee listened to testimony and arguments from the attorneys for two days and recommended by a vote of four to three that Crumbly keep his seat. The full Senate reassembled and concurred by a vote of twenty-one to twelve.

Even the majority on the committee and in the Senate said the evidence proved that fraud and irregularities were rampant in the election. They found a "blatant and flagrant disregard for the democratic process as guaranteed by the Constitution and laws of our State and Nation."

"Furthermore," the senators concluded, "it is our opinion the evidence and testimony presented during our hearing unveils a chilling and alarming pattern of disregard for state election laws in a cavalier and irresponsible manner."

But since there was no evidence that poor Crumbly personally did anything wrong and they couldn't determine from their own shallow hearing exactly what the correct final vote was, the senators decided that Crumbly, whom they had got to know and like, should keep the seat for the duration of the term. No attempt was made at the hearings to identify how the illegal votes had been counted.

The minority took the view that the courts would almost certainly have embraced if given the chance. Since far more votes than were needed to put the election in doubt had been proved to be illegal, there was no legitimate winner in the election. The election result should have been voided and the voters given a fresh chance to choose their delegate to the Senate.

The authority of the Senate to act was never reviewed by the supreme court, and its orders were never acted upon. I am still dumbfounded at this turn of events, and I am incensed by the resulting ambiguity when we were so close to clarity on what to do about voter fraud. Since it was never appealed, the circuit judge's decision in the Crumbly case is not binding precedent and the supreme court's last opinion is the prevailing law, but his error provides dangerous ammunition for future election-fraud cases.

The Crumbly case was just about my last, and certainly the last in the field in which I had spent so much of my life's labor. It was a particularly dispiriting way to go out, but I do not think the courts will permit that absurdity to prevail. There inevitably will be another case, and I hope that someone will take the time to read my comments here and take the steps to clarify that the voters, through the good offices of the courts, will always determine who will represent them.

I prefer to reflect now upon the progress that the state made, at least judicially, in giving people honest elections and some reasonable assurance that they can fix those that are not.

EPILOGUE

Having set out to record historical episodes of election fraud, quite a number of which engaged my poor skills as an investigator and lawyer, I worry that it is now expected of me that I say what it all meant. If it is not altogether historical and is still a problem, what can we do about it now? I would like to be able to say that technology, better laws, heightened scrutiny, a public that is less tolerant of the schemes of the vote thieves and, in our state, the arrival of a vigilant two-party system have made serious and widespread fraud impossible. I do think that Winthrop Rockefeller was right in 1964 when he said that fifty thousand votes could be manipulated in a statewide election, and I believe that fraud on such a scale now is quite unlikely.

But not impossible.

The possibilities are not scarce, only riskier. It does not take fifty thousand votes but only a fistful of fraudulent ballots to swing an election for county coroner, governor or president of the United States. When passions move elections, as they increasingly do, winning at all cost is the guiding impulse. The urge to go the extra mile to put your man in office or keep him there is eternal. I do not know but suspect that every judge or clerk who ever stuffed a ballot box, altered a return or filled out a fake absentee application and ballot felt a patriotic impulse. You believe it is important to put the best man, your man, in office, and that whatever risks you take to achieve it are for the public good. If there is will, there usually is a way. Four years ago, they were able to rig an election for a state senator in east Arkansas under the watchful gaze of a smart and determined opponent and a unanimously disapproving supreme court. They got away with it.

Laws now are in place to prevent it. What is still missing is the will to enforce the laws, which was always the central problem. If people who break the law, even to elect the princeliest of men, were to be punished swiftly and resolutely there would soon be few with the will to do it. Love, hate, and money will drive men to take terrible risks, but not so the election of a municipal judge or state senator. Fudging on the casting and counting of ballots has never entailed much risk in Arkansas.

The machinery of modern elections, which registers and counts the votes of people swiftly and mechanically or digitally, is an advancement, but it carries risks, too. The unlettered rubes who managed the ballot boxes in George Fisher's cartoons may be daunted by machines on which people vote or that electronically read a voter's ballot, but voting technology is not foolproof and I am not convinced that it will ever be. No one tried to cheat people out of their votes in Florida when machines and then individual voting officials were confused by the "hanging chads" that voters failed to punch out altogether in the punch-card machines. That innocent quandary may have changed the outcome of a presidential election and sharply altered the course of history.

The unsophisticated election clerks in Morrilton's First Ward may not be a threat to manipulate the equipment to thwart the will of the voters there, but there is not enough genius in the world of high technology to prevent a clever hacker somewhere, maybe a junior high school student with a cheap laptop, from breaking the code, and spreading havoc across the country and the world. If a lone agent can put the banking system or national security at risk, why not an election that rests on the reliability of computerized voting systems? There is the possibility of voting fraud, undetectable fraud, on a scale that we have never known. It need not be on a big scale to do cataclysmic injustice. Fraud in a handful of boxes in Ohio, Florida, or Nevada in national elections dilutes the votes of people in Blue Ball, Arkansas, and robs the country of the just expression of its will.

I worry about it a lot.

INDEX

Numbers in italics refer to illustrations.

Eaton, John, 181–4
Edens, Max J., 42
Eighth US Circuit Court of Appeals, 153
Eisele, G. Thomas, 54, 57, 85, 99, 100–102, *101*, 111, 138, 150
El Dorado, Ark., 64, 150, 160
El Dorado Wildcats, 149
elections, of 1868 on a Reconstruction constitution, 6–7; of 1872, 7; of 1888 for state and local offices and for Congress, 7–13; of 1913 for governor, 14; of 1946 for Garland County offices, 15–16; of 1950 for sheriff of Conway County, 105–7; of 1954 in primary runoff for governor, 36; of 1958 for Congress in the Second District, 39–40; of 1960 for state senate in Prairie and Lonoke counties, 4–6; of 1960 for the Wonderview school board and Morrilton form of government, 108; of 1962 for Conway County school boards, 110; of 1964 for state representative in Marion County, 29–30; of 1964 for state offices, 31–32; of 1964 on casino gambling and the poll tax, 33–34; of 1964 in Madison County, 35–39; of 1964 and absentee ballots, 39–46; of undetermined year for library millage in Poinsett County, 40; of 1966 for state and local offices and the "Throw the Rascals Out" campaign, 58–61; of 1968 for governor, 67–69; of 1968 for prosecuting attorney of Pope and Conway counties, 174–6; of 1970 for governor, 16–17, 75–79, 118–19; of 1972 and the American Party initiative campaign, 85–92; of 1972 for mayor of Plumerville, 120; of 1972 for governor, 124; of 1974 for the US Senate and governor, 94–95, 124–5; of 1974 for sheriff in Lee County, 96; of 1974 for US representative from the Second District, 119; of 1974 for US representative in the Third District, 177-9; of 1974 for lieutenant governor, 79; of 1975 for vacancy in the state senate from Conway, Faulkner and Van Buren counties, 123–34, and aftermath, 137–63; of 1976 in Conway County, 166–73; of 1976 in Searcy County, 180–86, 188; of 1978 for chancery judge in Pulaski County, 195–7; of 1982 for the Arkansas Court of Appeals, 198–9; of 1982 for governor, 79; of 1986 for the Arkansas Supreme Court, 199–200; of 1986 on a wet-dry proposition in Conway County, 208–9; of 1999 for municipal judge in Ouachita County, 210–11; of 2006 for state senate from Crittenden, Lee, St. Francis and Phillips Counties, 211–14; of 2000 and 2004 for president, x
Election Research Council, 42, 44-47, 51, 54, 56, 62, 63, 68, 83, 107, 121, 123, 200, 306, 320
Elkins, Mrs. E. E., 25
Elliott, Fern, xi, 181
Elliott, Rex, xi, 180–81, 187
English, Fred, 196
Enid, Okla., 23
Enola, Ark., 124
Epperson, Susan, 203–4

"Fanne Foxe." *See* Annabella Battistella
Farm and Ranch, 86
Farmer, E. L., 89
Farmer, R. G., 89
Fathers for Equal Rights, 196
Faulkner County, xi, 43, 71, 85, 121, 124–25, 133, 145, 155–56, 158–60, 172, 196, 201
Faulkner County Circuit Court, 85
Faulkner County Election Commission, 160
Faubus, Alta, 48, 77
Faubus, Doyle, 50
Faubus, Farrell, 38, 77
Faubus, Orval E., 16–17, 24–25, 31–36, *32*, *35*, 41, 44–47, 49–53, *52*, 55, 59–65, 68, 70–71, 73, 75–78, *78*, 81, 94–95, *95*, 100, 118–19, 124, 126, 132, 137, 174

Faubus, Sam, 31
Faulkner County, xi, 43, 71, 85, 121, 124,
    125, 133, 145
Faulkner, Robert W., 83
Fawcett, Farrah, 190
Fayetteville, Ark., xiii, 21, 36, 37, 38,
    62, 149
Federal Bureau of Investigation, 38, 89,
    141, 153, 179, 189–91, 206
Fendler, Oscar, 168
Fifth Amendment, US Constitution, 186
Fifth Judicial District, 112, 120–21
First Amendment, US Constitution,
    178, 194
First Baptist Church (Conway, Ark.), 124
First State Bank of Morrilton, 106
Fisher, Bob, 25
Fisher, George, xii, 59, 65, 196, 216
Fogleman, John A., 204
Ford Foundation, 96
Ford, Gerald, 153–54
Foreman, Ark., 68
Fort Smith, Ark., 3, 25, 64, 166, 179,
    191, 194
Foster, Phillip, 210
Fourteenth Amendment to the US
    Constitution, 93, 151, 181, 194
Fourth US Circuit Court of Appeals, 153
Freedom of Information Act, 151
Fulbright, J. William, 68, 76, 94, 95, 98,
    125, 154
Fussell, Bobby, 154
Futrell, J. Marion, 14–15

Galyean, Rev. Roy, 34
gambling, 11, 34, 45, 46, 51, 66
Gardner, Jack, 65
Garland, Augustus H., 7
Garland County, 15–16, 34, 43
Gaspard, Joe, 36
General Publishing Co., 85
George, Charlie, 6
Gist, Warfield, 44
GI revolt, 15
Gladden, Clair Reece, 67
Glaze, Amy, xiii
Glaze, Dick, 19

Glaze, Harry "Slick," 19–20, 23, 195
Glaze, Harry, Jr., 19
Glaze, Larry, 19
Glaze, Mamie Rose Guterman, 20–21
Glaze, Mike, xiii
Glaze, Phyllis Laser, xiii, 194, 206
Glaze, Steve, xiii
Glaze, Susan Askins, 23, 194
Goggin, Will, 178, 179, 185
Goldwater, Barry, 50
Goodman, W. Ward, 71
Gordon, Edward, 148
Gordon, Helen, xi, 117–19, 129, 151
Gordon, Nathan, 59, 61, 111, 147–48,
    155, 162, 170
Gordon, Virginia Frances, 148
Goss, Pat, 149
Govar, Robert, 130–31
GPW Nursing Home, 45
Grand Prairie, 4
Gray, Richard J., 13
Gray, Rosie, 194
Great Depression, 14, 19, 20, 104, 117,
    179, 180, 184
"Great Society," 50
Green Bay Packaging Inc., Arkansas
    Packaging Division, 117
Greenwood, Ark., xii
Gregory, Elmer, 184
Gremillion, Jack P. F., 64
Gulf of Tonkin, 24
Gunter, Joe T., 4–6, 27

Hagood, G. E., 89
Haines, Hank, 169
Haley, John H., xii, 24–27, 29, 31, 36–37,
    40–41, 53, 62
Ham, Everett, 55–56
Hammerschmidt, John Paul, 177–79
Hamner, Ralph C., Jr., xii, 96, 141, 149
Hamner, Ralph C., Sr., 141
Hanna, W. S., 13
Harmon, John T., 67
Harriet, Ark., 190
Harris, Carleton, 147, 155, 203
Harris, Katherine, 93